ESPECIALLY FOR

....

FROM

....

DATE

....

Daily Wisdom
FOR WOMEN

2025
DEVOTIONAL
COLLECTION

BARBOUR
PUBLISHING

Printed in China.

Introduction

And now, just as you accepted Christ Jesus as your Lord, you must continue to follow him. Let your roots grow down into him, and let your lives be built on him. Then your faith will grow strong in the truth you were taught, and you will overflow with thankfulness.

Colossians 2:6–7 NLT

To make our way with God victoriously as we journey through this life, we must develop a strong, resilient faith. That means growing our roots down into Jesus and building our lives up from Him.

To become more *rooted* in Jesus, it's essential to spend time studying God's Word, meditating on His promises (hearing, teaching, worshiping in song), praying continually, practicing gratitude and contentment. Building our lives *up* from Him means asking for guidance in life's decisions—both big and small. It means trusting in God's goodness even when life is hard and we don't know what He's doing. It means following His commands willingly, giving with a joyful heart, fellowshipping with other believers, putting the needs of others before our own, and living to bring glory to Him every day.

Growing and building this kind of faith will help us survive and thrive every moment, especially when the troubles of life come. To help you get there, four writers bring you the the *Daily Wisdom for Women 2025 Devotioanl Collection*. May the devotions that follow give you the strength and resiliency to not only survive but thrive every day!

Genesis 1–2 / Matthew 1 / Psalm 1

The Same Spirit

God's angel spoke in the dream: "Joseph, son of David,
don't hesitate to get married. Mary's pregnancy is Spirit-
conceived. God's Holy Spirit has made her pregnant."
MATTHEW 1:20 MSG

Are you ready to go deeper in your faith this new year? There's no better place to start than with the Holy Spirit.

One of the defining characteristics of Jesus' life on earth was the presence of the Holy Spirit. It was the Holy Spirit who caused a Jewish virgin to become pregnant with Jesus. As Jesus grew physically, spiritually, and mentally into a man, it was the same Spirit who enabled Him to perform miracles, boldly teach wisdom, follow God's perfect plan, and lead and love others. And when Jesus was accused, betrayed, tortured, killed, and buried in a tomb, it was the power of the Holy Spirit that brought Him back to life three days later.

It's inspiring and empowering to realize that it's this same miracle-working, wisdom-granting, beyond-understanding, life-giving Holy Spirit who also lives inside each believing heart. Today, ask the Spirit to move inside you. Ask for wisdom and understanding and a renewed joy of what it means to live in God's grace and freedom. The Spirit can and will lead you to a stronger faith that's rooted in and built on the love of Jesus!

Holy Spirit, please help me to grow in faith, to gain new understanding
of God's Word, and to be used for the glory of Jesus. Amen.

Genesis 3–4 / Matthew 2 / Psalm 2

God's Chosen King

*For the Lord declares, "I have placed my chosen king
on the throne in Jerusalem, on my holy mountain."*

PSALM 2:6 NLT

Jesus is in charge.

These four words can be empowering to a Christian who is actively seeking God's will. It's an encouraging, hope-sustaining truth if we've surrendered everything and allow Jesus the ultimate say in our decisions. But what about when we struggle to let go of control?

Scripture tells us in Philippians 2:9–11 that God put Jesus in charge of everything. Today, some people recognize that fact, but others don't. One day, *everyone* will bow down before Jesus and acknowledge that He is Lord over all.

If your life feels out of control today, if you're white-knuckling your to-do list and everything feels held together by an unraveling thread, the way to true peace is to lay it all down at the feet of Jesus. Because of God's great love for us, we can find freedom and blessings in surrendering fully to Jesus, God's chosen King, who will be the kind and benevolent ruler of our hearts and lives. Psalm 2:12 even promises us joy when we submit to His lordship, let go of control, and take refuge in Him.

*Jesus, I asked You to be the Lord of my life when I became
a Christian, but I need to surrender my life and will to You
every day. You are my chosen King now and forever.*

Genesis 5–7 / Matthew 3 / Psalm 3

Noah's Obedience

*"Make the boat 450 feet long, 75 feet wide, and 45 feet
high. Leave an 18-inch opening below the roof all the way
around the boat. Put the door on the side, and build three
decks inside the boat—lower, middle, and upper."*

GENESIS 6:15–16 NLT

The instructions God gave Noah for building the ark in Genesis 6
read like a DIY manual. Have you ever wished God would provide
a step-by-step guide for what He wants you to do? Do you yearn for
God to speak as clearly and specifically as He did to Noah? How was
it that Noah received such detailed instruction from the Creator of
the universe? Because God knew Noah would obey Him.

Noah had a close relationship with the Lord (v. 9). During one
of their conversations, God revealed His plans to destroy the earth
(v. 13), but God also promised Noah that his family and two of every
living creature would survive on an ark that he was to build (vv. 14–20).
What did Noah do with this instruction? "Noah did everything exactly
as God had commanded him" (v. 22 NLT).

If you long for God's instruction in your life, lean into your
relationship with Him. Ask Him for guidance and wisdom in any
situation. "If you don't know what you're doing, pray to the Father.
He loves to help" (James 1:5 MSG).

*Father, I need Your help. Let me hear Your voice,
Your clear instructions, and I will do exactly as You say.*

The Year of Waiting

*God remembered Noah and all the wild animals and
livestock with him in the boat. He sent a wind to blow
across the earth, and the floodwaters began to recede.*

Genesis 8:1 nlt

More than a year passed from the time the rain started until Noah left
the ark. Noah was already 600 years old at this time, so being cooped
up in the ark with animals and family members couldn't have been
easy or comfortable. Scripture doesn't record the conversations between
Noah and God during that time. Yet it seems the ark builder waited
patiently. He continued to follow God's plan—acting neither hastily
nor impulsively—obeying God and waiting for further instruction.

What can we learn from Noah's year of waiting? God's timing
is often different than ours (2 Peter 3:8), but we can trust that His
timing is always perfect. The Lord will bless and renew us in the
waiting (Lamentations 3:25; Isaiah 40:31), and He will make all
things work together for our good (Romans 8:28).

Noah's waiting ultimately resulted in the reboot of life on earth
when God said, "Leave the boat. . . . Release all the animals. . .so
they can be fruitful and multiply throughout the earth" (Genesis
8:16–17 nlt).

*Lord, I don't like to wait. But I trust that You are working in
every situation in my life and that Your timing—even when
I don't understand it—is perfect and worth waiting for.*

Genesis 11–13 / Matthew 5:1–20 / Psalm 5

Trailblazer God

Lead me in the right path, O LORD. . . .
Make your way plain for me to follow.
PSALM 5:8 NLT

Hiking on a well-established wilderness trail is a beautiful way to experience God's creation. But often the more remote the trail—the more unused it is—the more difficult the path may be to see and follow. And the less confident the hiker is of the right way to go. Even trail markers and maps can be confusing and unclear. The only foolproof way to hike such a difficult path is to closely follow someone who knows the way.

God is faithful to lead you through the journey of life. His is always the best, right path, and when you're walking closely behind Him—growing in your relationship with Him and learning to trust Him fully—He can show you and tell you the best way to navigate tricky parts of the journey. When you recognize God's voice, if you make a wrong turn, He will lead you back to the trail. And when a section of the path is impassable, He will guide you around or through it, just like He did for the Israelites when He parted the Red Sea for them to escape on dry ground from the Egyptians.

He is the waymaking, trailblazing God you can trust to lead you here on earth and into eternity with Him in heaven.

The way ahead looks treacherous, Lord, so instead
of worrying, I will keep my eyes on You!

Genesis 14–16 / Matthew 5:21–48 / Psalm 6

More Like Christ

You have been taught to love your neighbor and hate your enemy.
But I tell you this: love your enemies. Pray for those who torment you
and persecute you—in so doing, you become children of your Father in
heaven. He, after all, loves each of us—good and evil, kind and cruel.
MATTHEW 5:43–45 VOICE

The Jews listening to Jesus teach in Matthew 5 probably knew Leviticus 19:18 (NLT): "Do not seek revenge or bear a grudge against a *fellow Israelite*, but love your neighbor as yourself" (emphasis added). But the Messiah took this Old Testament law a step further by instructing His followers to extend love to *everyone*, even—or especially—people who oppose them and are different from them.

Is this easy to do? No. Will you be perfect at it? Absolutely not. But if your desire is to become more like Jesus in every way, you will work to bring God's love and grace to everyone.

Even the apostle Paul, a giant of the faith and leader in the early church, wrote of his continual effort to learn to be more like Jesus in Philippians 3:12 (MSG): "I'm not saying that I have this all together. . . . But I am well on my way, reaching out for Christ, who has so wondrously reached out for me."

Jesus, when my faith is growing stronger, I know I'm
on the right track. And nothing will stop me from
pursuing my goal of becoming more like You!

Authentic Prayer

"And when you pray, do not keep on babbling like pagans, for they think they will be heard because of their many words. Do not be like them, for your Father knows what you need before you ask him."
MATTHEW 6:7–8 NIV

There's a big difference between an informational exchange between coworkers and a heart-connected conversation between good friends over a cup of coffee. Both conversations result in communication, but only the latter has the power to encourage, refresh, and rejuvenate hearts and spirits.

Prayer, approached incorrectly, can be just a string of requests that we rattle off at God—empty words that babble on with no real intention other than to make us feel spiritual and to convince God to give us what we want. But authentic prayer is how we can express our honest emotions with God—the good, the bad, and the desperate. He won't shy away when we tell Him how we feel. For God is present with us in our struggles, welcomes our questions, and wants to give us good things. And He uses this one-on-one time to reveal His character to us.

Prayer is when we pour out ourselves so God can pour Himself into us. The great mystery of prayer is that it changes things by changing us from the inside out. There we gain the right perspective—His.

*Father, I'm here for a heart-connected talk with You.
Help me feel Your mighty presence as we spend
time together. Give me more of You.*

Genesis 19–20 / Matthew 6:19–34 / Psalm 8

God of the Heavens

I look up at your macro-skies, dark and enormous,
your handmade sky-jewelry, moon and stars mounted
in their settings. Then I look at my micro-self and wonder,
why do you bother with us? Why take a second look our way?

PSALM 8:3–4 MSG

Shepherd, king, and psalm-writer David had the universal experience of gazing up at a beautiful, expansive night sky and feeling small. . . overwhelmed with the enormity and complexity of God's creation and wondering why God would think of him at all.

That's one of the amazing mysteries of your Creator. The same God who set the outer boundaries of the galaxies also placed each star and planet and set it on its course. The same God who crafted the delicately balanced ecosystem of earth to allow life to thrive also designed the intricacies of you—your body, mind, and spirit.

But God didn't just create you and set you on your way to wander aimlessly through life. No, He loved you into being, and His all-encompassing love for you continues. Before you were born, God made a way for your salvation through the death of His Son (Romans 5:8). God delights in you (Zephaniah 3:17). He cares about your thoughts and feelings and wants to remove your anxiety (1 Peter 5:7). He will work to ensure all things come together for your good (Romans 8:28).

Father, I am in awe of the way You love me.
Thank You for being my Creator and friend.

Faith, Focus, Follow-Through

*Just ask and it will be given to you; seek after it and you
will find. Continue to knock and the door will be opened
for you. All who ask receive. Those who seek, find what they
seek. And he who knocks, will have the door opened.*

MATTHEW 7:7–8 VOICE

Have you ever given up asking God for something after a few
halfhearted attempts to pray, assuming that God either wasn't listening
or hearing you? Effective prayer happens when you approach God's
throne with a heart full of faith, focus, and follow-through.

Praying requires faith in the promise that God will listen and
respond (Isaiah 65:24). An effective prayer is accompanied by a hopeful
expectation that you will receive what you're seeking (Mark 11:24).
When your prayer is focused on the details of your situation, God
will help guide your thoughts, heart, and perspective to align with
His. And when you follow through and continue to ask again and
again (and again!), you're obeying the Bible's instruction to "never
stop praying" (1 Thessalonians 5:17 NLT).

An effective prayer life is one of the best ways to develop a deeper
relationship with God. And the more you talk with God, the more
you'll recognize His actions and His voice when He answers.

*Thank You, Father, for the privilege of prayer. I praise You for
Your faithful promises to hear my asks—both big and small—
knowing You will reward me when I earnestly seek You.*

Genesis 24 / Matthew 7:12–29 / Psalm 9:9–20

Built on Bedrock

"Anyone who listens to my teaching and follows it is wise, like a person who builds a house on solid rock. Though the rain comes in torrents and the floodwaters rise and the winds beat against that house, it won't collapse because it is built on bedrock."

MATTHEW 7:24–25 NLT

There are good reasons why homebuying usually involves a once-over by a home inspector. From termites and mold to basement walls that warn of future collapse, a qualified inspector can inform buyers about the house from the foundation up.

A strong foundation is key to the longevity of a house, and just like laying a solid foundation of faith, it starts with intention. In Matthew 7, Jesus uses the analogy of two home builders. On the outside, the lives of these two may look the same, but the difference between them is that the wise builder obeys Jesus' teaching and the foolish builder does not.

Nobody intentionally builds their life on a flawed foundation, but it could be that they never considered the future. Every choice will eventually have a consequence—either good or bad. Obeying God's teaching anchors our faith foundation deep into the bedrock, the solid, immovable rock beneath the loose surface layer.

A person deeply rooted into the bedrock wisdom of God can weather the big storms of life as well as the shifting gravel and loose soil of day-to-day life.

Jesus, with Your help, I intend to build my life on the wisdom of Your Word.

Genesis 25–26 / Matthew 8:1–17 / Psalm 10:1–11

Immediate Satisfaction

"Look, I'm dying of starvation!" said Esau.
"What good is my birthright to me now?"
GENESIS 25:32 NLT

Esau had just returned from hunting in the wilderness, exhausted and hungry. To him, it was an I-must-eat-now-or-I-will-die emergency. He was desperate enough to trade his birthright as the firstborn son of Isaac for his twin brother Jacob's stew!

For the immediate satisfaction of filling his belly, Esau gave up a double portion of the family inheritance, the honor of one day becoming the family's leader, and the spiritual blessing tied to his grandfather Abraham's covenant with God. He chose instant gratification with no thought for the long-term consequences.

It's easy to judge Esau's actions harshly. If he had just paused for a moment to think, considered the result, or even had a shred of common sense, he never would've made the trade. But the truth is that we all make bad decisions sometimes. No one lives without regrets from a rash action—words said in anger, big impulse purchases, overindulging in a vice of choice, falling prey to temptation.

So what can you do to avoid an Esau-esque pitfall? Before acting or reacting, take a breath. Weigh the short-term satisfaction and long-term consequences. Sleep on big decisions. Seek advice from trusted friends. Pray and literally ask God what He wants you to do and how your actions can glorify Him.

Lord, help me act wisely in every decision—
both in big and small things.

Genesis 27:1–28:9 / Matthew 8:18–34 / Psalm 10:12–18

The Calmer of Storms

*Then Jesus got into the boat and started across the lake with his
disciples. Suddenly, a fierce storm struck the lake, with waves
breaking into the boat. But Jesus was sleeping. The disciples went
and woke him up, shouting, "Lord, save us! We're going to drown!"*

MATTHEW 8:23–25 NLT

Sudden, strong storms often descend upon the Sea of Galilee. It's a
relatively small body of water (13 miles long, 7 miles wide), but it's
also 150 feet deep and surrounded by mountains. So when Jesus and
His disciples started across the lake, there likely was no sign that bad
weather was coming.

Prior to this storm, the disciples had seen Jesus perform miracles.
Earlier in Matthew 8, He'd healed a man with leprosy, a paralyzed
man from afar, and Peter's mother-in-law's fever. He'd also delivered
many from demon possession. But this episode on the Sea of Galilee
showed Jesus' followers what true, personal faith means.

Afraid for their lives, the disciples shouted Jesus awake in a panic.
With a word, God's Son calmed the storm and sea. Even though their
faith had wavered, Jesus was faithful to save them.

Living, active faith believes that Jesus controls both the storms of
nature and the storms of life. His power that calmed the sky and sea
can also help you with the problems you face, even the most difficult.
All you have to do is ask.

Jesus, I praise You for being the powerful storm calmer You are.

Praying for Others

Some people brought to him a paralyzed man on a mat.
Seeing their faith, Jesus said to the paralyzed man,
"Be encouraged, my child! Your sins are forgiven."

MATTHEW 9:2 NLT

We don't know much about the people who brought this paralyzed man to Jesus. We don't know how many there were or how they knew the disabled man. What we do know is that Jesus recognized their faith.

As believers, we have the privilege of praying for not only our own needs but also the needs of others. . .both believing friends and family and those who may not know Jesus yet. There's great power in multiple people talking to God about the same person. Is someone sick? Pray for healing. Discouraged? Ask God to show how you can build them up. Struggling through a difficult season? Pray for their hope and perseverance. Wavering in their faith? Ask God to anchor them in His truth.

Because of the faith of his friends, Jesus healed this man spiritually by forgiving his sins and physically by making him walk. Imagine how encouraging this must've been as the man jumped up from his mat and went home. Not only was he healed, but he was surrounded by people who loved him enough to take him to Jesus.

Father, I will be faithful in praying for the people
around me. Open my eyes to the needs of others,
and please use me to help in whatever way I can.

Genesis 30:1–31:21 / Matthew 10:1–15 / Psalm 12

Pure Words

The words of the LORD are pure words, as silver
tried in a furnace of earth, purified seven times.
PSALM 12:6 SKJV

Sincerity and pure motives are often hard to come by in this world. Perhaps you've questioned the truth of what someone said to you. . . you've wondered if you're being taken advantage of. . .you've received a compliment and gotten the feeling there's an ulterior motive behind the flattery.

King David, the author of this psalm, certainly faced deception, flattery, and insincerity in his life, especially when people tried to win his favor and gain advancement in his court. But even when David didn't know whom to trust, he knew he could trust the truth of God.

God's Word and the promises therein are pure and tried and true. He has no angle, ulterior motive, or deceit. There's no fine print or tricks to make us believe one thing when He really means another. God doesn't fast talk and He doesn't upsell. What God says, He means. And He wants the same from us.

In Matthew 5:33 (MSG), Jesus said, "Don't say anything you don't mean. . . . Just say 'yes' and 'no.'" And in verse 37 He said, "When you manipulate words to get your own way, you go wrong." Today, examine your motives and your words, and align them with God's truth.

Father, I never have to wonder if You really mean what You
say, and that makes me feel so secure in Your love.

Genesis 31:22–32:21 / Matthew 10:16–36 / Psalm 13

Prepare for Conflict

Rescue me now, please, from the hand of my brother, from the grip of Esau. I am afraid that he may come and crush us all, the children alongside their mothers. Remember You told me, "I will make good things happen for you and make your descendants as many as the grains of sand on the shores, which are too numerous to count."

GENESIS 32:11–12 VOICE

Jacob was shaking in his sandals. The last time he and Esau were together, Esau had been ready to kill Jacob for stealing the family blessing (Genesis 25:29–34; 27:1–45). And it wasn't the I'm-gonna-beat-the-snot-out-of-you kind of brotherly tussle—Jacob had to flee the country to avoid being murdered by Esau.

Now, about twenty years later, Jacob was returning to his homeland where Esau still lived, and he had no idea how his twin brother would react to his homecoming. Worst case scenario? Esau's army of four hundred men headed toward Jacob and his family would wipe them all from the earth. Best case? Well, anything but that.

Throughout your life, you've probably faced times of deep personal conflict. Perhaps you had no idea how a hard conversation would end. When that's the case, it's essential to pause and pray, just as Jacob did, asking for confidence as God works through you in any situation.

Father, I believe You work all things together for my good. Please give me Your wisdom to work through conflicts.

Genesis 32:22–34:3 / Matthew 10:37–11:6 / Psalm 14

Jacob's Persistence

The man said, "Let me go; it's daybreak." Jacob said,
"I'm not letting you go 'til you bless me."
GENESIS 32:26 MSG

Life requires persistence. When you learned to walk as a toddler, you tumbled to the ground many times, but you stood back up and tried again. To get your first big job, you probably sent a slew of inquiries and résumés and sat through multiple interviews. But you kept pushing, kept going until your efforts resulted in success.

Here in Genesis 32, we read about Jacob's persistence during an all-night wrestling match with God. Even after He had wounded Jacob's hip, Jacob refused to yield his tight grip on God until He blessed him.

God encourages and will reward your persistence too. Jesus taught His followers to pray continually (Luke 11:9–10; 18:1–8). And elsewhere God's Word tells us to persevere through trials (James 1:2–4; Romans 12:12; Hebrews 12:1–2).

God blessed Jacob's persistence and renewed his purpose and life through a transformative name change to Israel. Where in your spiritual life do you need to develop more persistence? It's never easy, but the results are worth it. Remember that God promises to hear and answer your constant prayers, help you grow a strong character from your persistence in trials, and gain true hope grounded in Christ.

Father, when I feel like giving up, remind me that Your
Spirit makes me powerful to persist in any situation.
Renew me and build me up to keep going no matter what.

Genesis 35–36 / Matthew 11:7–24 / Psalm 15

God's Standards

*Eternal One, who is invited to stay in Your dwelling?
Who is granted passage to Your holy mountain? Here is
the answer: The one who lives with integrity, does what is
right, and speaks honestly with truth from the heart.*

PSALM 15:1–2 VOICE

We live in a world of shifting standards. What's right or wrong, acceptable or unacceptable, fashionable or hideous, cool or cancelled can leave our heads spinning. The world says what's right is based on feelings, personal preference, what's most pleasurable. The world wants no direction from God.

But God's standards of right and wrong never change, and Psalm 15 gives us concrete examples of what pleases Him: integrity, honesty, speaking truth, and refusing to gossip or harm or speak ill of others. God says it's good to honor the righteous living of others, keep promises even when it's hard, give generously, and refuse bribes.

The depth and strength of our faith can be measured by how well we live out God's standards in everyday life. If you struggle in any of these areas, know that progress is more important than perfection. God's grace covers every slip-up and lapse, but God also wants you to experience the freedom that comes with right living. Ask the Holy Spirit to help you become more and more like Jesus every day.

*Holy Lord, I am thankful You have immovable standards.
Help me stretch and grow toward them every day.*

Genesis 37–38 / Matthew 11:25–30 / Psalm 16

Sleepless Nights

I will bless the Lord who guides me;
even at night my heart instructs me.
PSALM 16:7 NLT

When you're well in mind, body, and spirit, the overnight hours are a respite from the challenges of the day—a time for rest, restoration, and rejuvenation. But if you're struggling emotionally, physically, or spiritually, nighttime might be a huge challenge. Thoughts in the dark can turn desperate and negative as lengthy hours stretch on.

David, the writer of Psalm 16, probably had his share of sleepless nights. Whether he was running for his life from King Saul, leading his troops into battle, or struggling with guilt over his extramarital affair with Bathsheba, David clung to the promise that even in his sleeplessness, God would grant him peace and safety (Psalm 4:8).

The next time you find yourself staring at the ceiling in the middle of the night, instead of counting sheep, try counting God's blessings in your life by praying the psalms. "I know the Lord is always with me" (Psalm 16:8 NLT). "Every good thing I have comes from you" (Psalm 16:2 NLT). "Let my soul be at rest again, for the Lord has been good to me" (Psalm 116:7 NLT).

Father, even if I struggle with sleeplessness, I know You are
with me. Please calm my heart and mind. Please help my
body relax and rest in You so I can sleep deeply and awake
rejuvenated, with a fresh perspective as I greet the day.

Genesis 39–40 / Matthew 12:1–29 / Psalm 17

He Hears and Listens

I am praying to you because I know you will answer,
O God. Bend down and listen as I pray. Show me your
unfailing love in wonderful ways. By your mighty power
you rescue those who seek refuge from their enemies.

Psalm 17:6–7 NLT

The words *hear* and *listen* may have similarities in their definitions, but there are significant differences between them too. Hearing is one of our five natural senses and is the involuntary, physiological act of observing sounds. It takes no effort on our part to hear a noise—our ears just do what they were designed to do. Listening, on the other hand, is an active, thoughtful attention to words and sounds to understand their meaning in order to respond.

King David's prayer in Psalm 17 includes a statement of belief that God will hear and listen closely to his pleas and answer his prayer. David humbly asks God to bend down to listen—something you may do with a young child so you can really hear what he's saying.

God is faithful to do the same for you. Yet the truth is He already knows your needs before you do, and He's already working them out. "I will answer them before they even call to me. . ." He said in Isaiah 65:24 (NLT), "I will go ahead and answer their prayers!"

Father, I believe scripture's promise that You hear my prayers.
Thank You for listening to my heart and answering me.

Genesis 41 / Matthew 12:30–50 / Psalm 18:1–15

The Lord Is My. . .

*I love you, LORD; you are my strength. The LORD is my rock,
my fortress, and my savior; my God is my rock, in whom
I find protection. He is my shield, the power that saves
me, and my place of safety. I called on the LORD, who is
worthy of praise, and he saved me from my enemies.*

PSALM 18:1–3 NLT

David, the writer of Psalm 18, sang this song on the day God rescued him from his enemies, including King Saul, who was hunting him to murder him. David chose some of the strongest language he could muster in his praise of his rescuer. Rather than singing, "you strengthen me," or "you're my source of strength," he said God *is* his strength, implying he is powerless without God and that he relies on Him fully.

David goes on to say that the Lord is his rock, fortress, Savior, shield, saving power, and safe place. Any one of those truths is enough to make God worthy of praise; but on top of that, David said, God answered his prayer.

What is God for you today? The Lord is your hope. Your joy. Your defender. Your advocate. Your peace. Your new start. Your rest. Your salvation. Your encouragement. No matter your need, He can and will fill it. Just ask.

*God, I praise You for always being
everything I need, exactly when I need it!*

Genesis 42–43 / Matthew 13:1–9 / Psalm 18:16–29

Deep Waters

He reached down from heaven and took hold of me; He pulled me out
of deep waters. He rescued me from my powerful enemy and from those
who hated me, for they were too strong for me. They confronted me in
the day of my distress, but the LORD was my support. He brought me
out to a spacious place; He rescued me because He delighted in me.

PSALM 18:16–19 HCSB

David understood just how helpless and defenseless he was when he was attacked by his enemies. Yet God kept David from drowning in the "deep waters" of his troubles. Even though David's foes were stronger than he, God helped him and supported him through the difficult confrontation and battle. David may have been backed into a corner for a while, but God was always with him and helped him escape because, David said, God delighted in him.

If you've ever prayed for change—for God's rescue—in a difficult situation (and who hasn't?), remember that He may choose to miraculously deliver you *or* He may be your support as you go through even the deepest waters (Isaiah 43:2). Whatever the case, be assured that God cares about what you're going through, and He will bring you out on the other side, to your own "spacious place" of peace and safety, because He delights in you too.

Lord, I believe Your promise that You will never
abandon me [Deuteronomy 31:6]. Please lead
me through to a better tomorrow.

The Truth about Growth

God arms me with strength, and he makes my way perfect.
He makes me as surefooted as a deer, enabling me to stand on
mountain heights. He trains my hands for battle; he strengthens
my arm to draw a bronze bow. You have given me your shield of
victory. Your right hand supports me; your help has made me great.

PSALM 18:32–35 NLT

One frustrating truth of life and faith is that real, lasting growth happens as a result of hard times. The more difficult things you face, the more you can learn about yourself and God. The Bible tells us in James 1:2–4 (MSG):

> *Consider it a sheer gift, friends, when tests and challenges come at*
> *you from all sides. You know that under pressure, your faith-life is*
> *forced into the open and shows its true colors. So don't try to get out*
> *of anything prematurely. Let it do its work so you become mature*
> *and well-developed, not deficient in any way.*

The truth is that God doesn't promise to eliminate every challenge. If He kept you away from every hard thing, you wouldn't grow. Instead, He will give you strength to make it through, just like He did for David. The Holy Spirit is inside you, teaching and strengthening you to be more like Him.

Father, when I see that Your path is up and over the mountain,
please give me the strength to climb to new heights with You.

Genesis 46:1–47:26 / Matthew 13:24–43 / Psalm 19

Proclaim God's Glory

The heavens proclaim the glory of God. The skies display his craftsmanship. Day after day they continue to speak; night after night they make him known. They speak without a sound or word; their voice is never heard. Yet their message has gone throughout the earth, and their words to all the world.

PSALM 19:1–4 NLT

What's your favorite sky view? Whether it's sunrise on a clear morning, puffy clouds set against an azure sky, gorgeous hues painted across the sunset, or a million points of light circling a harvest moon, God reveals Himself in creation every moment of every day. Look up and you can see His power, His love, His infiniteness, and His care. His design for the heavens and earth clearly points to a creative God who values beauty, order, intricacy, and wonder.

Yes, there's much that nature can reveal about God, but as His witnesses, we are called to build on nature's message to tell others *more* about who He is—His love, mercy, grace, forgiveness, and salvation. How can you do this? One way is to follow the teaching of 1 Peter 3:15–16 (NLT) that says "If someone asks about your hope as a believer, always be ready to explain it. But do this in a gentle and respectful way." What can you do today to proclaim the hope you have and the glory of God in your life?

Lord, today I'm joining Your creation to share You with the world!

Genesis 47:27–49:28 / Matthew 13:44–58 / Psalm 20

Joseph's Perseverance

Joseph is a fruitful plant that grows beside a spring,
its fruitful branches reaching over the wall. The archers fiercely
attacked him, shot at him, and pressed hard against him. But
his bow remained taut and strong, his arms firm and agile.
They were made so by the strong hands of God—by the Mighty
One of Jacob, by the Shepherd of the Rock of Israel.

GENESIS 49:22–24 VOICE

Near the end of Jacob's life, he bestowed a blessing on each of his twelve sons. When he got to Joseph, Jacob highlighted the difficult circumstances that Joseph had endured throughout his life. He was abused and harassed by not only his brothers but by people in Egypt during his enslavement. Yet Joseph remained faithful to God, and his perseverance led to growth and strength that resulted in victory for himself, for the Israelites, and ultimately for God.

Several mighty rulers descended from Joseph's line. Joshua—the man who led the Hebrews into the promised land—as well as judges Deborah, Gideon, and Jephthah came from the man Jacob described as "a prince among his brothers" (Genesis 49:26 NLT).

God is looking for faithful followers who are willing to persevere through challenges. When you face difficult times, remember what God did for Joseph. God can and will use any situation for your good and His glory—supplying blessings for generations to come!

God, make me adaptable like Joseph. Give me the strength
to persevere no matter what. Use me for Your glory!

Genesis 49:29–Exodus 1:22 / Matthew 14 / Psalm 21

Distractions All Around

*"Yes, come," Jesus said. So Peter went over the side of the boat and
walked on the water toward Jesus. But when he saw the strong
wind and the waves, he was terrified and began to sink. "Save me,
Lord!" he shouted. Jesus immediately reached out and grabbed him.
"You have so little faith," Jesus said. "Why did you doubt me?"*

MATTHEW 14:29–31 NLT

Perhaps Peter thought the hardest part of faith was stepping out of
the boat, onto the water toward Jesus. But that was the easy part. It
was the distractions of the storm around him that caused Peter to
doubt Jesus' power.

Maybe your faith is strong enough for you to step out of the
boat. You know that everything is possible because you believe (Mark
9:23). But then something doesn't go the way you planned. Naysayers
get in your head. Your emotions dictate your doubt, and instead of
focusing on Jesus, life's distractions turn your thoughts negative—and
you begin to sink.

But there's hope. Follow Peter's example and cry out for help in
prayer. Jesus won't hesitate in reaching out and grabbing you, just like
He did for Peter. Ask Him for His perspective on the wind and the
waves—the doubt you're feeling and the emotions you're experiencing.
Fix your eyes on Jesus, and He will sustain Your faith and feet on
the water.

*Jesus, help me to fix my eyes and thoughts on You no
matter what's going on around me and inside me.*

Exodus 2–3 / Matthew 15:1–28 / Psalm 22:1–21

Time to Act

*Years passed, and the king of Egypt died. But the
Israelites continued to groan under their burden of
slavery. They cried out for help, and their cry rose up to
God. God heard their groaning. . . . He looked down on
the people of Israel and knew it was time to act.*

EXODUS 2:23–25 NLT

God told Jacob not to be afraid to move his large family to Egypt,
that He would make them into a "great nation," be with them there,
and one day take them home to Canaan again (Genesis 46:3–4). But
after Jacob and his twelve sons died, that plan seemed to go sideways.
The Israelites—growing in numbers in every generation—were forced
into slavery (Exodus 1:11–14) that lasted nearly four hundred years.

Had God forgotten His promise to Jacob? No. Did God care
about the suffering of His people? Yes. But as we see time and time
again in scripture, God's timeline is often different than our own.

God's rescue doesn't always come the moment you say "amen."
Seasons of waiting allow you to practice persistent prayer—prayers
that may come out like the "groaning" of the enslaved Hebrews. God
hears your cry, and He is with you and always working. He will not
waver in His perfect plan. Be encouraged that He knows when it is
time to act.

*Lord, please be near to me as I wait for change.
I trust You are working even when I can't see it.*

Exodus 4:1–5:21 / Matthew 15:29–16:12 / Psalm 22:22–31

He'll Do It Again

*[Jesus] called his disciples and said, "I hurt for these people.
For three days now they've been with me, and now they have
nothing to eat. I can't send them away without a meal—they'd
probably collapse on the road." His disciples said, "But where in
this deserted place are you going to dig up enough food for a meal?"*
MATTHEW 15:32–33 MSG

In the previous chapter in Matthew, Jesus fed more than five thousand people with five loaves of bread and two fish. After such a miracle, it might be surprising that the disciples have no clue how Jesus could feed this crowd of four thousand with seven loaves and a few small fish. It's like the story in Matthew 14:13–21 never happened.

Just like the disciples, we often forget that the same God who provided for us yesterday will do it again today. Jesus tells us in Matthew 6 that the Lord feeds the birds and beautifully dresses the wildflowers. And because God loves us even more than birds and flowers, we can be confident He will provide for our needs as well (vv. 26–29).

If you're worried about a need you currently have, take an inventory of times God has met your needs in the past. God may work the same way again, or He may provide in a completely different, unexpected way—but rest assured that He *will* provide.

Lord, thank You for being my provider in every way.

Exodus 5:22–7:24 / Matthew 16:13–28 / Psalm 23

What Gives, God?

Moses went back to GOD and said, "My Master, why are you treating this people so badly? And why did you ever send me? From the moment I came to Pharaoh to speak in your name, things have only gotten worse for this people. And rescue? Does this look like rescue to you?"

EXODUS 5:22–23 MSG

Moses' prayer in Exodus 5 reveals his perfectly logical frustration. After all, Moses never wanted to be the one to lead God's people out of slavery in Egypt. When God commissioned him from the burning bush, Moses made every excuse he could think of to get out of it (Exodus 3–4:17). Now, after he'd followed God's instructions, the Hebrews were suffering even more.

Although Moses resisted God's call, he trusted in the great I AM who sent him to Egypt. So now that things seemed to be going wrong, he turned to God and asked, "What gives?"

What can you learn from Moses' prayer? God can handle your questions, frustrations, fear, and doubts. Don't be afraid to pray honestly and frankly. God won't get defensive or panic when things aren't going the way *you* expect them to. He will listen and provide the strength you need. After Moses' honest prayer, God says that the force of His strong hand will soon come down on Pharaoh, reassuring Moses that He remains in control of the situation. Just as He remains in control of yours.

God, thank You for listening to my prayers—
even my prayers of frustration!

Exodus 7:25–9:35 / Matthew 17:1–9 / Psalm 24

The Persistent Ask

"Go back to Pharaoh," the LORD commanded Moses.
"Tell him, 'This is what the LORD, the God of the Hebrews,
says: Let my people go, so they can worship me.'"
EXODUS 9:1 NLT

Have you ever had to make a request more than once? Maybe it's a chore you've asked your husband to do. . .or a reminder to your kids to take the clean laundry to their rooms. . .or a carefully worded email sent to an absentminded coworker to get her to complete a task. Asking once or twice may not send you over the edge, but by the fifth time? Look out.

This was the fifth time God sent Moses to Pharaoh with the demand "Let my people go." We can only imagine how tired and discouraged Moses must've been by this point, but regardless, he continued to obey God.

Do you get tired and discouraged when it comes to doing good? To persistently pray? To continuing to believe that God actually is working? The Bible tells us that God rewards perseverance and persistence. So when you're making a request or facing a difficult situation for the fifth time or the fiftieth time, don't give up doing the right thing. As Moses discovered and Paul wrote to the Galatian church, "At just the right time we will reap a harvest of blessing if we don't give up" (Galatians 6:9 NLT).

> *Lord, please give me the strength to obey You*
> *again and again. . .just like Moses did.*

Exodus 10–11 / Matthew 17:10–27 / Psalm 25

Trustworthy Guidance

*Show me the right path, O LORD; point out the road for me
to follow. Lead me by your truth and teach me, for you are the
God who saves me. All day long I put my hope in you.*

PSALM 25:4–5 NLT

Road atlases, once a mainstay in every glove compartment, are now
a relic because of the map app that comes installed on nearly every
smartphone. Simply type in a business name or address and through
the magic of the internet and GPS satellites, you'll get step-by-step
directions, a highlighted path from start to finish, and even audible
instructions of where and when to turn.

Here in Psalm 25, David is earnestly seeking God's direction
in his life. "Show me the right path," he humbly asks, "point out the
road for me to follow." David doesn't just want God to point him in
a general direction. He's asking for specific, turn-by-turn guidance.
"Lead me by your truth and teach me"—David knew God's way was
the best way, and he fully submitted to His map.

God knows the way for your life too. He *created* the way, He holds
the keys to life and eternity, He is the victor over death and evil. Put
your hope in God, who is going before you, faithful in blazing the
trail in any terrain, leading you with unfailing love and faithfulness
(Psalm 25:10).

*I will follow You, Lord, because You know
the way. I trust You with all my heart.*

Childlike

The disciples came to Jesus and asked, "Who is greatest in the Kingdom of Heaven?" Jesus called a little child to him and put the child among them. Then he said, "I tell you the truth, unless you turn from your sins and become like little children, you will never get into the Kingdom of Heaven. So anyone who becomes as humble as this little child is the greatest in the Kingdom of Heaven."

MATTHEW 18:1–4 NLT

Nearly every child daydreams about what she'll become when she grows up. Learning, growth, new experiences—these are all part of maturing from infancy to adulthood. But we live in an imperfect, fallen world and along with all the beautiful, life-giving things that come with growing up often come disappointments that can lead to cynicism, distrust, and pride.

When Jesus' disciples asked Him who would be the greatest in His kingdom, Jesus explained that the qualities He valued most were like those of children, who tend to be trusting, sincere, humble, loving, and forgiving.

If you're feeling the weight of adulthood today, if the concerns of life have left you worried and jaded, pray and ask God to restore your outlook and faith to what they once were. Humbly admit that you don't know everything, and be willing to learn from Jesus. His unending love for you will rejuvenate and renew your sense of childlike wonder and sincerity.

Jesus, soften my heart and make me more open, sincere, trusting, loving, and forgiving.

Exodus 13–14 / Matthew 18:21–35 / Psalm 27

Confident Faith

I am confident I will see the LORD's goodness while I am
here in the land of the living. Wait patiently for the LORD.
Be brave and courageous. Yes, wait patiently for the LORD.
PSALM 27:13-14 NLT

When you're running from a perceived challenge or danger, be assured that the God who brought you where you are is still with you. He's also going *ahead* of you to lead the way every moment of the day and night (Exodus 13:20–22).

Because your God is always with you, you are forever safe from danger and confusion. Even if you feel there's no way out of a particular situation or challenge, you can rest assured He will make a way where there seems to be none (Exodus 14).

At the beginning of Psalm 27, its author, David, bases his faith on the fact that God is his light amid the darkness, his rescue in times of trouble. So he need not fear (v. 1). God surrounds him with a fortress of protection. Thus, nothing should cause him alarm (v. 1). By the last two verses, the psalmist's confidence in God had grown to such an extent that he *knew* he would experience God's goodness.

You can live with this same confidence. Today, remind your soul to be brave and courageous. Know that you will see God's goodness! He cannot help but deliver!

Lord, You are my rock, confidence, and hope, my forever
God and guide! On Your presence I build my faith and life.

God the Song

The Eternal is my strength and my song.
EXODUS 15:2 VOICE

It's hard to sing a song well if you don't know the tune or are unfamiliar with the lyrics; nor can you adequately experience the emotion, the truth of the song.

It's the same thing with faith. If you don't understand who God is or what His people had to sing about, you'll only have a surface faith. You may be able to go through the motions of a believer or have memorized a few God-inspired words, but your heart and soul aren't in Him or them.

To understand who God is and what He has done for you and other believers, you need to sink your heart into each line and verse of the Bible. To allow His truth to lead you into His presence. Then one day you too will be able to join in the chorus of all those followers of faith who have gone before you. You will find yourself singing, on key: "The Eternal is the source of my strength and the shield that guards me. When I learn to rest and truly trust Him, He sends His help. This is why my heart is singing! I open my mouth to praise Him, and thankfulness rises as song" (Psalm 28:7 VOICE).

May I know You, Lord, as my Lord and Shepherd
[Psalm 28:9], my strength and song.

On Eagles' Wings

*"You have seen what I did to the Egyptians. You know how
I carried you on eagles' wings and brought you to myself."*
EXODUS 19:4 NLT

You haven't seen with your own eyes what God did to Pharaoh and the Egyptians on behalf of His people. You didn't suffer "all the hardships they had experienced along the way and how the LORD had rescued his people from all their troubles" (Exodus 18:8 NLT). But you have access to the account. You can read about it in the Bible. In that way you can "see" all that God did; you can in some way experience all His people went through.

You too have had your own suffering in life. You have seen how God worked things out for your good in many instances. In that way, you can know how God, in His miraculous way, carried you on eagles' wings and brought you to Himself.

Find some time each day to remember what God has done in the history of humankind and in your own personal history. Remember how He has continually rescued you from all your troubles. Then close your eyes and allow God to carry you on eagles' wings and bring you to Himself. Linger there. In love. In prayer. In peace.

*Thank You, Lord, for continually rescuing me from my troubles.
I pray You would now carry me away on eagles' wings so that
I can experience Your presence and linger in Your peace.*

Exodus 20–21 / Matthew 20:1–19 / Psalm 30

Turning Back

*When things were quiet and life was easy, I said
in arrogance, "Nothing can shake me." By Your grace,
Eternal, I thought I was as strong as a mountain;
but when You left my side and hid away, I crumbled in fear.*

PSALM 30:6–7 VOICE

There may be times in our lives when things are going well. We think we can stand in our own power. We close God's Word and stop seeking Him. We begin to rely on ourselves, taking our strength from other people or things. Our prayers become stilted, or we stop praying altogether.

In not relying on God, we find ourselves turning away from Him. We stop rooting ourselves in Him. Yet He still is with us. Lingering in the shadows. Waiting for us to come back to Him, to remember He alone is the source of all we need, want, and desire, that He alone gives us the strength, courage, and confidence to carry on.

If you are in that place, if you have turned away from God, turn back. Humble yourself before Him. And you will find Him. Focusing on Him, depending on Him alone, you will become unshakable.

Lord, forgive me for the times that I turn away from You and begin relying on my own strength. For it is You alone who gives me the power to stand, to live, to grow, to become the woman You created me to be.

Exodus 22–23 / Matthew 20:20–34 / Psalm 31:1–8

Going Before You

Look! I am going to send a heavenly messenger before you
to protect you during your journey and lead you safely to the
place I have prepared for you. Pay attention to all he shows
you. . . . Jesus had compassion on them and touched their eyes.
Immediately they could see, and so they followed Him.

EXODUS 23:20–21; MATTHEW 20:34 VOICE

God's angel goes before you. He's there to not only scope out what
lies ahead but to protect you as you go, to safely lead you to the place
God has already prepared for you. Your job is to keep your eyes open.
To pay attention.

Are your eyes open? Have you told Jesus you want to see with
the eyes of faith?

In Matthew 20, two blind men were sitting on the roadside. They
heard the rumble of the crowd coming down the street, Jesus leading the way. They cried out to Him, asking for His mercy. So Jesus
took them aside. He asked what they wanted. They said, "Lord, we
want to see" (Matthew 20:33 VOICE). Jesus, feeling their pain, seeing
their desire, touched their eyes. In that moment their eyes opened.
Their sight regained, they followed Him.

Know that God goes before you. That you're safe on your journey
with Him. That He'll lead you to the place He's prepared. That He'll
increase your vision, aligning it with His. Ask Him to show you all.

Lord, as You go, I shall follow, eyes open wide. Lead on.

Exodus 24–25 / Matthew 21:1–27 / Psalm 31:9–18

In the Center

*Jesus was in the center of the procession, and the people
all around him were shouting, "Praise God for the Son
of David! Blessings on the one who comes in the name
of the LORD! Praise God in highest heaven!"*

MATTHEW 21:9 NLT

When Jesus is in the center of your life, you cannot help but be affected.
The light of His presence makes everything clear. It illuminates the
past, present, and future. It shows you the pathway, the route you're
to take, the road you're to walk.

Some may tremble with excitement at Jesus' presence. Others
may be agitated, shaken. And more than a few may turn away in fear
or anger. Which are you?

Hopefully, you'll be the one in the crowd that's not just caught
up in the *moment* but immersed in the *movement*—the movement of
love for God, self, and others. Because when you walk with Jesus, a
life centered in love is the only true path forward. Love alone, Jesus
alone, becomes your motivating factor.

Today, walk in the presence of the Lord, keeping Him at the center
of your life. Ask Him to illuminate your life. Tell Him you love Him
above everyone and everything. Then take in all the love He has for
you. Use it to bless the lives of others, loving them as He loves you.

Lord, my love and light, be my center.

God's Plan

*"You are to set up the tabernacle according to the plan
for it that you have been shown on the mountain."*
EXODUS 26:30 HCSB

God always has a plan. It's not a secret. It's in His Word. There He reveals the road you're to walk, the way you're to live your life.

Sometimes God gets into the nitty gritty details of His plan, as when telling Moses how to build the tabernacle. He tells him not only how many curtains to make but what their length and width should be, how many loops each should contain, even how to sew them up together (Exodus 26).

God has done the same thing with His church. He's devised a pattern His people are to follow. First, He sent John the Baptist "to show you the straight path, the path to righteousness" (Matthew 21:32 VOICE). John was followed by Jesus—the pattern we're to follow. The apostle Peter writes, "This is the kind of life you've been invited into, the kind of life Christ lived. He suffered everything that came his way so you would know that it could be done, and also know how to do it, step-by-step" (1 Peter 2:21 MSG).

Step by step, follow Christ. Dig deep into the Word. Allow Him to become the pattern you follow. Live your life according to His specific plan for you. And all God's blessings will find you.

*Lord, help me to pattern my life after Jesus.
Help me walk according to Your good plan.*

Love

" 'Love the LORD your God with all your heart, all your soul, and all your mind.' This is the first and greatest commandment. A second is equally important: 'Love your neighbor as yourself.' "

MATTHEW 22:37–39 NLT

Love springs from God (1 John 4:7). In fact, it's who God is (1 John 4:8).

It's God's love that sent Jesus to rescue you. It's God's love that pulls you to Him. It's God's love that made the Word available to you so you could find your way.

All that's required of you is to love God entirely with everything you are—your heart, soul, and mind. Just as important is loving yourself. For you must do that before you can love your neighbor.

Having trouble loving? Soak yourself in God. Dig deep into His Word so that you can see how much He has done, is doing, and will continue to do to rescue you, to keep you safe, to provide for you, to help you see who you were always meant to be.

And as night falls at the end of each day, rest easy, knowing that you, "the one who trusts in the Eternal is wrapped tightly in His gracious love" (Psalm 32:10 VOICE).

I breathe easy, Lord, knowing You are the personification and source of love. Pour Your love into me so I can learn to live and love Your way and find the peace that doing so brings.

Exodus 29 / Matthew 23:1–36 / Psalm 33:1–12

Meet and Speak

"These burnt offerings are to be made each day from generation to generation. Offer them in the LORD's presence at the Tabernacle entrance; there I will meet with you and speak with you. . . . I will live among the people of Israel and be their God."

EXODUS 29:42, 45 NLT

God is not some far-off entity, one that cannot be reached or approached. He is a living supernatural force in everything around you—including you—and He is closer than your next breath. He patiently waits for you to come to Him, to bear your soul, pour out your heart, or just chat.

The Lord wants to be active in your life, included in your day-to-day activities, not just on the occasional Sunday or religious holiday. He desires to speak with you, walk with you, talk with you, spend time with you.

You need not travel to any special place to meet with the God of all creation. All you need to do is open His Word, spend time in prayer, and get to know Him in all His wonder, power, gentleness, and strength.

Today, meet with God. Tell Him what's on your mind. Then listen to Him speak into your heart and soul as you allow Him into your life.

Lord, may I make a conscious effort to not only meet and speak with You every day but to integrate You into my life.

The Wonder of His Wings

*"How often I have wanted to gather your children together
as a hen protects her chicks beneath her wings, but you
wouldn't let me. . . ." "You will hear of wars and threats
of wars, but don't panic. . . ." The LORD watches over those
who fear him, those who rely on his unfailing love.*

MATTHEW 23:37; 24:6; PSALM 33:18 NLT

Yes, the world's a dangerous place. But God doesn't want you to panic. He doesn't want you to worry or feel uneasy. But what He *does* want is for you to come to Him, to allow Him to gather you up so you can take shelter beneath His wings. He wants you to trust Him with your life, to understand He'll never stop loving you.

Jesus Himself tells you to trust God with everything. To not be alarmed when you hear about wars or the threats of wars, school shootings, financial failures, political upheaval, sexual assaults, murders, and disastrous weather events.

How do you build up trust in God so that you remain unshaken no matter what's happening? By rooting yourself in Jesus, the mother hen who spreads her wings so you can take refuge beneath her. By remembering that God watches over you and will never stop loving you.

Intentionally choose to trust in God, look to Jesus, and walk with the Spirit each day. And let God be God.

*Lord, I turn to You for love, protection,
and peace. Swoop me under Your wings.*

A Personal Invitation

*"I will personally go with you. . .and I will give
you rest—everything will be fine for you."*

EXODUS 33:14 NLT

Thinking you're walking this road of life all alone? Think again.

God goes with you. He's made it His personal mission to travel with you. He promises to give you the rest you need as you sleep at night and His peace as you awaken with the dawn. He wants you to be assured in your mind, heart, spirit, and soul that everything will be fine.

Yes, you may see some hard times. But God softens them with His presence. Yet how do you keep His presence in your mind and heart so you can live every moment knowing all is and will be well? Simply acknowledge He's beside you, loving you, protecting you, watching over you, standing between you and the darkness. Keep His eternal Word close, knowing that although heaven and earth may pass away, His "words will never disappear" (Matthew 24:35 NLT).

Friend, God is with you. All is and will be well. Keep His Word in your heart and mind, knowing He's your help, stay, support, comfort, peace, and strength. Understand that "those who look to him for help will be radiant with joy" (Psalm 34:5 NLT).

*Thank You, Lord, for personally walking with me.
I know that with You by my side, all is and will be well.*

Exodus 34:1–35:29 / Matthew 25:1–13 / Psalm 34:8–22

Worship Opens Doors

Open your mouth and taste, open your eyes and see—how good
GOD is. Blessed are you who run to him. Worship GOD if you
want the best; worship opens doors to all his goodness.
PSALM 34:8–9 MSG

There are so many advantages to worshiping God, to revering Him, respecting Him for who He is. Such worship, such reverence for God, sings the psalmist, "opens doors to all his goodness"!

When you look to God, recognizing Him and His power, His will and His way, His angel will surround you and deliver you. God will fill you with Himself, His presence naturally prompting you to guard your tongue and turn from sin.

When you open your mouth and taste, open your eyes and see how wonderful He is, God's goodness will sweep its way into your life. You'll sense Him not only watching over you but picking up on every moan and groan that rises from your mouth. You'll understand He is forever ready to rescue you. Even "if your heart is broken, you'll find GOD right there; if you're kicked in the gut, he'll help you catch your breath" (Psalm 34:18 MSG).

Today, sing your praises to God. Worship Him morning, noon, and night. Feel His presence, power, protection, and peace surround you.

I praise Your name, Lord! I praise Your love, Word,
and presence helping me along this road of life. To You alone,
I run. As I worship You, open doors to Your goodness.

Exodus 35:30–37:29 / Matthew 25:14–30 / Psalm 35:1–8

Crafting Joy

*"Let all who are gifted with wisdom and skill come and make
these things the Eternal One has instructed." . . . "Well done,
good and faithful slave! You were faithful over a few things;
I will put you in charge of many things. Share your master's joy!"*

EXODUS 35:10 VOICE; MATTHEW 25:23 HCSB

God invites you to use the talents, skills, and wisdom with which
He has blessed you to make things. To answer the call of the inner
craftswoman.

Because the Lord has made you in His image, you, like Him,
have a creative side. You can brighten the world by using your unique
gift to spread God's goodness and to help others. You can use your
talents in a way that would bring praise and glory to Him. When you
do, He will not only put you in charge of something even bigger but
ask you to share His joy!

If you aren't sure where your talents lie, ask God for direction. Ask
Him to help you find your God-given gift and how He would have
you use it. The chances are that whatever task gives you joy—whether
it be writing, construction, keeping house, drawing, cooking, helping,
teaching, raising children, sewing, painting, crocheting, knitting,
nursing, or running a company—is where your gift lies. So use it—and
bring yourself, Him, and the world joy!

Lord, show me what gift I may use to bring us both joy!

Exodus 38–39 / Matthew 25:31–46 / Psalm 35:9–17

Blessed in Love

*"Then the King will say to those on his right, 'Come,
you who are blessed by my Father, inherit the Kingdom
prepared for you from the creation of the world.'"*

Matthew 25:34 NLT

God provided you a place in His kingdom. Through His death, Jesus purchased it for you. And the Spirit has prepared it. Wondering how to get there? Simply ground yourself in Jesus. Then use the blessings He's given you to bless others, who will, in turn, bless Him!

Jesus promises to richly reward you for feeding those who hunger, slaking the thirst of those who are parched, welcoming the stranger into your home, clothing the naked, nursing the sick, and visiting those imprisoned. Because when you love others by performing such tasks, it's as if you are doing it for Jesus.

There are so many needs to be tended to, gaps to be filled, people to be cared for. Those who actively seek to tend the needs, fill the gaps, and care for others will not only be personally rewarded but eternally rewarded by God.

Who can you bless today? Whose need can you satisfy? Who needs your love?

*Thank You, Lord, for the privilege of serving You and
others with the love and blessings You pour upon
me. What a rich reward—for Thee and me!*

Exodus 40 / Matthew 26:1–35 / Psalm 35:18–28

Trusting God to Lead

*Whenever the Cloud lifted from The Dwelling, the People of
Israel set out on their travels, but if the Cloud did not lift,
they wouldn't set out until it did lift. The Cloud of GOD was
over The Dwelling during the day and the fire was in it at
night, visible to all the Israelites in all their travels.*

EXODUS 40:36–38 MSG

To develop a strong and resilient faith, it's important to practice
trusting God and His goodness, especially when life is hard and you
don't know what He's doing. That's what the Israelites had to do when
they wandered in the wilderness. They followed God wherever He
led, stopped when He stopped, rested when He rested, and rose when
He rose. What comfort His constant presence must have supplied.

You too have that presence. God and His light reside within you.
He prompts you as to which way He'd have you go. There may be
times when you don't understand what He's doing or why or what
He's waiting for, moments when you're filled with questions. So ask.
And listen for God's reply. Above all, trust Him to lead you in the way
He's already planned you're to go. And as you follow, you'll become
the woman He created you to be.

*Lead me on, Lord. Prompt me to stop when
You stop, to go when You go, to rest when You rest,
to trust You with all I am and hope to be.*

Leviticus 1–3 / Matthew 26:36–68 / Psalm 36:1–6

At a Distance

*The people who had arrested Jesus led him to the home of Caiaphas,
the high priest, where the teachers of religious law and the elders
had gathered. Meanwhile, Peter followed him at a distance
and came to the high priest's courtyard. He went in and sat
with the guards and waited to see how it would all end.*

MATTHEW 26:57–58 NLT

When we begin to distance ourselves from Jesus, whether out of fear
or anxiety, we and others can see we are no longer trusting God, no
longer believing Jesus can do all He said He can do. We find ourselves
keeping company with unbelievers, those gearing up to attack or mock
Jesus rather than become one of His disciples.

Peter was perhaps more courageous than the other disciples who
dispersed in the first panic during Jesus' arrest. Yet he is not courageous
enough to admit to anyone that he was a follower of Jesus and ends
up lying to those who questioned him.

Today, consider where in your life you may have distanced yourself
from the Lord. Then ask God for the courage to draw close once more.

*Forgive me, Lord, when I may have distanced myself from
You. Give me the courage to stand with You, through good
times and bad, no matter where I am or who's with me.*

Leviticus 4:1–5:13 / Matthew 26:69–27:26 / Psalm 36:7–12

Soul Awakened

Your strong love, O True God, is precious. All people run for shelter under the shadow of Your wings. In Your house, they eat and are full at Your table. They drink from the river of Your overflowing kindness. You have the fountain of life that quenches our thirst. Your light has opened our eyes and awakened our souls.

PSALM 36:7–9 VOICE

True riches can be found in God's love. When you feel alone, hurt, rejected, afraid, anxious, or blue, run for shelter in God's Word. Rest beneath His wings. Take into your deepest part His great affection for you, allowing it to lift you, inspire you, heal you, calm you, strengthen you, and shelter you.

There, in God's presence, you can be filled with all you need to leave the past behind and greet the light of the present moment. You will begin looking forward to tomorrow, no matter what it may bring. For God Himself, the creator of the world, re-creates you in His presence. He opens your eyes to a world of possibilities. You begin to see the world through His eyes, your soul envisioning Him within every snowflake, leaf, sunrise, and twilight.

Today, shelter in the Lord, allowing Him to melt His Spirit with yours and give you the peace He alone can bring.

I come to You, Lord, to shelter in the shadow of Your wings and the light of Your endless love. Awaken my soul to Your presence.

Leviticus 5:14–7:21 / Matthew 27:27–50 / Psalm 37:1–6

Great Expectations

*Believe in the Eternal, and do what is good—live in the land
He provides; roam, and rest in God's faithfulness. Take great joy
in the Eternal! His gifts are coming, and they are all your heart
desires! Commit your path to the Eternal; let Him direct you. Put
your confidence in Him, and He will follow through with you.*

PSALM 37:3–5 VOICE

Psalm 37:1–6 provides you with a way of looking at the world, a way of avoiding getting dragged down by news reports of terrorism, inflation, political discord, murders, pandemics, etc. It begins by telling you to not worry about those who do or act evil. For soon they will wither away like grass and plants in the summer sun.

Instead of focusing on what's wrong in the world, focus on God, believing in Him with all your heart, mind, and strength. Do what's good in His eyes. Take joy in Him and how He blesses you day after day after day.

Rather than living in dread of the world's evil, live with a sense of great expectation, knowing God's gifts are on the way. Be confident that He will fulfill your desires and help you go the way He would have you go. Believe in the God who loves you, staying strong and confident in His promises, knowing what He says He will do—and more!

*Lord, help me to keep my faith in and my eyes on You,
expecting good to come today and tomorrow.*

Leviticus 7:22–8:36 / Matthew 27:51–66 / Psalm 37:7–26

No-Fall Assurance

Be still in the presence of the LORD, and wait patiently for
him to act. . . . The LORD directs the steps of the godly. He
delights in every detail of their lives. Though they stumble,
they will never fall, for the LORD holds them by the hand.

PSALM 37:7, 23–24 NLT

Imagine witnessing Jesus being crucified, looking on at the man of God you had followed faithfully for the last few years, the one in whom you'd put your hope.

Matthew 27:55 (NLT) tells us, "Many women who had come from Galilee with Jesus to care for him were watching from a distance." Unlike the disciples, these women hadn't turned and run when Jesus was arrested and hung on the cross. Instead, they were still in His presence, waiting for Him to act.

When Jesus was declared dead, these faithful females continued to let His words and Father God lead them, direct their steps. They knew deep within their spirits, the ones Jesus had kindled with His light, that He would not let them fall but would continue to guide them. How He would do this was still a mystery, one that would be revealed in the coming days.

If you're going through a rough patch, keep watching for God to work. Be still in His presence, knowing He will act. He will not let you fall. That's His no-fall assurance.

In You, Lord, I live, pray, hope, and wait.

Leviticus 9–10 / Matthew 28 / Psalm 37:27–40

As He Said He Would

*The glory of the Lord [the Shekinah cloud] appeared. . .
[as promised]. . . . Do not be alarmed and frightened, for I know
that you are looking for Jesus, Who was crucified. He is not here;
He has risen, as He said [He would do]. . . . I am with you all
the days (perpetually, uniformly, and on every occasion).*
LEVITICUS 9:23; MATTHEW 28:5–6, 20 AMPC

God's glory appeared to Moses and God's people just as He said it
would. Jesus rose again just as He said He would. Look to these and
other biblical instances and know for certain that God keeps His word.
Allow that truth to get you through the bleakest and darkest of days.

Some of God's promises may seem like impossibilities. That's
because our finite minds cannot take in all God can do, all the ways
He can bring His promises to fruition. So as farfetched as it might
seem on those days when you cannot see the rainbow in the cloud,
when it looks like the end is indeed near, when you can neither catch
your breath nor garner energy, remember that God is on your side.
That "the Eternal saves His faithful; He lends His strength in hard
times" (Psalm 37:39 VOICE). He stands with you. You can stake your
eternal life on it.

*I stake my life, Lord, on You keeping Your
promises and will grow my life up from there.*

Leviticus 11–12 / Mark 1:1–28 / Psalm 38

Cared For

*After that the Spirit compelled Him to go into the wilderness,
and there in the desert He stayed for 40 days. He was tested by
Satan himself and surrounded by wild animals; but through these
trials, heavenly messengers cared for Him and ministered to Him.*

MARK 1:12–13 VOICE

We live in a dangerous wilderness. But we, like Jesus, need not fear
when we keep ourselves close to God, when we hide ourselves in the
refuge of His Word. For it is there we find the faith, strength, and
protection we need to keep us from temptation and trouble.

Along with finding refuge in God's Word, we have the power
of prayer to help us stay secure in the Lord. By just linking fingers,
bowing our heads, mumbling under our breath, or speaking silently
to God within our minds, we can plead to the source of all aid and
comfort, "Eternal One. . .my True God, don't be far from me. . . .
I need Your help now—not later. O Lord, be my Rescuer" (Psalm
38:21–22 VOICE).

God will respond. He will come to our aid. He will send angels
to care for us, bind our wounds, tame the wild animals surrounding
us, and minister to us.

God sees you as His child, His precious daughter. See Him as
the Father who can and will do anything and everything to keep you
safe in Him.

*Lord, stay close. Hear my prayer.
Make me strong. Keep me safe in You.*

A Quiet Place to Pray

*Early in the morning, Jesus got up, left the house while it was
still dark outside, and went to a deserted place to pray.*

MARK 1:35 VOICE

After spending the previous day preaching and the evening working
miracles, Jesus went off by Himself. He left all behind—His disciples
as well as the multitudes—and went to a lonely, deserted place to
spend quiet time with His Father.

We, who are instructed to do as Jesus did and walk as He walked
(1 John 2:6), are to also go off by ourselves and find quiet places to
pray. To leave our work and friends behind and seek God's strength,
guidance, energy, power, and path. Yet how often do we make a
point to do so? How often do we turn away from our cell phones,
laptops, televisions to seek God's face? To hear His voice? To simply
spend time in His presence, soaking up His light and love?

If you truly want to hear God's voice and spend time in His
presence, if you truly want to develop a resilient faith, find a way
to escape from the hubbub of life and into the peace of the Spirit.
Whether that means walking to the park, shutting your bedroom
door, or stepping into church, find a way to pray, to listen, to seek, to
meet up with God and become rooted in Him.

*"Hear my prayer, O Lord, and give
ear to my cry" [Psalm 39:12 AMPC].*

Leviticus 14 / Mark 1:40–2:12 / Psalm 40:1–8

Strong and Steady

He reached down and drew me from the deep, dark hole
where I was stranded, mired in the muck and clay. With a
gentle hand, He pulled me out to set me down safely on a
warm rock; He held me until I was steady enough to continue
the journey again. As if that were not enough, because of Him
my mind is clearing up. Now I have a new song to sing.

PSALM 40:2–3 VOICE

When you feel stuck, as if you are stranded all alone in a dark place, go to God. No matter how far you may have sunk, He can draw you out of the darkness and back into His light.

Knowing God will treat you gently, pull you out of the cold, clingy mud and on to a warm rock, a place of comfort and safety, can give you the hope you need in any difficulty. For in God, in His presence, in His love, you are protected. There you can linger until you are strong and steady enough to start again, to move forward, to find your footing, to take first one step, then another, and another, walking where He would have you go.

Need a clear head? Need some light and love? Need to find a place of comfort and safety? Go to God. Listen to His voice. Then sing His praises as you move on down the road.

Thank You, Lord, for always being there
to help me, hold me, and give me hope.

Leviticus 15 / Mark 2:13–3:35 / Psalm 40:9–17

Constant Readiness

*He told His disciples to have a little boat in [constant] readiness
for Him because of the crowd, lest they press hard upon Him
and crush Him. For He had healed so many that all who
had distressing bodily diseases kept falling upon Him and
pressing upon Him in order that they might touch Him.*

MARK 3:9–10 AMPC

You may not have crowds of people coming to you for healing. But you probably have days where you feel as if everyone wants something from you. And you have nothing left to give.

That's why you need to make sure you "have a little boat in [constant] readiness" standing by 24/7. Its name? Jesus.

When life is crowding in on you, when your energy is sapped, when you have trouble thinking clearly, when you are doing so much for others that you feel as if you have lost yourself, step into your Jesus boat. Allow Him to take you away, to guide you to the still water, to restore and refresh you, to give you the time to take a deep breath, to regroup and recharge.

Keeping Jesus, your ark, your place of safety and replenishment, your strength and peace, continually on standby will help you get through the hardest and busiest of days.

*Thank You, Jesus, for being my place of
rest and refreshment. Let's sail away!*

Good Ground

*And those sown on the good (well-adapted) soil are the ones
who hear the Word and receive and accept and welcome it and
bear fruit—some thirty times as much as was sown, some sixty
times as much, and some [even] a hundred times as much.*

MARK 4:20 AMPC

Jesus tells the people a parable about a farmer sowing seeds (the Word). Some fell by the wayside along a path and so couldn't take root within the people. Some fell on the stones. This time the Word did take root but not deeply enough, so when trials came, their faith quickly withered. Some seed was sown among the thorns. The Word within these people was choked out by the cares, temptations, idols, and anxieties of the world.

Lastly is the group God would have you be in. The one where the Word is sown and takes deep root. These are people who hear the Word and embrace it by spending time seeking God's face, listening for His voice, and walking His way. Among these followers, the Word cannot be choked out. And because the Word is so deeply rooted, their life becomes amazingly fruitful.

Today and every day, look to the Lord and His Word. Ask Him to help your heart become good ground.

*Lord, help me stay deeply rooted in You and Your Word so that
no matter what comes, my life cannot help but bear fruit.*

Leviticus 18–19 / Mark 4:21–41 / Psalm 41:5–13

Be Still!

He arose and rebuked the wind and said to the sea,
Hush now! Be still (muzzled)! And the wind ceased
(sank to rest as if exhausted by its beating) and there
was [immediately] a great calm (a perfect peacefulness).
MARK 4:39 AMPC

You are a woman accompanied by Jesus. And chances are good that in your travels you will come across some terrifying storms—squalls that will rock your boat, making you, an experienced sailor, feel as if you are powerless against them. But have no fear! With you is the one who can still the storms within and without. At one cry from you, He will rise up and quiet the sea and wind. With a few words, He will invoke His will, bringing a great calm, a perfect peace to settle upon you.

It matters not how little or great your faith is. You can remain fearless because Jesus is in your boat. And He who has already saved your life will do so over and over again.

When troubles strike, when you feel powerless, when anxieties begin to build, turn to Jesus. Rush to His side. Know that He can still the fiercest wind and the tallest waves. Then allow His calm to settle upon you.

Amid the storm, I come to You, Lord, knowing that
in Your presence I will find the great calm I need,
the perfect peace I desire and require.

Leviticus 20 / Mark 5 / Psalm 42–43

Go in Peace

It's all right. Don't be afraid; just believe.
MARK 5:36 VOICE

One touch, made in faith, can turn a life around or completely restore it. Such was the case of the woman who had an issue of blood. She'd spent all her money on doctors who couldn't help her. And then she heard about Jesus. And she sought Him out.

Thinking to herself, "If I can just touch his robe, I will be healed" (Mark 5:28 NLT), the woman with an issue reached out and touched Jesus. "Immediately the bleeding stopped, and she could feel in her body that she had been healed of her terrible condition" (Mark 5:29 NLT).

Jesus felt His healing power going out from Him. He asked who'd touched Him and kept looking around to see who'd done it. Finally, the woman confessed. His response: "Daughter, your faith has made you well. Go in peace. Your suffering is over" (Mark 5:34 NLT).

No matter what your malady—anxiety, fear, trauma, illness, worry, pain, stress, depression—Jesus has the power to rid you of it. All you need is the faith and courage to reach out for Him, and He will give you peace.

"Despite all my emotions, I will believe and praise the One who saves me and is my life" [Psalm 42:5 VOICE].

Leviticus 21–22 / Mark 6:1–13 / Psalm 44

Keep It Simple

Jesus called the Twelve to him, and sent them out in pairs.
He gave them authority and power to deal with the evil
opposition. He sent them off with these instructions: "Don't
think you need a lot of extra equipment for this. You are the
equipment. No special appeals for funds. Keep it simple."

MARK 6:7–9 MSG

You don't need a whole lot of equipment to do what God has called you to do. As Jesus told His disciples, "*You* are the equipment (emphasis added)."

You need only keep your head and heart in God's Word. To follow Jesus and walk His way. Remember that God is surrounding you with His wall of protection. It is He who can and will empower you, strengthen you, equip you, and use you. And the Spirit within you will prompt you as to where you are to go, what you are to say, who you are to be.

In other words, keep your walk and life simple. Remember, God is really all you need. Allow Him to handle all your battles, to help you overcome all the obstacles in your way, to stand up to the challenges before you. Knowing you have the Holy Trinity within you, surrounding you, leading you, you can shrug off all that may hinder "and be on your way" (Mark 6:11 MSG).

Lord, help me to always remember to keep things simple—
that in this walk with You, I am the equipment.

Leviticus 23–24 / Mark 6:14–29 / Psalm 45:1–5

Check Out of the World. . . Check in with God

*"Work six days. The seventh day is a Sabbath, a day of
total and complete rest, a sacred assembly. Don't do any
work. Wherever you live, it is a Sabbath to GOD."*

LEVITICUS 23:3 MSG

Are you obedient in taking a real rest? The "complete rest" mentioned in the book of Leviticus isn't just a night that involves eight hours of blissful, uninterrupted shuteye. Nope. This kind of rest involves *so much more* than a good night's sleep.

Here in Leviticus 23, God commands we take a *different* kind of rest. A Sabbath rest is a solemn rest. A Sabbath rest involves meeting together and connecting with other believers. A Sabbath rest is wholly centered on faith while being fully disconnected from life's everyday interruptions.

What does *your* Sabbath look like? Do you begin the day with good intentions only to become distracted by your daily to-do list? Is it difficult to turn your outward focus inward and upward so you can fully rest in God and His Word? Do you make it a weekly habit to spend time with fellow Christ followers?

Whatever your Sabbath looks like, ask the Creator to guide and help you be obedient to Him in your day of rest. As you faithfully follow Him, your soul will be revived and refreshed.

*Father God, help me to check out of the world and
check in with You. I want You to have my full focus.*

Leviticus 25 / Mark 6:30–56 / Psalm 45:6–12

Fear-Free Resilience

*The boat was far out at sea. . . . [Jesus] could see his men struggling
with the oars, the wind having come up against them. At about
four o'clock in the morning, Jesus came toward them, walking on
the sea. . . . They thought it was a ghost and screamed, scared to
death. Jesus was quick to comfort them: "Courage! It's me. Don't be
afraid." As soon as he climbed into the boat, the wind died down.*

MARK 6:47–51 MSG

Imagine you're on a small boat in the middle of the sea at night. Your
only means of control are the oars in your hands. The wind is whipping,
waves are lapping over the side of the boat, and you're struggling to
keep afloat. You're holding on for dear life. And then you see the
silhouette of a person—a man—and he's walking on water toward
your boat! Your fear escalates to a whole new level. You're terrified!

Suddenly, you hear the voice of Jesus. "Courage! It's me. Don't
be afraid." He climbs into your boat, and immediately the turbulent
winds and seas grow calm. You're safe and secure.

Every time you face adversity, cling to Jesus—the calmer of storms.
He's got *everything* in His capable hands.

*Jesus, I give my fears and troubles to You. Instead of looking
down into the depths of life's difficulties, I will look up to You
. . .to the light! With You, Lord, I am resilient and fear-free.*

When Hope Falters

If you walk in My decrees and keep My commandments. . .
I will grant you plenty of rain. . .and. . .abundant crops. . . .
Your grain threshing will last until the time of the grape
harvest. . . . You will fill your bellies with food. . . . I will
see to it that you have peace in your land. You will be able
to go to bed at night without a worry on your mind.

Leviticus 26:3–6 voice

Every day our already-strange world seems to grow a little bit stranger, a little more volatile, a little more unsettling. And when we're inundated with troubles, turmoil, and terror everywhere we look (sometimes in our own backyards!), it's hard to keep hold of hope.

When hope seems lost, what's a woman of God to do? God *is* the hope of the world (Romans 15:13), isn't He? And so, all is not lost.

When you're feeling hopeless, remember that when you do life *with* God and *for* Him, then you have an all-access pass to His beautiful promises, including rain when you need it, abundant crops, a full belly, safety and security, peace, and a worry-free life. With Him in the lead, you can survive and thrive—even in a weird, wayward world.

God, it's comforting to know that when the world spirals out of control, I have the hope of Your promises. You are so good to me!

Leviticus 27 / Mark 8 / Psalm 46

Sure and Fearless

God is our shelter and our strength. When troubles seem near,
God is nearer, and He's ready to help. So why run and hide? . . .
When the earth spins out of control. . . When mountains crumble
and the waters run wild. . . Even in heavy winds. . .we are
sure and fearless. . . . You know the Eternal, the Commander
of heavenly armies, surrounds us and protects us.
PSALM 46:1–3, 11 VOICE

Some people try to run from their problems. Maybe you know someone like that—or perhaps that someone is you.

But if we're being honest, that whole problem-avoidance strategy doesn't work very well. In fact, running often makes things much worse. Then our troubles begin to compound, one on top of the other, until we're eventually surrounded with no escape in sight.

That's where the beauty of Psalm 46 comes in. God is our shelter and strength when life is hard. He's always near, always willing to help. So, there's never a need to run and hide—not even in the direst circumstances. If God can bail us out when the earth is spinning out of control, when the mountains crumble, when the winds and waters rage—and He can!—He can bail us out of anything. With Him, we are secure and fearless!

When troubles are near, remember "God is nearer." Run toward His sure shelter and protection.

Heavenly Father, when troubles come,
guide me into Your loving embrace.

Numbers 1–2 / Mark 9:1–13 / Psalm 47

Just One of Those Days

Come, everyone! Clap your hands! Shout to God with joyful praise!
For the LORD Most High is awesome. He is the great King of all
the earth. . . . He chose the Promised Land as our inheritance,
the proud possession of Jacob's descendants, whom he loves.

PSALM 47:1–2, 4 NLT

Certainly, you've experienced "just one of those days." Maybe it was today. Your car wouldn't start, and you were late for work. You spilled coffee and stained your favorite blouse. You missed an important appointment that you had scheduled months in advance.

"Those days" happen to all of us. And while it's easy to become discouraged, we have a choice: we can either allow temporary troubles to overwhelm our hearts and become discouraged, or we can choose to rest our souls in the King of kings and Lord of lords and become encouraged by His promises. The Lord Most High has good plans for you, even on your worst days. He has promised you a wonderful inheritance if you only stick with Him!

If your mood needs a boost today, take the wise advice from the psalmist to heart and "Clap your hands! Shout to God with joyful praise!" When you live with a grateful heart, fully focused on Your heavenly Creator, "those days" will be powerless to keep you down!

Thank You, Father, for Your good plans for me.
Help me to deal with my temporary troubles and
move on—with a lighter, more grateful heart.

Numbers 3 / Mark 9:14–50 / Psalm 48:1–8

Preservatives

"If your hand or your foot gets in God's way, chop it off. . . . You're
better off maimed or lame. . .than the proud owner of two hands
and two feet, godless in a furnace of eternal fire. And if your eye
distracts you from God, pull it out and throw it away. You're
better off one-eyed. . .than exercising your twenty-twenty vision
from inside the fire of hell. Everyone's going through a refining
fire sooner or later, but you'll be well-preserved, protected from
the eternal flames. Be preservatives yourselves. Preserve the peace."

MARK 9:43–50 MSG

When you preserve something, you keep it going—you keep it fresh
and alive or safe and protected from harm.

"Preserving" is what Jesus required of His followers in these
passages from the book of Mark. You too can be a preserver and
help grow and protect God's kingdom when you:

1. Look out for yourself. Be honest. Is anything distracting
   you from God? Is anything getting in the way of your
   relationship with Him? If so, get rid of it!
2. Look out for others. Welcome them into your circle. Lead
   by example.

When you're all-in for Christ and allow His Word to guide your
speech and actions, your godly influence will remain healthy and
strong—for life!

Father God, show me where I can do better with my
influence and how I can work to preserve Your kingdom.
Help me to always have a warm, welcoming spirit.

Love-in-Action

We pondered your love-in-action, God. . . . Your name,
God, evokes a train of Hallelujahs wherever it is spoken,
near and far; your arms are heaped with goodness-in-action.
Be glad. . . . Dance. . . . He does what he said he'd do!
PSALM 48:9–11 MSG

Have you ever thought about God's "love-in-action"? You've certainly read scriptures about His love for you. The Bible is overflowing with His *words* of love (John 3:16; 1 John 3:1; 1 John 4:10; Romans 5:8; 2 Thessalonians 2:16; Ephesians 1:3–11).

But what if the Bible were only words with no action to back them up? What if you could never see or experience God's love for yourself? God would seem quite impersonal and unknowable, wouldn't He?

Thankfully, we serve a very personal God. And we can always experience His love-in-action. If you've followed God for any length of time, you know "he does what he said he'd do!" You don't ever have to wonder, *What if He doesn't come through?*

God says He loves us, forgives us, listens (and answers) when we pray, is there for us through every high and low, and is preparing a home for us in heaven. . .and He 100 percent, without a doubt, will do *all* of it! Because He is the ultimate promise-keeper, His love-in-action will lead us to a remarkable, unshakable, resilient faith!

Promise-keeper, my faith is resilient because of You and
Your love-in-action. Whatever You say You'll do, You'll do!

Numbers 5:1–6:21 / Mark 10:35–52 / Psalm 49:1–9

Before the Miracle

Bartimaeus. . .was sitting by the roadside begging. . . .
He [shouted], "Jesus, Son of David, have mercy on me!" . . .
What do you want me to do for you?" Jesus asked him.
The blind man said, "Rabbi, I want to see." "Go," said Jesus,
"your faith has healed you." Immediately he received his sight.
MARK 10:46–47, 51–52 NIV

To survive, the blind Bartimaeus sat in the streets and begged for money. His life, in no uncertain terms, was difficult and riddled with mistrust and doubt. People were likely cruel to him. Yet, in a moment, everything changed.

That day must have begun like any other. Bartimaeus was sitting in the dusty street, hoping for a coin or two to be tossed his way. But then he hears Jesus is coming. And, without missing a beat, Bartimaeus begins shouting for Jesus, telling Him that he wants to see. Jesus' response? "Go. . .your faith has healed you." Immediately, Bartimaeus could see!

Bartimaeus had faith *before* he received his miracle. What about you? Are you in a season of waiting? For healing? For a relationship to be restored? For a financial crisis to be resolved? If your faith is wavering, ask God to help you believe even before you get your miracle!

Father, I am growing weary as I wait for my miracle.
Strengthen my faith. Help me to trust You no matter
how You choose to answer my request.

Numbers 6:22–7:47 / Mark 11 / Psalm 49:10–20

Only the Very Best

*GOD spoke to Moses: "Tell Aaron and his sons, This is how you
are to bless the People of Israel. . . . GOD bless you and keep you,
GOD smile on you and gift you, GOD look you full in the face
and make you prosper. In so doing, they will place my name on
the People of Israel—I will confirm it by blessing them."*

NUMBERS 6:22–27 MSG

Are there people in your life who *don't* want the best for you? Sadly,
people like this are everywhere. They themselves are miserable, and
it would delight their souls if you were miserable right along with
them. These people don't want to see you showered with heavenly
blessings. They'd rather watch you struggle and falter in your personal
life and your faith.

Fortunately, there is one who wants nothing but the very best
for you. He gifts you full access to His blessings. And He's the *only
one* who matters!

When others wish for your downfall, God will lift you up.
When others seek to hurt, He will heal.
When others lash out, He will comfort.
When others abandon, He will save.
When others disrespect, He will favor.
When others take, He will provide.
When others curse, He will bless.

If you haven't already, say *yes* to the heavenly Father's invitation
of salvation today and experience the resilient faith your soul craves!

Heavenly Father, my answer to You is always YES!

Numbers 7:48–8:4 / Mark 12:1–27 / Psalm 50:1–15

A "Thankfulness" Sacrifice

*"Make thankfulness your sacrifice to God, and keep the vows
you made to the Most High. Then call on me when you are in
trouble, and I will rescue you, and you will give me glory."*

PSALM 50:14–15 NLT

In Bible times, sacrifices of thanksgiving were made to honor God for
something He had done in a person's life. Healing. Saving. Providing.
Helping. Forgiving. These "thanks" offerings weren't given without
thought. They involved acknowledgment of God's work and sincere
gratitude for His undeserved goodness.

How are you in this area of your faith, friend? Are you consistent
to offer up praises of thanksgiving to almighty God? Or do you give
it very little thought? When God works in your life, how do you
typically respond? Do you respond at all?

Our relationship with the heavenly Father should be filled with
an ongoing, back-and-forth interaction. God gives, and we respond in
praise. God loves, and we give Him all the glory. God rescues, and we
honor Him. An ever-present attitude of gratitude. . .*that's* the proper
response to God's blessings in your life!

*God, You are so very good to me, and I am so thankful. When
my faith falters from time to time, transform my thoughts so I
am wholly focused on Your generosity and love. When I fix my
thoughts on good things, my faith will follow suit. My heart is
filled with gratitude, Lord, for all You do. . .for who You are.*

Numbers 8:5–9:23 / Mark 12:28–44 / Psalm 50:16–23

Sacrificial Giving

Jesus sat down opposite the treasury. . .and He watched. . . .
Many rich people threw in large sums of money, but a poor
widow came and put in only two small coins. . . . Jesus (calling His
disciples together): Truly this widow has given a greater gift than
any other contribution. All the others gave a little out of their great
abundance, but this poor woman has given God everything she has.

MARK 12:41–44 VOICE

One day, Jesus sat and watched the Temple tithers. The rich were tossing large sums of money into the treasury; but a widow tossed in only two coins. Honestly, her offering didn't make a difference—not financially speaking. Regardless, this widow's contribution got Jesus' attention. Why? Because she gave despite her obvious need. She didn't have a savings account or investment income. She had *only* two small coins—and she tossed *both* into the treasury. This poor widow, who had every reason to make an excuse for *not* giving, showed complete faith and trust in giving *all she had*.

Dear one, are you giving from your surplus? Or are you giving despite your need? Ask the heavenly Father for guidance as you learn to trust Him through your giving. Ask Him to help you see what you can't afford to keep for yourself!

Heavenly Father, help me trust You so completely that my giving
becomes a reflection of my immovable faith in You, my provider.

Dance in Delight

*I am fully aware of all I have done wrong, and my guilt is. . .
staring me in the face. . . . I have done what You say is wrong. . . .
But. . .You show me wisdom. Cleanse me. . .and I will be clean.
If You wash me, I will be whiter than snow. Help me hear joy and
happiness as my accompaniment, so my bones. . .will dance in delight.*
PSALM 51:3–4, 6–8 VOICE

Do you ever get stuck in your sin and guilt, your mind playing every
offense on repeat? When we're overwhelmed by guilt, it becomes
difficult to imagine God's forgiveness when we can't even forgive
ourselves. And so, we hole up and hide away, living in a perpetual
state of shame and regret. But the good news is we don't need to stay
there—not today, *not ever*!

When we know Jesus as Savior, two things are certain: (1) we'll
make mistakes sometimes (we'll never be perfect this side of heaven),
but (2) Jesus will always forgive our mistakes—the big and the small.
So, when you mess up, take a cue from the psalmist and confess it.
Ask God to give you wisdom and joy, to forgive you, to erase your
guilt. He can. He will!

*Father God, free me from my sin and shame. I want
to be full of Your joy so I can dance in delight!*

Numbers 12–13 / Mark 13:9–37 / Psalm 51:10–19

Now Is the Time

*"You will be handed over to the local councils. . . . You will
stand trial. . .because you are my followers. But this will be
your opportunity to tell them about me. For the Good News
must first be preached to all nations. . . . Just say what God tells
you. . . . Everyone will hate you because you are my followers.
But the one who endures to the end will be saved."*

MARK 13:9–11, 13 NLT

Jesus warned His disciples of what would happen in a fallen world—a
world that has turned its back on Him and closed its eyes and ears to
the truth of His Word. Christ followers will be mocked, mistreated,
maligned. Those who oppose Christianity will do everything in their
power to silence truth.

Jesus' warning sure hits close to home, doesn't it? Turn on the
evening news. . .scroll through social media. . . . Christians certainly
aren't being embraced by the world. Perhaps you've even been ridiculed
for your faith. And while it might be tempting to pack up and head
home—keeping Christ to yourself—*now is the time* to share Him
with anyone who will listen!

If you're feeling world-weary today, ask God to give you His
strength so you can persevere and be "one who endures." With Him
in the lead, *nothing* can silence the gospel of Jesus!

*Father God, I need Your almighty strength so I can keep going,
keep sharing, keep loving. Thank You for leading me!*

Numbers 14 / Mark 14:1–31 / Psalm 52

All the Difference

But I am like an olive tree flourishing in the house of God;
I trust in God's unfailing love for ever and ever. For what you
have done I will always praise you in the presence of your faithful
people. And I will hope in your name, for your name is good.

PSALM 52:8–9 NIV

Have you ever had a glimpse into the life of a person who doesn't know Jesus? If so, you've probably seen the telltale signs. Someone who doesn't have a relationship with Christ lacks peace and purpose, hope and security, love and contentment. This person has a gaping emptiness that nothing in the world can fill, and yet she keeps trying to fill it with stuff—only to grow even more dissatisfied and insecure. It's a vicious cycle of discontent.

Now contrast this with a Jesus-filled life—a life celebrated by the psalmist David, who compares himself to an olive tree, a tree known for its strength and resilience especially when faced with adverse weather conditions. The olive tree can survive things most other plants and trees cannot. The olive tree is nothing if not resilient.

When you trust Christ as Lord and leader of your life, friend, you'll be resilient too! You'll be strong, productive, hopeful, loved, forgiven, joyful, and more! A life with Christ makes all the difference!

Lord of my life, I thank You. For saving me. For giving me
the gift of eternal life. For loving me without condition.

"Tassel" Reminders

*The LORD said to Moses, "Speak to the Israelites and say. . .
'Throughout the generations to come you are to make tassels
on the corners of your garments, with a blue cord on each
tassel. You will have these tassels to look at and so you will
remember all the commands of the LORD, that you may
obey them. . . . Then you will remember. . .and will be
consecrated to your God. I am the LORD your God.'"*

NUMBERS 15:37–41 NIV

The Israelites had tassels sewn onto their clothes with blue cord.
Every time they looked at these tassels, they thought of God and
their obedience to His commands. Through their obedience, they
strengthened their relationship with the Lord. In return, the Lord
would fulfill His promises to His people.

Is there something that serves as a constant reminder of your
relationship with God? Perhaps a meaningful piece of art hanging
on the wall reminds you of your connection to the heavenly Father
. . .or a Bible passed down to you from a close family member or
friend draws you closer to God whenever you open its cover. . .or
maybe a special plant reminds you of the goodness of the Creator.
Whatever serves as a reminder of your special connection to God,
say a prayer of thanks for those things today.

*God, thank You for "tassel" reminders. I want to always
be surrounded by things that make me think of You.*

Overcomer

*God comes to rescue me; the Lord is my valiant supporter. . . .
God has pulled me out from every one of the troubles
that encompass me, and I have seen what it means
to stand over my enemies in triumph.*

PSALM 54:4, 7 VOICE

Overcomers are people who persevere despite life's circumstances. They believe who God says they are. They stick close to God (no matter what). They trust God with all they have, with all they are. They obey God's commands. They stand firm in their beliefs and lean into their faith when the going gets tough. They are generous in love and grace.

The psalmist David was an overcomer. Despite the odds being stacked against him time and time again, he never gave up on life or on his God. (You can read David's story in the books of 1 and 2 Samuel.) And, because of his ongoing walk with the heavenly Father, he knew without a doubt that God, his "valiant supporter," would come to his rescue in every single battle he faced.

Whatever challenge or heartache you're experiencing right now, lean into the one who supports, the one who rescues, the one who triumphs. And trust that your resilient heart will be strengthened and comforted.

> *Father God, thank You for coming to my
> rescue. Whenever I call, I know You'll answer.
> With You by my side, I am an overcomer!*

The Good Life

*GOD will help me. At dusk, dawn, and noon I sigh deep
sighs—he hears, he rescues. My life is well and whole,
secure in the middle of danger. . . . God hears it all.*

PSALM 55:16–19 MSG

What words would you use to describe your life? If life has been mostly easy for you, perhaps you'd choose words like blessed, happy, abundant, satisfying, and peaceful. If you've had a life of hardship or tragedy, words you might choose include chaotic, stressful, sad, difficult, and unpleasant. But did you know that even if your life isn't chock-full of sunshine, rainbows, and cuddly kittens, you could still have a life that is well and whole and secure? You could still have what others would describe as "the good life."

How is that possible?

It's possible because God, who made heaven and earth and you, is a good God. He has nothing but the very best in mind for you (Jeremiah 29:11). And no matter your circumstances, He will help, He will heal, He will rescue. When God is for you, nothing can triumph against you (Romans 8:31). That's the very best life there is!

*Thank You, God, for allowing me to live the good life.
When hard times come, I can hold on to Your hope
and joy through it all. I trust You will rescue me and
bring me through to the other side. . .victorious!*

"In God I Trust!"

When I am afraid, I put my trust in you. In God,
whose word I praise—in God I trust and am not
afraid. What can mere mortals do to me?

PSALM 56:3–4 NIV

Ask any number of women what they're afraid of, and their responses will differ wildly. Spiders. Snakes. Clowns. Heights. Crowds. Public speaking. Aging. Mice. Illness. Flying. The future. Truth is, most of our fears are quite small, though we feel them *quite large* within our souls.

When fear grips your heart and mind, how do you cope? Do you freeze up? Cower in the corner? Experience a full-blown panic attack? Or do you stand up and stare fear directly in its face because you are fully connected to the one who sees all, controls all, and promises to deliver you from all harm (Psalm 121:7–8)?

Today, make a mental note—or a list—of the things that strike terror in your heart. Then, one by one, give them to God. You can trust Him to deliver you, to fill your soul with courage and grit. When you can honestly say, "In God I trust and am not afraid," you will experience the delightful freedom of fearless living.

Lord, I am so grateful to be connected to You, my heavenly fear-crusher. I give You every single one of my fears—and today,
I boldly proclaim, "In God I trust and am not afraid!"

Numbers 21:1–22:20 / Luke 1:1–25 / Psalm 56:8–13

On Time. . .God's Time

*Zachariah said. . . , "Do you expect me to believe this? I'm an old
man and my wife is an old woman." But the angel said, "I am
Gabriel. . .sent especially to bring you this glad news. . . . Every
word I've spoken to you will come true on time—God's time." . . .
It wasn't long before [Zachariah's] wife, Elizabeth, conceived.*

LUKE 1:18–20, 24 MSG

Unbelievable! Nutso! Preposterous! While these weren't the words
Zachariah spoke in response to Gabriel, we can surmise he was
thinking them! When the angel came to deliver the message that
Zachariah and his wife would become parents, it was no surprise that
he reacted in disbelief. People in their golden years didn't have babies!
And Zachariah and Elizabeth were *well* into their golden years.

Yet, the angel assured him, saying, "Every word I've spoken to you
will come true on time—God's time." And, true to God's promise,
Zachariah and Elizabeth became first-time parents just as the angel
had said. (Read their full story in Luke 1.)

Is there a promise you're waiting on God to fulfill? Do you have
doubts? Are you wrestling with feelings of hopelessness and despair?
If so, remember Zachariah and Elizabeth. With God, *nothing* is
impossible (Luke 1:37). You only need to trust in His perfect timing!

*Promise-keeper, I trust You. Help me hold tight to that
trust and be patient as I wait on Your perfect timing.*

Numbers 22:21–23:30 / Luke 1:26–56 / Psalm 57

The Guardian of Your Life

May Your mercy come to me. . .for my soul is safe within
You, the guardian of my life. I will seek protection in the
shade of Your wings until the destruction has passed. I cry out
to God, the Most High. . .who always does what is good for
me. Out of heaven my rescue comes. He dispatches His mercy
and truth and goes after whoever tries to run over me.

PSALM 57:1–3 VOICE

What if you woke up every morning with the assurance that a heavenly guardian was watching over you? And this divine protector offered you safety, goodness, mercy, truth, and more. How might that change your attitude and outlook for the day? Would you be more optimistic? Would your worries take a backseat to your hopes and dreams? Would you have an extra spring in your step?

If so, friend, then you'll be glad to know this isn't some far-fetched fantasy—it's your marvelous reality! Just as David relied on the mercy and protection of God while he was being pursued by his enemies, you can rely on the heavenly Father too. In the best of times, even—and most importantly—in the worst of times, the Most High will rescue you and keep you safe from harm. Ask Him to wrap you in His loving protection today.

Guardian of my life, I praise You—my rescuer,
my Savior, my friend and loyal protector.

Numbers 24–25 / Luke 1:57–2:20 / Psalm 58

Best News Ever

*[God's] angel said, "Don't be afraid. I'm here to announce a
great and joyful event. . .for everybody, worldwide: A Savior
has just been born in David's town, a Savior who is Messiah
and Master.". . . [The shepherds] left, running. . . . They told
everyone they met what the angels had said. . . . [They]. . .
let loose, glorifying and praising God for everything.*

LUKE 2:10–11,16–18, 20 MSG

Have you ever received awesome news? Not just *any* good news, but the *very best* news of your life? This kind of news brings tears of joy to your eyes. You want to shout from the rooftops so everyone can celebrate with you!

One night long ago, some shepherds received news just like that. And, even better, the good news they received was for *all* people: the long-awaited Messiah had come! The shepherds' reaction did not disappoint. They left, "*running.*" They couldn't wait to see the Christ child for themselves. They shared the news with "everyone they met." They were so excited that they "let loose" praising God.

When you reread the story of angels announcing the Christ child's birth, does your heart leap with the same overwhelming joy the shepherds felt? The Messiah who came some two thousand years ago for the shepherds in the field came to save the whole world! This, friend, *is* the best news ever.

*Heavenly Father, thank You for sending
Your angels to share the best news ever!*

Numbers 26:1–27:11 / Luke 2:21–38 / Psalm 59:1–8

Trusting through the Wait

*Anna. . .had been married seven years and a widow
for eighty-four. She never left the Temple area. . . . At the
very time Simeon was praying, she showed up, broke into an
anthem of praise to God, and talked about the child to all who
were waiting expectantly for the freeing of Jerusalem.*

Luke 2:36–38 msg

Is your faith resilient enough to withstand an extremely long wait? Not your run-of-the-mill frustrating wait for your morning coffee or a return phone call or the end of a very long winter, but the kind of wait that may not be resolved in your lifetime?

Most young women who lived in Bible times were married in their teenage years, so we can assume Anna had married young. Sadly, after only seven years of marriage, Anna's husband passed away. Anna then turned her entire focus on her heavenly Father. She worshiped at the Temple and prayed day and night.

Anna spent *most of her life* learning and *waiting* for the promised Messiah. Yet nowhere is it recorded that she gave up hope. What scripture does tell us is that day after day, Anna kept trusting God would make good on His promise. And, in her very old age, Anna *finally* met the Christ child face-to-face!

What are *you* waiting for today, friend? Ask God to help you trust Him through the wait.

*Father God, even in unusually long
waiting seasons, I will cling to my faith.*

Numbers 27:12–29:11 / Luke 2:39–52 / Psalm 59:9–17

Faith-Check

The LORD said to Moses, "Climb one of the mountains. . .
and look out over the land I have given the people of Israel.
After you have seen it, you will die like your brother, Aaron,
for you both rebelled against my instructions in the wilderness. . . ."
Moses said. . . "Please appoint a new man as leader. . . .
Give them someone who will guide them. . .so the community
of the LORD will not be like sheep without a shepherd."

NUMBERS 27:12–17 NLT

That glorious land God had promised the Israelites? Moses would never get to experience it for himself. Instead, he'd climb a mountain, take in a faraway view of the land, and then die.

Moses had led God's people for many years. Didn't he deserve to enjoy the promised land even for a short while? But God's words were clear and to the point. Moses and his brother had not followed God's direction in the wilderness, so the divine judgment wasn't up for debate.

Moses accepted God's decision without argument, without anger or attitude. Instead, he asked God to appoint his replacement— someone who would guide the people well. Moses modeled a resilient faith, even as his time on earth was coming to an end.

Have you done a faith-check lately? Ask God where your faith needs strengthening, then invite Him to come alongside you to reinvigorate your hope and trust in Him.

God, strengthen my faith today.

Numbers 29:12–30:16 / Luke 3 / Psalm 60:1–5

Keep the Faith

*God, You have turned away from us; You have shattered us into
a million tiny pieces; You have boiled with anger. Now put us
back together, and refresh us with Your mercy. You have made
the earth shake; You have cracked it open effortlessly. Heal the
fissures in the earth. . . . So that Your treasured ones may be
saved, rescue us with Your right hand, and answer our pleas!*

PSALM 60:1–2, 5 VOICE

Have you ever experienced complete confusion in your relationship
with God? Maybe you were walking closely with Him; and yet, He
didn't seem to come through for you. You suffered disappointment,
defeat, difficulty—and it felt, for a season, like God had shaken up
your world. You were uncertain and afraid.

This is how the Israelites felt when they were defeated in battle.
God was supposed to be on their side! Yet, He allowed their enemy to
persevere. The Israelites hadn't seemed to be in disfavor with God, but
they felt His wrath. It seemed God had given them a good shaking
up. However. . .

The Israelites held on to hope. They showed confidence in God's
ability—and willingness—to heal, to help, to rescue. And, friend, we
can trust Him to do the same. So don't lose hope. Don't give up. Keep
believing He will come through!

*Father God, You are my healer, my helper, my rescuer. I need
You! And so I will keep trusting, keep believing, keep hoping.*

Numbers 31 / Luke 4 / Psalm 60:6–12

Mighty Things

*Oh, please help us against our enemies, for all human
help is useless. With God's help we will do mighty
things, for he will trample down our foes.*

PSALM 60:11–12 NLT

If you were facing insurmountable odds, would you want to forge ahead
with God or without Him? Seems like an absurd question, doesn't it?
And yet, many people choose to fight alone, determined to win life's
battles in their own strength and fortitude. But humans *alone* aren't
enough. We aren't powerful enough, wise enough, or brave enough.

David, in Psalm 60, even writes about people and their inability
to help others during trials and troubles. He says, "All human help is
useless." This is a tad surprising coming from David, who had stood
on many battlefields and saw firsthand some of the bravest men go to
war. But David, in his wisdom, knew that victory on the battlefield—
and in life—was only certain with total dependence on God. Yes, we
must participate in the fight, but we fight *through* Him!

When God is on our side, we can trade in our weak, uncertain,
timid selves for the strong, courageous, confident women He created
us to be. So never choose to fight alone, dear one. Choose total
dependence on God. With Him, we can do mighty things!

*God, today I choose total dependence on You. In every
battle I face, I want You by my side, providing the strength,
courage, and confidence I need to be victorious.*

Numbers 32–33 / Luke 5:1–16 / Psalm 61

"Because You Say So"

*[Jesus] said. . . "Put out into deep water, and let down the
nets for a catch." Simon answered, "Master, we've worked
hard all night and haven't caught anything. But because
you say so, I will let down the nets." . . . They caught such
a large number of fish that their nets began to break.*

LUKE 5:4–6 NIV

You can sense the doubt in Simon's words. When Jesus told the
fishermen to put their nets out in deep water, Simon first replies with
an excuse: "Master, we've worked hard all night and haven't caught
anything." But then he says, "But *because you say so*, I will let down the
nets" (emphasis added). Simon's obedience, reluctant though it was,
resulted in the catch of a lifetime!

Have you ever made an excuse when God told you to do something?
You *want* to obey, *but* you also have reason to doubt—life experience
has taught that things don't always go as planned. And while we
question and wonder and doubt, we'd do well to acknowledge that
our human experience falls quite short when we stack it up against
the divine plans of the Creator.

Friend, how many times have you missed out on "the catch of a
lifetime" due to an ill-informed excuse? May your response to God
always be a faith-filled "but because You say so. . ."!

*Heavenly Creator, I don't want to miss another
blessing from You. Because You say so. . .I'll do it!*

Numbers 34–36 / Luke 5:17–32 / Psalm 62:1–6

Visible Faith

Jesus was teaching. . . . Some men came. . .carrying a paralyzed
man on his bed pallet. . . . The house was so packed with people that
they couldn't get in. So they climbed up on the roof and pulled off
some roof tiles. Then they lowered the man by ropes so he came to
rest right in front of Jesus. . . . Their faith was visible to Jesus.
LUKE 5:17–20 VOICE

Imagine the surprising disruption Jesus and the people in the house experienced! One minute Jesus is talking, the people hanging on His every word; the next, a paralyzed man is being lowered into the room! (What a story everyone must have shared around the dinner table that night!)

When the men arrived at the house, they couldn't get their friend in because it was packed with people. Undeterred, they decided to lower him with ropes—through the roof! The men's belief in the healing power of Jesus was obvious. . .because, while it certainly wasn't easy to lower the paralyzed man into the house, it would have been *much* harder to pull him back up! Jesus recognized their bold faith, so He healed the man then and there!

Do *you* have an unrelenting faith? When there's a roadblock, do you give up or persist, looking for another way? Jesus sees your heart. May it always overflow with persistent faith!

Lord Jesus, help me have a visible faith!

Deuteronomy 1:1–2:25 / Luke 5:33–6:11 / Psalm 62:7–12

Wilderness Wandering

GOD, your God, has blessed you in everything you have done.
He has guarded you in your travels through this immense
wilderness. For forty years now, GOD, your God, has been
right here with you. You haven't lacked one thing.

DEUTERONOMY 2:7 MSG

Little did the Israelites known what lay ahead, that their "quick" journey to the promised land would take forty years! Undoubtedly, they experienced a myriad of moments along the way that felt more like punishment than God's good promise. Their journey—their wandering in the wilderness—was difficult. And yet, in every year of their wandering, God cared for them.

He *blessed.*   He *was present.*
He *guarded.*   He *provided.*

Although our current life circumstance might bear little resemblance to our once-hoped-for future, we can still find comfort in the heavenly Father's promises. It would do us good to keep our eyes on Jesus and off the obstacles in our path. Because, with our eyes on Him, we can remain fully focused on His promises. With the heavenly Father by our side, He will lead us around and through anything that stands in the way of His good plan for us.

In the meantime—in all our "wilderness wanderings"—we must trust and believe that God is faithful, because He is (Hebrews 10:23)!

Father God, every year You prove Yourself faithful
to me. You bless and guard; You are ever-present and
always provide. Thank You for never failing me!

Deuteronomy 2:26–4:14 / Luke 6:12–35 / Psalm 63:1–5

Extraordinary

Keep loving your enemies. . . . Keep doing good to those who hate you. Keep speaking blessings on those who curse you. Keep praying for those who mistreat you. If someone strikes you on one cheek, offer the other cheek too. . . . If you want to be extraordinary—love your enemies! Do good without restraint! . . . Don't expect anything in return!

LUKE 6:27–29, 35 VOICE

Has anyone ever stolen from you, mistreated you, cursed you, hurt you? If so, how did that person make you feel? If you answered angry, confused, upset, frustrated, afraid, or insecure, you're not alone.

Human nature tends to feel *all the feels*—good and bad—and then react from those raw emotions. However, our emotions are terrible taskmasters. Just think of a time when you reacted from an emotional state with no thought of the consequences. Probably not your best moment, right? The better way is to follow God's guide for managing relationships with our less-than-favorite people: love them; speak blessings on them; do good to them; pray for them; give them what they need; always act from a place of kindness; never expect anything in return. And do all these things "without restraint"!

"If you want to be extraordinary," say yes! You'll never be sorry when you trade your unreliable human emotion for the unending, unconditional, uncommon love of the Savior.

Father God, I want to love others with an extraordinary love!

Deuteronomy 4:15–5:22 / Luke 6:36–49 / Psalm 63:6–11

Yesterday, Today, Forever

*If you seek GOD. . .you'll be able to find him if you're serious,
looking for him with your whole heart and soul. When troubles
come. . .you will come back to GOD. . .and listen obediently to what
he says. GOD. . .is above all a compassionate God. In the end he
will not abandon you, he won't bring you to ruin, he won't forget
the covenant with your ancestors which he swore to them.*

DEUTERONOMY 4:29–31 MSG

No matter what our relationship with God looks like on the outside, there are times we slip away from Him—probably a little farther than we'd like to admit. Such was the case of the Israelites who were wandering and waiting to enter the promised land. Although they were God's people—and He had made a promise that He would fulfill in His perfect timing—they often demonstrated rebellious unbelief. Nevertheless, God kept His promise.

The same goes for you and me. Whether we get tripped up, tempted, or troubled—no matter what poor choices we make now or in the future, God will *never* stop being our God. His compassion will never end. He will never abandon or wreck us. He'll never renege on His promises to us. And when we reach for Him—and come running back to Him—He'll lovingly receive us with arms wide open.

*God, I am so glad You never change. Yesterday, today,
forever. You love me and accept me as Your own!*

"Simple" Trust

When [Jesus] was still quite far from the house, the captain sent friends to tell him, "Master, you don't have to go to all this trouble. I'm not that good a person. . . . Just give the order and my servant will get well. . . ." Taken aback, Jesus addressed the accompanying crowd: "I've yet to come across this kind of simple trust anywhere in Israel, the very people who are supposed to know about God and how he works." When the messengers got back home, they found the servant up and well.

LUKE 7:6–7, 9–10 MSG

How would you describe your trust in God? Would you say it's uncertain? Situational—dependent on what's happening in the moment? Solid? What about *simple*?

The word *simple* often gets a bad rap. *Simple* is plain, boring, lackluster, ordinary. However, when Jesus referred to the captain's "simple trust," it was anything *but* ordinary. His trust was so pure, so certain, that he just *knew* Jesus could give an order, and whatever He commanded would happen—no fanfare or ceremony necessary. The man had *zero* doubt. In fact, his trust ran so deep that even Jesus was "taken aback"!

Friend, does your trust run as deep? If so, say a prayer of thanksgiving right now. If your trust is weak, ask the heavenly Father to help you grow a "simple trust" today.

Heavenly Father, thank You for being trustworthy. Great is Your faithfulness!

Deuteronomy 8–9 / Luke 7:18–35 / Psalm 64:6–10

How Will You Live?

*The righteous will delight in the Eternal and will take shelter
in Him. All those with an honest heart will glorify Him!*

PSALM 64:10 VOICE

Every day we get to choose how we will live. Will we follow the
ways of the world, hoping to stay relevant and trendy? Will we seek
acceptance from others to validate our worth? Will the goal be to fit in
and stand out? Or will we instead pursue righteous living that delights
the heart of the Father even though it may be in stark contrast with
those around us? Will we wake each day infused to let our words and
actions bring glory to God?

As believers, we're invited to find hope and healing in the Lord as
we lean into Him for our needs. We'll find shelter, wisdom, confidence,
and peace as our heart connects daily with His. As we spend time in
prayer and in the Word, we'll find the courage and endurance necessary
to live in godly ways. And as we choose to follow God, the roots of
faith will naturally grow deeper, helping us navigate each day with
purpose and passion.

*Lord, help me choose You today and every day.
I want to delight You through my demonstrated faith,
looking for ways to glorify Your Holy Name.*

Deuteronomy 10–11 / Luke 7:36–8:3 / Psalm 65:1–8

Blessed or Cursed

*Look, you've got two choices: you can be blessed, or you can
be cursed. If you obey His commands, which I'm giving you
today, you'll be blessed. If you don't obey His commands—
if you leave the path I'm showing you today so you can worship
other gods who are foreign to you, then you'll be cursed.*

DEUTERONOMY 11:26–28 VOICE

As you read today's verse, you may wonder how this would even be
a decision one needs to make. Wanting to receive blessings seems
like the obvious answer, right? But notice the role you're to play in
this divine equation. God requires obedience, and that isn't always
so simple. Even though we know He will give us the wisdom and
strength to follow Him, we still must reject what our flesh wants the
most. And how do we do that when the pull is so strong?

Without a disciplined faith, it's almost impossible. Unless
we are willing to spend time growing our relationship with God
through studying His Word, meditating on His promises, and
praying continually, we'll lack the courage and confidence to obey
His commands. Ask God for help to follow His will and ways, and
you will find it.

*Lord, of course I want to receive Your blessings
because I know all good things come from You.
Help me choose obedience every time.*

Deuteronomy 12–13 / Luke 8:4–21 / Psalm 65:9–13

When the Good-Hearted Hear

"But the seed in the good earth—these are the good-hearts who seize the Word and hold on no matter what, sticking with it until there's a harvest."

LUKE 8:15 MSG

Like He often did, Jesus was speaking to a great crowd, sharing the parable of the sower and how people react to hearing the Word of God. Some let the devil snatch it away from their heart. Some have no roots and can't hold on to it for long. Some become distracted by the world's offerings and the Word is choked out. But when it falls on an honest and good heart—one who grabs on to the truth and doesn't let go—it becomes something powerful. Let that be you, friend.

It takes perseverance for believers to develop a resilient faith. It takes consistency to continue growing through the ups and downs that life brings our way. And it's a daily decision to trust God's goodness when life brings new challenges and to trust His provision through persistent difficulties that make us feel hopeless. When we do, however, we'll experience a beautiful harvest that compares to nothing else.

Lord, let my heart be good and ready to receive Your Word today and always. I am committed to holding tight to You as I navigate this life.

Deuteronomy 14:1–16:8 / Luke 8:22–39 / Psalm 66:1–7

Experiencing Freedom

*The man who had been freed from the demons begged to go with him.
But Jesus sent him home, saying, "No, go back to your family, and
tell them everything God has done for you." So he went all through
the town proclaiming the great things Jesus had done for him.*

LUKE 8:38–39 NLT

Imagine the freedom this man experienced after being held captive
by a legion of demons that had taken up residency within him.
Once cast out, they fled into a herd of pigs who ran over a cliff and
drowned in the lake below. In his deep gratitude, the man desperately
wanted to be with Jesus, but Jesus instead wanted him to go share
the good news. And he did.

Maybe you too have experienced life-changing freedom at the
hands of God. Maybe you were freed from an addiction or a season
of sinning or an abusive relationship and can relate to the depth of
this man's feelings. Unlike this once-possessed man, we, as believers,
are always in the Lord's presence. And it's just as important that we
also share our story with others. Not only will doing so keep our faith
strong and resilient, but God will use it to strengthen their faith as well.

*Lord, thank You for freedom in Christ. And thank You
for Your constant presence in my life. Let my story
help grow my faith as it encourages others.*

Deuteronomy 16:9–18:22 / Luke 8:40–56 / Psalm 66:8–15

Praise Is a Powerful Tool

*Everyone, bless our True God! Let praise-filled voices be
heard near and far—at home and on foreign soil! Praise
the One who gives us life and keeps us safe, who does not
allow us to stumble in the darkness. For You have put us to
the test, O God; You have refined us as silver is refined.*

PSALM 66:8–10 VOICE

Praise is a powerful tool in the hands of believers. Why? Because it
keeps our eyes focused on the Lord and His faithfulness rather than
looking at the tumultuous waters rising around us. When we obsess
over our marital struggles, parenting challenges, financial burdens,
health worries, and career crises, we forget how blessed we are. We
overlook His promise to keep us safe. We disregard His vow to keep
us from stumbling in the darkness. We let our faith wither.

Friend, take heart! It's in difficult times we need to cling to God
even more. This is when we dig deeper into the Word and spend
quality time in His presence through prayer. This is when we take
every thought captive and let God renew our minds each morning.
So, in confidence, praise Him today for what He's already doing
about tomorrow.

Lord, let my praise demonstrate the faith I have in Your goodness.

Deuteronomy 19:1–21:9 / Luke 9:1–22 / Psalm 66:16–20

The Reason We Confess

*If I had not confessed the sin in my heart, the Lord
would not have listened. But God did listen! He paid
attention to my prayer. Praise God, who did not ignore
my prayer or withdraw his unfailing love from me.*

PSALM 66:18–20 NLT

No one really likes to admit when they are wrong. It's often difficult
to acknowledge the times and places we fall short. But let today's verse
be a strong reminder of the value of confession. It's an important part
of a faith-filled life and something often overlooked. For unless we
keep short accounts with the Lord and admit our transgressions with
honesty and authenticity, our unconfessed missteps can affect our
communication with Him, turning them into an unwanted barrier.

As you grow deeper with God, let times of confession be quick.
Each day, make choices that keep your relationship moving forward
and developing deep roots that will hold you steady in hard times. If
you're a true believer, rest assured your sins have already been forgiven
because of Jesus' death and resurrection. But each time you come before
the Lord and humbly confess where you've messed up, be assured that
you and God will stay connected in meaningful ways.

*Lord, thank You that my sins have been forgiven, but keep
me in a position of humility so I am quick to confess and
walk in the freedom and goodness Jesus brings.*

Deuteronomy 21:10–23:8 / Luke 9:23–42 / Psalm 67

Why We Deny

If any of you want to walk My path, you're going to have to deny yourself. You'll have to take up your cross every day and follow Me. If you try to avoid danger and risk, then you'll lose everything. If you let go of your life and risk all for My sake, then your life will be rescued, healed, made whole and full.

LUKE 9:23–24 VOICE

To deny yourself doesn't mean to merely turn down certain "creature comforts" like eating your favorite food, shopping at your favorite store, or indulging in your favorite pastime. It's not just choosing to refuse the temptation to gossip, judge, or boast. Instead, Jesus is asking us to surrender personal control of our lives. We're to put ourselves into His capable and loving hands. This is what it means to walk Jesus' path, to live a life of faith.

If our goal is to fully embrace all that God has for us, then this decision to surrender ourselves and our lives to Jesus is a vital part of the equation. We've been controlling and manipulating for far too long, and it's exhausting. Today, dig in deeper with the Lord and let go of your will and ways, knowing you can fully trust His. Then watch as your faith grows into something marvelous.

Lord, I confess that I've been a control freak and have tried to make my own way in life. I now surrender my plans so I can follow Yours. Lead me down Your path.

Deuteronomy 23:9–25:19 / Luke 9:43–62 / Psalm 68:1–6

When God Is Your Source

*The True God who inhabits sacred space is a father
to the fatherless, a defender of widows. He makes a home
for those who are alone. He frees the prisoners and leads
them to prosper. Yet those who rebel against Him live in
the barren land without His blessings and prosperity.*

PSALM 68:5–6 VOICE

When you feel alone and abandoned—be it by choice or circumstance—know that God is with you. When you feel spent, you can find rest in His arms. When you feel bound by sin or situations, He'll bring freedom. When you feel broken, He'll bring restoration. Whatever you need for comfort, God will provide in abundance.

When you recognize the Lord as your source for all things, you cannot help but grow a more resilient faith and discover a newfound strength for your weary bones. Yet notice the consequences for those who rebel instead of obeying. These unfortunates will find themselves living in a barren wasteland.

The Bible is clear: there is a blessing that comes from following God's will. Such obedience will be rewarded. So, be quick to look to the Lord for provision. Let Him be the one to meet you right where you are. Being in His hands is the safest, most heartening place to be.

*Lord, what a comfort to know that no matter where
I am, You are there, willing and able to meet every
need with unfailing and unwavering precision.*

A Declaration

You have declared this day that the LORD is your God and that
you will walk in obedience to him, that you will keep his decrees,
commands and laws—that you will listen to him. And the LORD
has declared this day that you are his people, his treasured possession
as he promised, and that you are to keep all his commands.

DEUTERONOMY 26:17–18 NIV

To grow a deep faith in God, choosing a path of obedience is imperative. It would be difficult to speak of your great love for the Lord while simultaneously embracing a life of sin. It wouldn't make sense to proclaim His trustworthiness if you're always trying to find solutions in your own efforts. Amen?

Friend, declare this day that the Lord is your God. Then be intentional to walk in the ways He leads. Ask for discernment and wisdom to know His will. Ask for spiritual ears to better hear His voice. Ask Him to open your eyes to His direction. And let God's Holy Spirit grow your roots deep in the rich soil of faith so you can become the woman He created you to be.

Lord, thank You for being my Father in heaven who
I can follow and trust and serve. Help me show my
love to You through my obedience every day.

Deuteronomy 28:15–68 / Luke 10:21–37 / Psalm 68:15–19

The Call to Love

*And he replied, You must love the Lord your God with all your
heart and with all your soul and with all your strength and
with all your mind; and your neighbor as yourself. And Jesus said
to him, You have answered correctly; do this, and you will live
[enjoy active, blessed, endless life in the kingdom of God].*

LUKE 10:27–28 AMPC

Love is a constant theme throughout the Bible. And while it may
seem like a no-brainer command that takes little effort to walk out,
that couldn't be further from the truth. In reality, this call to love is
more challenging than we may realize. Why? Because it requires a
great measure of trust to humble ourselves so we can love others well.
It's an act of service as we choose to put the needs of others above our
own. And as we journey with God through this adventure in faith,
we will find a deeper desire to love sacrificially. Our pressing petition
will be to love the Lord with our heart, soul, and strength.

If this divine calling feels unattainable to you today, ask God
for a better understanding of today's verses from Luke. Ask that He
saturate His truth in the fertile soil of your heart and bring forth a
fresh revelation. Let God create in you a resilience to love without
condition.

*Lord, help me love You, myself,
and others in extraordinary ways.*

Deuteronomy 29–30 / Luke 10:38–11:23 / Psalm 68:20–27

When We're Worried

But the Lord said to her, "My dear Martha, you are worried and upset over all these details! There is only one thing worth being concerned about. Mary has discovered it, and it will not be taken away from her."

LUKE 10:41–42 NLT

Worry gets us nowhere. It doesn't fix any problems. It doesn't make us feel better. It doesn't right the wrong. And it doesn't change the outcome of the situation. In fact, worry only makes us feel hopeless and stressed out. Yet many struggle with it every day.

Today's scripture reveals that Martha was a worrier. She allowed a spirit of injustice to rise up within her heart. She felt that Mary's time at Jesus' feet was unfair because it left Martha in the kitchen alone. Martha partnered with stress and got tangled up in anxious thoughts.

Yet she didn't stew for long before she went right to the Lord. Her feelings—like ours—were real. In her mind, there was good reason to be upset. But rather than let her emotions spin out of control, she flexed her faith and confided in Jesus. Her motives may not have been pure, but she still went right to the one who could calm her heart and give her the focus and redirection she needed. She trusted Jesus with her worry. And friend, that is resilient faith.

Lord, remind me to bring every worry to You rather than try to handle circumstances on my own. Help me deepen my trust in who You are and what You promise to do.

Deuteronomy 31:1–32:22 / Luke 11:24–36 / Psalm 68:28–35

A Healthy Eye

"Your eye is like a lamp that provides light for your body.
When your eye is healthy, your whole body is filled with light.
But when it is unhealthy, your body is filled with darkness.
Make sure that the light you think you have is not actually darkness.
If you are filled with light, with no dark corners, then your whole life
will be radiant, as though a floodlight were filling you with light."

LUKE 11:34–36 NLT

As you spend time in God's Word, you will begin to see a transformation taking place. You will naturally find the ability to shift your perspective, to see things with an eternal focus.

When today's scripture talks about having a "healthy eye," it's describing someone who looks at life through the lens of faith. It's a direct blessing from a deep and meaningful relationship with the Lord. It's part of having the light of the Lord within. In contrast, an *unhealthy* eye symbolizes an evil way of looking at things. It's spiritual darkness that can't dwell within a true believer.

Be certain you're intentionally deepening your relationship with God daily. Grow deep roots of faith, and be transformed into an undeniable light that shines into the world.

Lord, if there's anything unhealthy in my spiritual
journey that will keep me stunted in my faith, please
reveal and heal it. My desire is to shine Your light.

Deuteronomy 32:23–33:29 / Luke 11:37–54 / Psalm 69:1–9

Weathering Every Storm

*Reach down for me, True God; deliver me. The waters have risen to
my neck; I am going down! My feet are swallowed in this murky
bog; I am sinking—there is no sturdy ground. I am in the deep;
the floods are crashing in! I am weary of howling; my throat is
scratched dry. I still look for my God even though my eyes fail.*

PSALM 69:1–3 VOICE

When you find yourself in crushing situations—ones that feel as if
they're going to overpower you—what do you do? What is your first
response when it seems you are sinking in your circumstances? Do
you look for God in the midst of the flood, crying out to Him, or
flounder in the waves threatening to overcome you?

As believers, we should be quick to remember that God is our
deliverer. He will bring us through every storm. And as we prioritize
growing daily in our faith, this truth will anchor us. It may take
intentionality to be in God's Word and spend time in prayer each
day, but it results in a beautiful maturity. It helps us become seasoned.
And then as we find ourselves caught in life's challenges, our faith
will drive us to seek the Lord. We'll cry out to Him before we do
anything else. We will be able to weather every storm with resiliency.

*Lord, it's only through You I am able to withstand the ups
and downs of life. Thank You for being the anchor I can
tether myself to when the waves come crashing in.*

Becoming Strong and Courageous

This is My command: be strong and courageous. Never be afraid or discouraged because I am your God, the Eternal One, and I will remain with you wherever you go.

JOSHUA 1:9 VOICE

Where do you need to be strong and courageous in life right now? Maybe your children have made choices that don't reflect the way you raised them. Maybe you recently discovered the secret life your husband has been living. Maybe you're worried about how you'll pay bills with inflation on the rise and money already tight. Maybe the doctor delivered an unexpected diagnosis, and you are terrified. Or maybe you're devastated by loss, frustrated by singlehood, or brokenhearted by barrenness. Regardless of the battle you're facing, God's command to Joshua is also His command to you.

Rest knowing that the Lord guarantees to be with you always. That He won't abandon you to figure things out alone. And if you're struggling to become strong and courageous, *no matter what,* make a concerted effort to spend time with God. Get deep into the Word. Pray continually. Meditate on His promises. Remember His goodness. Without exception, recognize God as your source. Then you'll find your roots growing deeper and your strength and courage blossoming more than you ever imagined possible.

Lord, help me become resilient in my faith so that being strong and courageous is my default.

Memorializing When God Showed Up

Then Joshua said to the Israelites, "In the future your children
will ask, 'What do these stones mean?' Then you can tell them,
'This is where the Israelites crossed the Jordan on dry ground.'
For the LORD your God dried up the river right before your eyes,
and he kept it dry until you were all across, just as he did at the
Red Sea when he dried it up until we had all crossed over."

JOSHUA 4:21–23 NLT

Our memory is a beautiful gift from God, and it plays a key role in helping to build a resilient faith. That's because each time we remember the Lord's goodness in our life, our belief is strengthened. Each recollection of His provision in lean times, protection in scary times, and progression in stuck times reinforce God's sovereignty. When we hear the stories of His defending and delivering others, our own faith is reinforced.

Joshua was spot on! Looking back to see the Lord's hand is important. It's important enough for us to take time to memorialize where He showed up in our lives. Whether it's stones from the Jordan or an entry in a journal, be diligent to document times with God so your faith will deepen.

Lord, remind me of Your goodness and the ways You stepped into my life or the lives of others. Doing so will not only shore up my faith but create resilience within me in the days to come.

Following His Plan

When the people heard the sound of the rams' horns, they shouted as loud as they could. Suddenly, the walls of Jericho collapsed, and the Israelites charged straight into the town and captured it. They completely destroyed everything in it with their swords—men and women, young and old, cattle, sheep, goats, and donkeys.

Joshua 6:20–21 NLT

The battle plans the Lord downloaded to Joshua were out of the ordinary. Circle the city. Blow trumpets. Give a great shout. You can imagine the people inside the city probably watched with confusion for six days, shaking their heads, giggling while the Israelites followed what God had prescribed. But on day seven, when the walls began to wobble and then collapsed, no one was laughing anymore.

When you have resilient faith, you'll do what the Lord asks no matter what. You will seek His direction and obey His voice with vigor, regardless of how outlandish His orders may seem. This is when the result of your time in the Word will shine forth. This is where you'll see the answers to the prayers you poured out before God. And these moments become memories that will remind you of His goodness again and again, resulting in deep roots of faith to hold you steady in the good and not-so-good times.

*Lord, help me obey You without question.
Let Your perfect track record in my life give me
the confidence to follow You no matter what.*

Joshua 8–9 / Luke 12:49–59 / Psalm 70

Desperate for His Presence

*But let those who pursue You celebrate and have joy because
of You. And let the song of those who love Your saving
grace never cease: "God is great!" But I am poor and in
serious need, so hurry to my side, God, because You are my
helper, my liberator. Eternal One, please don't wait.*

PSALM 70:4–5 VOICE

There are times when we are desperate for God's presence to surround
us. It could be a financial blow that hits swiftly or a friendship that
crumbles from betrayal. It could be deep insecurities bleeding into
every area of your life or the discovery of a moral failure that rocks
the foundation of your marriage. Maybe the medical treatment didn't
work, the hard conversation failed to bring the necessary changes, or
an overwhelming grief refuses to heal.

Friend, remember that God is great, and His timing is perfect.
He is your helper. He is your shelter. He is your comforter. And the
Lord will bring freedom and restoration to those who love Him. As
a believer, all that's required is to cry out for help and then wait for
God's leading. Then be steadfast in faith, knowing that God is working
on your behalf, that He sees your need and is already clearing the way.

*Lord, You are fully aware of what I lack and where
I'm struggling. I trust You to be everything I need.*

Joshua 10:1–11:15 / Luke 13:1–21 / Psalm 71:1–6

You Can Count on God

*I have found shelter in You, Eternal One; I count on You to
shield me always from humiliation and disgrace. Rescue and
save me in Your justice. Turn Your ear to me, and hurry to
deliver me from my enemies. Be my rock of refuge where I
can always hide. You have given the order to keep me safe;
You are my solid ground—my rock and my fortress.*

PSALM 71:1–3 VOICE

The psalmist knows God is trustworthy. He knows the Lord is his
shelter and shield. He knows the Lord will rescue and save. He believes
his pleas are heard in the heavens and will result in deliverance. He
recognizes God as his refuge and hiding place as well as his safety
and fortress. No doubt this psalmist has seen the Lord's promises
come to pass in his life and the lives of others. And his faith has been
strengthened through it. His faith is resilient.

How about you, friend? Do you have the same understanding
of God as the writer of this psalm does? Consider how you have
witnessed God's hand moving mightily in your life—when He has
delivered, been your refuge, and hidden you. Write down all the ways
the Lord has been your source; then view Him as such. Allow your
faith to be fortified because of His goodness.

Lord, I know I can count on You to be everything I need You to be.

Bear, Speak, Remind

*But I will keep hope alive, and my praise to You will
grow exponentially. I will bear witness to Your merciful acts;
throughout the day I will speak of all the ways You deliver,
although, I admit, I do not know the entirety of either.
I will come with stories of Your great acts, my Lord, the
Eternal. I will remind them of Your justice, only Yours.*

PSALM 71:14–16 VOICE

Today's passage of scripture reveals important elements that contribute
to believers having a hardy faith. Did you catch them? We're to *bear
witness* to God's goodness in our lives. We're to *speak of the ways*
we've seen His deliverance through our personal stories. And we are
to *remind* others of the Lord's justice. These acts not only keep our
minds focused on all He can do, but they also breed hope for those
around us.

In this crazy world, we all need powerful pictures of who our God
is and what He can do. We need reasons to hope and reasons to praise
because they are often a catalyst to creating a robust relationship with
the Father. So be quick to bear witness to God's good, to speak of the
ways He's worked in your life, and to remind others of His unerring
judgment. And when you need such encouragement in your own life,
be quick to connect with those who can offer it.

*Lord, help me keep hope alive through sharing and receiving.
Remembering Your goodness creates resilient faith in me.*

Joshua 14–16 / Luke 14:1–15 / Psalm 71:17–21

God Will Keep Every Promise Made

*"Now, as you can see, the LORD has kept me alive and
well as he promised for all these forty-five years since
Moses made this promise—even while Israel wandered in
the wilderness. Today I am eighty-five years old. I am as
strong now as I was when Moses sent me on that journey,
and I can still travel and fight as well as I could then."*

JOSHUA 14:10–11 NLT

In this passage where Caleb is asking Joshua for the land God promised, you can see the former's resilient faith demonstrated by his strong words. Caleb clearly sees the ways the Lord had sustained him throughout their journey, just as He said He would. What a case for faith he now has!

What about you? Can you see God's promises blooming in your own life? Has He restored a marriage that had been headed for divorce? Has He returned a prodigal? Has God repaired a family broken and mangled by anger? Has He repositioned you financially? Has the Lord revived a friendship dead from betrayal? The truth is that God keeps every promise made—whether it be one mentioned in the Bible or whispered into your soul. If He said it will be…then it will be.

*Lord, thank You that in a world where vows are broken all the
time, You guarantee a follow-through on what You promise.*

Joshua 17:1–19:16 / Luke 14:16–35 / Psalm 71:22–24

When We Can See It

*My lips will shout for joy when I sing praise to you—
I whom you have delivered. My tongue will tell of your
righteous acts all day long, for those who wanted to
harm me have been put to shame and confusion.*

PSALM 71:23–24 NIV

There is something so powerful and meaningful that happens to the heart of a believer when she's able to see God's deliverance in a situation. We read about it in the Bible. We hear stories from our friends. We see His hand move mightily in the lives of others. But when the veil is pulled back and we can see His goodness manifested in the circumstances we're having to navigate, it's a beautiful gift that strengthens our faith. Then just like those around us, we have accounts of the Lord's kindness and generosity to share.

Where has God shown up for you recently? How has He changed the trajectory, bringing much-needed hope to your weary heart? What is it that He did for you that no one else could have managed in their own abilities? These are the divine sharables that help create a resilient faith in believers. Be ready and willing to bring this kind of encouragement when the opportunity presents itself.

*Lord, thank You for being so present in my life
that I have stories of Your goodness to share.*

Joshua 19:17–21:42 / Luke 15:1–10 / Psalm 72:1–11

God Sees Your Value

*This is how it is in heaven. They're happier over one sinner
who changes his way of life than they are over 99 good and
just people who don't need to change their ways of life.*

LUKE 15:7 VOICE

Today's verse is the last line of the parable of the lost sheep. As Jesus was unpacking this story, tax collectors and sinners were drawing closer to listen because He was gaining popularity with them. Maybe they felt understood. Maybe they felt cared for. Or maybe Jesus was relatable because He saw the value in each person. He made it clear that everyone was worth going after and bringing back into the fold.

When you truly understand how much you mean to God, you will draw closer in relationship with Him. You will feel compelled to invest your time and effort, growing deeper roots of faith daily by reading God's Word, spending time in prayer, and meditating on scripture that encourages your heart. You will feel valuable, knowing you always have the Lord's attention, no matter what. And you will trust more fully that God will bring you back to Him because of His great love.

*Lord, knowing how much You love me makes
me want to know You more. What a wonderful
encouragement to be valued by my perfect Creator!*

Joshua 21:43–22:34 / Luke 15:11–32 / Psalm 72:12–20

God's Resilient Love

" 'I have forfeited any right to be treated like your son, but I'm
wondering if you'd treat me as one of your hired servants?' " So he
got up and returned to his father. The father looked off in the distance
and saw the young man returning. He felt compassion for his son
and ran out to him, enfolded him in an embrace, and kissed him.

LUKE 15:19–20 VOICE

Don't you love the resilient love displayed by this father?

As the parable goes, the youngest son asked for his inheritance
early and left home. (Chances are he didn't leave on good terms,
demanding what was not yet his.) Once on his own, he recklessly
squandered it. And as famine hit the land and the money was gone,
the son longed to be back at home. He didn't feel worthy, but he
decided to go anyway.

Notice the father's reaction. His love was so great that seeing
his prodigal return caused him to celebrate. He felt compassion and
embraced him tightly. In the same way, when we return to our faith
and dig in with passion and purpose, God is delighted. There is no
condemnation. We're not turned away. Instead, we are received with
open arms and hardy love.

Lord, what a blessing to receive Your compassion and
forgiveness when I make a mistake or reject You. Grow
my faith so I long to stay in Your presence always.

Choosing to Worship God

"If you decide that it's a bad thing to worship GOD, then choose a god you'd rather serve—and do it today. Choose one of the gods your ancestors worshiped from the country beyond The River, or one of the gods of the Amorites, on whose land you're now living. As for me and my family, we'll worship GOD."

JOSHUA 24:15 MSG

Faith is a choice. It takes an intentional decision to worship the Lord above all other things. That means putting Him first in your heart and letting your actions follow. It means choosing God at every turn, giving Him priority with your time, talents, and treasure. It means humbling yourself and submitting to the Lord's will and ways. For when you do, you'll see His hand at work in your life. Your eyes will be trained on Him, and your ears will listen for God's still, small voice. Your faith will grow deep roots, keeping you steady when the storms of discouragement and disappointment threaten. Your life will have meaning and purpose.

Friend, choose today who you will serve. Will you cling to the Lord for hope, or will you look to the world for direction? Will you waste your time on earthly promises that continually fall short, or will you trust God at all times, even when you're desperate? Every day, the choice is yours.

Lord, I choose You!

Judges 1–2 / Luke 16:19–17:10 / Psalm 73:10–20

The Size of Your Faith

*It's not like you need a huge amount of faith. If you just had
faith the size of a single, tiny mustard seed, you could say to
this huge tree, "Pull up your roots and replant yourself in the
sea," and it would fly through the sky and do what you said.
So even a little faith can accomplish the seemingly impossible.*

LUKE 17:6 VOICE

To God, the size of your faith isn't the issue. You don't need a Mount
Everest–sized amount to draw from. The depth or breadth isn't what's
important. Scripture says all we need is faith the size of a mustard seed,
which is tiny! What the Lord wants is for us to have faith, period.
With faith, what may seem impossible is possible.

The truth is that the more time we spend with God through prayer
and reading of the Word, the deeper the roots of our faith will grow.
And there is something so sweet about investing in your relationship
with Him. Doing so brings you calm. It ushers in a peaceful heart.
It creates resilience. It comforts in hard times. And while the size of
faith isn't important, tending to it daily empowers us to live in ways
that please the Lord and keep us hopeful that with God, anything
is possible.

*Lord, regardless of its size, let my
faith bless You and benefit us both.*

Judges 3–4 / Luke 17:11–37 / Psalm 73:21–28

A Joy-Sustaining Revelation

Even though I was angry and hard-hearted, You gave
me good advice; when it's all over, You will receive me into
Your glory. For all my wanting, I don't have anyone but
You in heaven. There is nothing on earth that I desire other
than You. I admit how broken I am in body and spirit,
but God is my strength, and He will be mine forever.
PSALM 73:24–26 VOICE

The psalmist understands the value of having a healthy relationship with the Lord. He knows there is nothing on earth that can satisfy in the miraculous ways God can. He recognizes his lack and brokenness, knowing the source of his strength is through faith. And while the writer doesn't share how he came about this joy-sustaining revelation, we know it comes from time in the Lord's presence. The same is true for us.

When we seek God's guidance in life's decisions, study His Word, meditate on His promises, worship through song, practice gratitude, fellowship with other believers, and pray without ceasing, our faith is secured. It creates in us a desire for His presence each day, and it produces a reliance in God for all we need.

Lord, thank You for loving me in spite of my shortcomings.
Thank You for the promise of eternity. And thank You for
blessing me with Your presence, for bringing me joy. Amen.

Judges 5:1–6:24 / Luke 18:1–17 / Psalm 74:1–3

The Simplicity of a Child

People brought babies to Jesus, hoping he might touch them.
When the disciples saw it, they shooed them off. Jesus called
them back. "Let these children alone. Don't get between
them and me. These children are the kingdom's pride
and joy. Mark this: Unless you accept God's kingdom
in the simplicity of a child, you'll never get in."

LUKE 18:15–17 MSG

Sometimes we tend to complicate things. Maybe we overpopulate our to-do list and push ourselves too hard. Maybe in an effort to be thorough, we add unnecessary steps and end up frustrated. Maybe we think more is better. But when it comes to faith, we're to accept God's gift of salvation with simplicity. We should not muddy the water with things that don't belong.

Let's be careful not to steep our relationship with the Lord in unnecessary confusion. Let's be mindful that we don't make growing our faith difficult and taxing. God wants us to come to Him with the simplicity of a child. Humble. Meek. Undemanding. Doing so will set a firm foundation of fertile soil where our faith can grow deep roots of resiliency.

Lord, I confess that at times I make things much more confusing
than need be. Help me remember Your desire for me to be
down-to-earth and uncomplicated when it comes to faith.

Asking for What We Need

Jesus stopped and ordered him to be brought over. When he had come near, Jesus asked, "What do you want from me?" He said, "Master, I want to see again." Jesus said, "Go ahead—see again! Your faith has saved and healed you!" The healing was instant: He looked up, seeing—and then followed Jesus, glorifying God. Everyone in the street joined in, shouting praise to God.

LUKE 18:40–43 MSG

The blind man had enough faith to ask Jesus for what he needed. He had confidence to share his desire with a deep sense of expectation. And by doing so, his sight returned, and he gave the Lord the glory. But it didn't stop there. His miracle affected others who'd witnessed the healing and joined in the praise.

Just like this man, our posture before Jesus should be one of expectation. Our hope should be huge, especially since *we*, unlike this blind man, have the means of deepening our faith through prayer and spending time in the Word.

Investing in our relationship with God will position us for resiliency. We'll be quick to look to Him for comfort and strength. We'll ask for what we need, having confidence in His goodness. And we'll find reasons to praise the Lord for blessings in abundance.

Lord, thank You for being generous in Your care and compassion toward me! May I always praise You for it!

Judges 8:1–9:23 / Luke 19:1–28 / Psalm 74:12–17

He Is a Big God

*The day is Yours, the night also is Yours; You have established
the [starry] light and the sun. You have fixed all the
borders of the earth [the divisions of land and sea and of
the nations]; You have made summer and winter.*

PSALM 74:16–17 AMPC

Simply put, God is bigger and better than anything the world can offer.
He is the most efficient and effective Creator. And He is in control of
it all. That means we can exhale a sigh of relief and surrender our need
to direct and manage everything and everyone. God has everything
in His very capable hands. And through faith, we learn to trust Him
more and more.

In this world, giving up control isn't easy to do, and to be honest,
there are times and situations it's unwise. But unlike the world, the
Lord is always a safe place. As you grow your roots of faith deeper,
releasing your grip on difficult circumstances and putting them into
His hands, you'll find your life easier to navigate. Over time, you'll
see God's perfect track record and be comforted in letting Him lead,
appreciating more and more the big God we serve every day.

*Lord, what a relief to know You are in control so
I don't have to be. Help me rest in You rather
than try to fix everything myself.*

Judges 9:24–10:18 / Luke 19:29–48 / Psalm 74:18–23

Choosing God Over the World

*The LORD replied, "Did I not rescue you from the
Egyptians, the Amorites, the Ammonites, the Philistines,
the Sidonians, the Amalekites, and the Maonites? When they
oppressed you, you cried out to me for help, and I rescued you.
Yet you have abandoned me and served other gods. So I will
not rescue you anymore. Go and cry out to the gods you have
chosen! Let them rescue you in your hour of distress!"*

JUDGES 10:11–14 NLT

God's desire is for His children to place their trust in Him and
embrace righteous living. He wants us to study the Word, ruminate
over His promises, seek guidance through prayer, live with gratitude,
find contentment through Him, have a servant's heart, and fellowship
with other believers. Yet many times we forget the ways we've seen
God's goodness in our lives and instead seek comfort in worldly
offerings. Just like the Israelites referenced in today's scripture, we
fail to have resilient faith.

What about you? Can you relate to God's people who abandoned
Him for earthly options? Are you seeking the Lord to sustain you
or are you investing time and money in the latest trends? Ask the
Holy Spirit to grow in you a joy-sustaining faith that will keep you
focused on God each day.

*Lord, let me always press into You. The world
simply cannot compare to Your magnificence.*

Judges 11:1–12:7 / Luke 20:1–26 / Psalm 75:1–7

Firm Foundation

"When the earth quakes and its people live in turmoil,
I am the one who keeps its foundations firm."
PSALM 75:3 NLT

An earthquake happens when two tectonic plates suddenly slip past one another. Our planet experiences thousands of earthquakes every year, some causing damage to property as well as a devastating loss of life. A minor earthquake can be traumatic, rocking the normally steady ground. But even the deepest seismic activity only travels less than halfway to the earth's core. Earthquakes are mostly a surface problem.

Since Adam and Eve first disobeyed God, every human has existed in sinful turmoil—the moral earthquakes in the world. No matter the personal hardship or broader societal problems that rock your world, the fact remains that God's power runs deeper and stronger than anything you face. Even better, He promises to be there through it all: "God is our refuge and strength, always ready to help in times of trouble. So we will not fear when earthquakes come and the mountains crumble into the sea" (Psalm 46:1–2 NLT).

A faith rooted in the power of God can tap deeper than the surface turmoil you experience. You may feel the rock and roll of the quakes. You may see mountains tremble and oceans rage (Psalm 46:3), but God is your forever-firm foundation.

God, when my world is lurching out of control, help me
and steady me. I will not fear because You are with me.

What's in a Name?

*Then Manoah asked the angel of the LORD, "What is your
name? For when all this comes true, we want to honor
you." "Why do you ask my name?" the angel of the LORD
replied. "It is too wonderful for you to understand."*

JUDGES 13:17–18 NLT

Manoah and his wife struggled with infertility. On top of that, they
and the rest of God's chosen people were in the middle of a forty-year
period of oppression under their enemies, the Philistines.

So when an angel appeared to Manoah's wife and told her that
she would soon become pregnant with a son who would "begin to
rescue Israel from the Philistines" (Judges 13:5 NLT), she ran to
tell her husband the exciting news. Later the angel returned and
answered Manoah's questions. . .mostly. When the soon-to-be father of
Samson asked the angel's name, the Lord said His name was too
wonderful for human minds to fathom.

Scripture says that God's name is a divine secret (Genesis 32:29;
Exodus 3:13–14). Although no human can fully know God this side
of heaven, the fact remains that God has known you by name since
before you were born. He planned your path before He knit you
together in your mother's womb, just as He did for Samson. Take
comfort in the fact that you are known intimately and perfectly by
your heavenly Father.

*Father, thank You for knowing the true,
authentic me and loving me fully and completely.*

Judges 15–16 / Luke 21:1–19 / Psalm 76:1–7

Giving All

*Just then he looked up and saw the rich people dropping offerings in
the collection plate. Then he saw a poor widow put in two pennies. He
said, "The plain truth is that this widow has given by far the largest
offering today. All these others made offerings that they'll never miss;
she gave extravagantly what she couldn't afford—she gave her all!"*

LUKE 21:1–4 MSG

The two coins the widow put in the collection plate were *lepta*,
worth about 1/64 of a day's minimum wage. (In today's terms, that's
little more than a dollar.) Luke's descriptor of "poor widow" was a
double whammy for this unfortunate woman. Not only did she have
little money, but as a widow she had very few options for earning
more. If anybody had a legitimate excuse for not giving an offering,
it was this woman. Her miniscule gift had little monetary worth, but
it was a great sacrifice that she gave willingly.

Jesus saw, recognized, and praised the spiritual worth of her
offering. While the others gave a small portion of their surplus, she
gave extravagantly from what she had. Although scripture doesn't tell
us anything more about this woman, we can be confident that her
selfless generosity pleased God and He blessed her because "God loves
it when the giver delights in the giving" (2 Corinthians 9:6–7 MSG).

*Jesus, I will be more like the poor widow and practice
extravagant giving because You supply all.*

Look Up

"What's happening to the world?" people will wonder. The cosmic order will be destabilized. And then, at that point, they will see the Son of Man coming in a cloud with power and blazing glory. So when the troubles begin, don't be afraid. Look up—raise your head high, because the truth is that your liberation is fast approaching.

LUKE 21:26–28 VOICE

"What's happening to the world?" might be a question you're regularly asking yourself these days. Some of the crazy, evil situations we hear about and face today may point to Jesus' imminent return, but regardless of when He comes back to earth, they are certainly evidence of sin's grip on the world.

The picture Jesus paints of the end times in Luke 21 is grim, but for a Christian, it is cause for great joy. When we see false messiahs, experience natural disasters, and endure persecution, we know that each passing day is one day closer to Christ's return. Rather than being fearful and anxious about what's happening in the world, we can choose to be confident in God's victory over sin and Satan. For Jesus will bring justice, peace, and restoration to us—His brothers and sisters.

Although two thousand years have passed since Jesus spoke these words, their truth remains. Don't be afraid. Look up. Your liberation is fast approaching.

Come quickly, Lord Jesus. I feel the chaos, but I trust in Your perfect plan. I will raise my head high and look for You!

Judges 19:1–20:23 / Luke 22:7–30 / Psalm 77:1–11

Wonderful Deeds

You don't let me sleep. I am too distressed even to pray!
. . . But then I recall all you have done, O Lord;
I remember your wonderful deeds of long ago.
PSALM 77:4, 11 NLT

Asaph, the writer of Psalm 77, was having a colossally bad night: "When I was in deep trouble, I searched for the Lord," he wrote. "All night long I prayed. . .but my soul was not comforted" (v. 2 NLT). As he focused on his woes, Asaph couldn't feel the presence of God.

Yet even though Asaph felt abandoned, he continued to think about God. He expressed his uncertainties and innermost feelings connected to his doubt: "Has the Lord rejected me forever? . . . This is my fate; the Most High has turned his hand against me" (vv. 7, 10 NLT). The turning point in his night came when his focus changed from his current state to memories of God's miracles and faithfulness in the past—like the parting of the Red Sea (Exodus 14). Asaph's distress morphed into authentic worship and thankfulness and peace.

What personal stories of God's "wonderful deeds" can you dip into when you're struggling with stress and doubt? Perhaps in the past you received unexpected blessings, encouragement from an unlikely source, a favorable test result, physical healing, or a restored relationship. Remember and celebrate God's faithfulness!

God, when I am down, pick me up with memories of
Your goodness. You are worthy of my praise!

Judges 20:24–21:25 / Luke 22:31–54 / Psalm 77:12–20

Wherever the Path Leads

*Your road led through the sea, your pathway through the
mighty waters—a pathway no one knew was there!*
PSALM 77:19 NLT

When Pharaoh and his army pursued Moses and the Hebrews, God's
chosen people fled on a path that dead-ended at the shore of the Red
Sea. Sure, they could turn right or left, but that would only result in
their capture and return to slavery in Egypt.

They needed some guidance—which way to go.

We've all needed this kind of help from time to time. An eighteen-
year-old needs help deciding on post-graduation plans. A dating
couple needs to decide on the next step in their relationship. Which
job is the right one to take? Which house is the wisest to buy? Life is
full of these diverging paths that feel big and momentous, especially
at the time we're deciding which way to go.

When God answers our prayers for guidance, we expect there's
already an established path wherever He will lead us. But just like
He did with the Israelites, God can make a way when there seems
to be no way through a situation. He will help us navigate difficult
decisions and lead us on to bigger and better things. But we have to
be willing to go where He leads and do what He tells us to do. Our
obedience and faith are what produce walk-through-the-Red-Sea-
on-dry-ground kinds of miracles!

*Lord, give me faith to follow You,
even if the path doesn't exist (yet)!*

Ruth 1–2 / Luke 22:55–23:25 / Psalm 78:1–4

No Longer an Outsider

"I. . .know about everything you have done for your mother-in-law since the death of your husband. I have heard how you left your father and mother and your own land to live here among complete strangers. May the LORD, the God of Israel, under whose wings you have come to take refuge, reward you fully for what you have done."

RUTH 2:11–12 NLT

By Old Testament standards, Ruth wasn't considered a child of God. She was a Moabite, and Moabites had tried to curse the Israelites during the exodus from Egypt (Deuteronomy 23:3–6), so even being friendly with them was discouraged.

But from the beginning of Ruth's story, it's obvious that God guided her and called her one of His own. She adopted the faith of her mother-in-law, Naomi, and after both women became widows, Ruth stuck with Naomi instead of staying in Moab.

Ruth exemplified God's love by caring for her mother-in-law, and her hard work and sacrifice led to her marriage to a kind and generous man named Boaz. But Ruth's blessings didn't end there; they continued for generations. Scripture lists Ruth as the great-grandmother of King David and the ancestor of Jesus (Matthew 1:5, 16).

If you ever feel like an outsider, remember the story of Ruth. God can and will do great things through a loving and obedient heart—no matter who you are or where you come from.

Lord, thank You for welcoming Ruth—
and me!—into Your story and family.

Ruth 3–4 / Luke 23:26–24:12 / Psalm 78:5–8

Generational Faithfulness

*Then Naomi took the child and laid him in her bosom and became
his nurse. And her neighbor women gave him a name, saying,
A son is born to Naomi. They named him Obed. He was the father
of Jesse, the father of David [the ancestor of Jesus Christ].*
RUTH 4:16–17 AMPC

Life is hard. Sometimes it seems impossible. But Ruth's story reminds us that even when life is tragic, terrible, and confusing, God is still faithful, powerful, and in control. It's a story worth revisiting often.

God generously rewarded Ruth's faithfulness and brought great blessings out of hers and Naomi's tragedy. When Ruth and Boaz told their son, Obed, about their own love story, they certainly would've talked about God's faithfulness to them. Then as Obed told his son, Jesse, Grandma Ruth's story, and Jesse told his son (the future king) David, they were already doing what it says in Psalm 78:4 (VOICE): "We will tell the coming generation all about the praise that is due the Eternal One. We will tell them all about His strength, power, and wonders."

Ruth's faith in God had a huge impact that and continued through generations. Take a cue from these giants of the faith and tell the children in your life about how you've experienced God's power, faithfulness, blessings, and unending love.

*God, give me opportunities to share stories of Your
strength, power, and wonders with the kids in my
life. We will honor You in every generation!*

1 Samuel 1:1–2:21 / Luke 24:13–53 / Psalm 78:9–16

Awe and Wonder

*Then the two from Emmaus told their story of how Jesus had
appeared to them as they were walking along the road, and how
they had recognized him as he was breaking the bread. And just as
they were telling about it, Jesus himself was suddenly standing there
among them. "Peace be with you," he said. But the whole group
was startled and frightened, thinking they were seeing a ghost!*

LUKE 24:35–37 NLT

Jesus' appearance to His followers on the road to Emmaus sounded
every bit like a ghost story. His resurrected body wasn't a figment of
the disciples' imaginations, yet when He suddenly appeared among
them, spoke to them, reassured them, and showed them His hands
and feet, they "stood there in disbelief, filled with joy and wonder"
(Luke 24:41 NLT).

Perhaps they stood taking it all in, jaws dropped. Maybe some
slow-blinked or shook their heads to clear out the cobwebs. Jesus'
resurrected body, perfect and immortal, seemed too good to be true.
Soon confusion was replaced with belief and understanding (v. 45),
and as they saw Jesus ascend to heaven, they worshipped Him (v. 52).

This side of heaven, there are amazing truths and wondrous
possibilities that are impossible to grasp. So, when you can't understand
the mysteries of Jesus, when things seem too good to be true, turn
your joy and wonder into praise and worship.

*Thank You for being a God so big that
my imagination can't hold You.*

1 Samuel 2:22–4:22 / John 1:1–28 / Psalm 78:17–24

Family Resemblance

No one has ever seen God, but the one and only Son,
who is himself God and is in closest relationship
with the Father, has made him known.

JOHN 1:18 NIV

"You sure remind me of your mom." If you've never heard someone say something like this, maybe you've looked in the mirror and said it to yourself. But you and your mom are different people, and when someone spends time with your mom, it's not the same as spending time with you.

No one has ever seen God. Some have experienced His glory. Many have felt His presence. Lots of people have communicated with Him. But no one living today has ever laid eyes on Him.

That's one reason why Jesus is God's greatest gift to the world. In Him God revealed His nature and essence in a man who people could see and touch. Jesus is both God as well as the Father's unique, human Son, and He is the living picture of the God who makes Him accessible to us. Jesus has firsthand knowledge of God. . .and He *is* God. When we read about Jesus in scripture, when we see how He treated the weak, sick, and vulnerable, when we hear Him talk about and demonstrate love, we see God.

Jesus, You sure remind me of Your Father. Thank You
for bringing Your kingdom to the world in a tangible
way. Thank You for becoming a human so I can
understand and know my heavenly Father better.

1 Samuel 5–7 / John 1:29–51 / Psalm 78:25–33

Your Potential

Then Andrew brought Simon to meet Jesus. Looking intently
at Simon, Jesus said, "Your name is Simon, son of John—
but you will be called Cephas" (which means "Peter").

JOHN 1:42 NLT

The first time Jesus met Simon, He renamed him *Cephas* (in Aramaic)
or *Peter* (in Greek)—both of which mean "rock." In reality, Peter
wasn't very solid or steady. He often spoke rashly and passionately
(Mark 8:32; John 13:8) and acted without thinking (John 18:10).
His biggest failure was his three denials of knowing Jesus (John
18:15–18; 25–27). Yet despite his shortcomings, Peter grew into
his new name "rock," and God used him in amazing ways to build
Christ's church.

Just like He did for Peter, Jesus sees you and knows who you
are now, but He also knows who you can become. He created your
innermost being (Psalm 139:13) and He knows every detail about
you (Matthew 10:30). What does Jesus see in your future? Courage.
Faith. Loyalty. Peace. Compassion. Generosity. Wisdom. Discernment.
Patience. Kindness.

Jesus loves you just as you are, but He loves you entirely too much
to leave you there. If you've ever wondered what Jesus sees in you,
know this: the same Savior who used a flawed Peter can use you to
do great things too.

Thank You for seeing me through the eyes of love, Lord.
Use me and grow me to my full potential—to be more like You.

1 Samuel 8:1–9:26 / John 2 / Psalm 78:34–41

From Ordinary to Extraordinary

Standing nearby were six stone water jars, used for Jewish
ceremonial washing. Each could hold twenty to thirty
gallons. Jesus told the servants, "Fill the jars with water."
JOHN 2:6–7 NLT

The servants were desperate. So much preparation had gone into the weeklong wedding feast—every detail planned and calculated—yet somehow they ran out of wine. This was more than embarrassing. It would bring shame on the newlyweds because it broke the unwritten laws of hospitality. So when Jesus' mother, Mary, told Him of the emergency, Jesus responded to the couple's heartfelt need by telling the servants to fill six stone jars with water.

There was nothing extraordinary about these six jars. Old Testament law said that Jews became symbolically unclean by touching everyday objects, so prior to eating, people used water from the jars to wash their hands. Yet Jesus used these ordinary jars to show extraordinary love and care to the bride and groom—He turned common water into high-end wine.

If you ever feel ill-equipped, too ordinary, to do something extraordinary for God, remember Jesus' first miracle. His great power and creative resourcefulness mean He can use anyone and anything for God's glory. All it takes is faith and obedience to fill the jars with water.

Jesus, Your first miracle shows how much You care about
the details of my life. Give me the confidence to step out
in faith and love others in extraordinary ways.

1 Samuel 9:27–11:15 / John 3:1–22 / Psalm 78:42–55

Nicodemus

*There was a man named Nicodemus, a Jewish religious leader who
was a Pharisee. After dark one evening, he came to speak with
Jesus. "Rabbi," he said, "we all know that God has sent you to teach
us. Your miraculous signs are evidence that God is with you."*

JOHN 3:1–2 NLT

Nicodemus had much to lose by meeting with Jesus. He was a Pharisee
and member of the Jewish council, the Sanhedrin. Most of his fellow
Pharisees were both skeptical and intensely jealous of Jesus because
He undermined their authority. Yes, Nicodemus had much to lose
politically, but he had so much more to gain from Jesus spiritually.

What made Nicodemus different? He was searching, and he
came to Jesus with a sincere heart and desire to learn. Even in his
uncertainty, Nicodemus took a step of faith toward Jesus and humbly
admitted that he didn't understand all of Jesus' teaching. Jesus honored
Nicodemus' humility and shared some of the great mysteries of
faith. Jesus even shared with Nicodemus the very core of the gospel
message in John 3:16 (NIV): "For God so loved the world that he
gave his one and only Son, that whoever believes in him shall not
perish but have eternal life."

Follow Nicodemus' example and come to Jesus with an open,
humble heart, and He will give you new understanding of the deep
truths of God.

*Jesus, I don't have the answers, but I know You do.
Please teach me as You taught Nicodemus.*

1 Samuel 12–13 / John 3:23–4:10 / Psalm 78:56–66

Jesus above All

If you are confused, consider this: the groom is the one with the bride.
The best man takes his place close by and listens for him. When he
hears the voice of the groom, he is swept up in the joy of the moment.
So hear me. My joy could not be more complete. He, the groom, must
take center stage; and I, the best man, must step to His side.

JOHN 3:29–30 VOICE

In many ways, John the Baptist's ministry linked the Old and New Testaments. He was a "voice shouting in the wilderness, 'Clear the way for the LORD's coming'" (John 1:23 NLT; see also Isaiah 40:3). The days of the ancient prophets as God's messengers were over, so John's bold declarations of the coming Messiah confused many, but he also garnered his own devoted disciples. Yet even with this popularity, John always elevated Jesus above himself.

The world today needs more people who, like John the Baptist, are pointing to Jesus. How can you adopt this attitude in your life? First comes humility. Realize that whatever talents and blessings you have are gifts from God. Second, serve others sincerely, doing "nothing out of rivalry or conceit, but in humility consider others as more important than [yourself]" (Philippians 2:3 HCSB). Finally, tell others about Jesus. Talk about what He's doing in your life, the difference He makes, and the hope you have because of what He did on the cross.

I need more of You, Jesus, and less of me.

1 Samuel 14 / John 4:11–38 / Psalm 78:67–72

One Conversation

*Jesus said, "Everyone who drinks from this water will get thirsty
again. But whoever drinks from the water that I will give him will
never get thirsty again—ever! In fact, the water I will give him will
become a well of water springing up within him for eternal life."*

JOHN 4:13–14 HCSB

The Samaritan woman probably didn't make eye contact with the
Jewish man resting beside the well. But she soon realized *this* Jew
wasn't like the others.

He first asked for a drink, which surprised her. As they continued
to talk, you can imagine the cartoon question marks above her head.
Living water? And if I drink it, I'll never be thirsty again? So she asked
Him for a drink of that kind of water. Then, throughout the course of
their conversation, the woman slowly realized who Jesus was. First,
He was merely a Jew (v. 9), then He was "sir" (v. 11), next He was the
Messiah (v. 29), and finally the Savior of the world (v. 42).

In *one* conversation, the Samaritan woman understood who Jesus
was—even His disciples took longer than that! But each of us is on
our own timeline of growth in our relationship with Jesus. Press into
Jesus, knowing He's the one who grants understanding and is faithful
to lead you to the truth of who He is.

*Lord, I want to know You more and more. Please let our
relationship grow ever deeper, wider, and stronger.*

1 Samuel 15–16 / John 4:39–54 / Psalm 79:1–7

Spiritual Anointing

Samuel took his flask of oil and anointed [David],
with his brothers standing around watching.
The Spirit of God entered David like a rush of wind,
God vitally empowering him for the rest of his life.

1 SAMUEL 16:13 MSG

Saul was legally still the king of Israel, but when Samuel anointed David with oil, the shepherd boy was set apart as holy—to be used for God's service. Each king and high priest of Israel was anointed in this way, and this act appointed David as God's representative to His people. David was changed forever, empowered by the Holy Spirit of God. He had no idea what the future held, but God had big plans for his life.

Although anointing with oil is relatively uncommon in the twenty-first century, God's spiritual anointing is as real today as it was in ancient Israel. Sometimes it comes in the form of a mentor or a parent who helps you figure out God's calling on your life. Sometimes it's a mountaintop experience when God calls you to do something specific for Him. And sometimes spiritual anointing comes as a prompting from the Holy Spirit. No matter the size and shape of the anointing, God will change you—as He changed David—when you are willing to listen to and learn from the Spirit.

Father, prepare my mind and heart for whatever You call me to do.
Change me and mold me into a proper vessel for Your Spirit.

1 Samuel 17 / John 5:1–24 / Psalm 79:8–13

Facing Giants

*"The LORD who rescued me from the claws of the lion
and the bear will rescue me from this Philistine!"*

1 SAMUEL 17:37 NLT

David's father had put him in charge of sheep and goats from a young age, so David knew what it took to fight off big predators. "When a lion or a bear comes to steal a lamb from the flock, I go after it with a club. . . ," David explained to King Saul in 1 Samuel 17:34–35 (NLT). "If the animal turns on me, I catch it by the jaw and club it to death."

But on this day, David took on a different kind of threat—it wasn't a lion staring him down from the top of the food chain but rather a nine-foot-tall Philistine warrior named Goliath who was taunting the Israelites and—even worse—mocking God.

To face Goliath, David summoned courage from his past experiences and trusted God to rescue him again. But it wasn't just saving he needed—he wanted God to display His mighty power for His glory.

As David squared off against Goliath, he knew the battle wasn't his—it was the Lord's. And He was faithful to make David victorious. What Goliaths do you face today? Give them to God and He will fight for you, just as He did for David.

> *Lord, no matter what dangers I face,
> I trust that You will lead me to victory.*

1 Samuel 18–19 / John 5:25–47 / Psalm 80:1–7

Again and Again

*Turn us again to yourself, O God. Make your face
shine down upon us. Only then will we be saved.*
PSALM 80:3 NLT

The writer of Psalm 80 repeated this request two more times—in verses 7 and 19—asking the Lord to turn His people to Him again. This psalm is a desperate cry from the Israelites who remember the blessings God provided—escape from Egypt, home in the promised land, prosperity—but who have suffered because they angered the Lord by choosing to worship idols instead of the one true God.

God longs to hear prayers of repentance from us when we have turned away from Him. He is faithful to turn us toward Him, but that also means that we must turn *away* from our own selfish desires. The challenge of repentance is that our sinful nature will tempt us to turn away from God—again and again. When we give in to that temptation and turn away, we can't see Him—even in our periphery. And when we can't see Him, we may start to doubt God's nearness and love.

Ask God for His help. Ask Him again. And again. Put in the work to demolish the stronghold of sin that causes you to turn away from Him. When you repent, He pulls you into His embrace, where you'll live an abundant life in His shining glory.

*God, I need Your help. . .I've messed up again.
Please turn me toward You and draw me close.*

1 Samuel 20–21 / John 6:1–21 / Psalm 80:8–19

Safe Arrival

*Soon a gale swept down upon them, and the sea grew very rough. They
had rowed three or four miles when suddenly they saw Jesus walking
on the water toward the boat. They were terrified, but he called out
to them, "Don't be afraid. I am here!" Then they were eager to let him
in the boat, and immediately they arrived at their destination!*

JOHN 6:18–21 NLT

Sudden storms are a common occurrence on the Sea of Galilee. The
fishermen disciples knew turbulent weather was always a possibility,
but they were miles from shore when this storm popped up. Although
the rough waters and high waves were a real threat to the boat and to
their lives, there wasn't much they could do but hold on.

We all experience spiritual or emotional storms where we're tossed
around by challenging circumstances—a scary diagnosis, relationship
problems, money worries, job stress—that leave us holding on for dear
life. Just like we read here in John 6, Jesus is present in our storms,
showing Himself in powerful ways, offering comfort, and reminding
us He is in control. Here, unlike the similar story in Matthew 8, Jesus
doesn't calm the storm. Instead He boards the boat and navigates His
friends safely across the turbulent sea.

Invite Jesus into your storm-tossed boat today, friend. He may
choose to calm the storm or He may steer you safely to your destination.
Either way, you are in capable hands.

Jesus, be the captain of my boat.

Friendship

*Then Saul's son Jonathan came to David in Horesh and
encouraged him in his faith in God, saying, "Don't be
afraid, for my father Saul will never lay a hand on you.
You yourself will be king over Israel, and I'll be your second-
in-command. Even my father Saul knows it is true."*

1 SAMUEL 23:16–17 HCSB

Anne Shirley, the beloved character from L. M. Montgomery's novel
Anne of Green Gables, had never experienced true, close friendship
until she met her "bosom friend" named Diana Barry. The two young
girls were kindred spirits who confided in each other and truly loved
each other.

David and Jonathan had a similar, close-knit relationship. First
Samuel 18:1 (VOICE) says that from the first time the two met, "Jonathan
was bound to David in friendship, and Jonathan loved David as he
loved himself." Throughout their relationship, Jonathan was a source
of encouragement to David. He saved David's life several times and
selflessly served both the current king and the future king of Israel.

Maybe today you can begin to grow into a Jonathan for someone
else. Who can you encourage in her faith? You can be a trusted
friend who will keep close confidences—a friend who is always
there, no matter what. Your friendship can be marked by loyalty,
care, compassion, and comfort. That is friendship that lives out Jesus'
commandment to love others as He loves us (John 15:12).

Father, let my friendships grow deeply rooted in You.

1 Samuel 24:1–25:31 / John 6:43–71 / Psalm 81:11–16

Uncanny Peace

*"May the LORD judge between us. Perhaps the LORD will
punish you for what you are trying to do to me, but I
will never harm you. . . . May the LORD therefore judge
which of us is right and punish the guilty one. He is my
advocate, and he will rescue me from your power!"*

1 SAMUEL 24:12, 15 NLT

When Saul entered the cave where David was hiding, the future king
had the perfect opportunity to take down the man who was hunting
to kill him. But instead of striking first, David spared Saul's life,
attempted to reconcile their relationship, and even promised never
to kill him or his descendants.

This isn't the first time David demonstrated an uncanny peace in
the face of great danger. In 1 Samuel 17:46–47 (NLT), we read David's
declaration to Goliath: "Today the LORD will conquer you. . . . And
everyone assembled here will know that the LORD rescues his people."

Why was David so calm in the face of great danger? He believed
in the power of God, trusted that God would do what He said He
would do, that God's plan was good and right; because of those things,
David was content to let God work.

*God, when I am gripping so tightly, trying to control
a situation, remind me of the peace awaiting me when
I yield to Your plan. You are good. Your ways are
perfect. Have Your way in me and in my life.*

Wise Words

"Thank God for your good sense! Bless you for keeping me from murder and from carrying out vengeance with my own hands."

1 SAMUEL 25:33 NLT

A crude and mean man named Nabal broke all kinds of Jewish hospitality protocol in his interaction with David, and the future king of Israel was mad. Murderously angry. Enraged to the point that he and four hundred of his men planned to kill Nabal and his entire household. But God used Nabal's wife, Abigail, to de-escalate David's anger. She not only saved herself and her family, but she also kept David from making a huge mistake.

Abigail's hospitality, generosity, humility, and God-honoring communication resulted in the best possible outcome. Even in the midst of seething, seeing-red anger, David was still willing to hear and listen to Abigail's wise words. First David praised God for sending Abigail (v. 32) and then he praised her for her good sense.

This story teaches us just how powerful our words are. Nabal and Abigail used the same twenty-two letters of the Hebrew alphabet, but where Nabal chose to speak words of cruelty and destruction, Abigail chose words of encouragement and life. Every day you have a choice to make too. What will you do with the twenty-six letters you have at your disposal?

Lord, help me to always choose words as Abigail did—words that build up and bring light and love into every situation. Give me Your wisdom to navigate every interaction with good sense.

1 Samuel 28–29 / John 7:25–8:11 / Psalm 83

Put in Position

Then Nicodemus, the leader who had met with Jesus earlier,
spoke up. "Is it legal to convict a man before he is given a hearing?"
he asked. They replied, "Are you from Galilee, too? Search the
Scriptures and see for yourself—no prophet ever comes from Galilee!"

JOHN 7:50–52 NLT

Jesus had been preaching at the Temple in Judea during the Jewish Festival of Shelters, and every time He spoke, the crowds were divided in their opinion of Him. The Pharisees and leading priests, however, seemed united in their thoughts: they hated Jesus and wanted Him arrested.

One outlier was Nicodemus, the Pharisee who had secretly met with Jesus (John 3:1–21). The fact that he indirectly spoke up on the Messiah's behalf indicates he became a secret believer. Since the Pharisees wanted to kill Jesus, Nicodemus took a big risk by sticking up for Him. His bold statement made the other Pharisees suspicious, and he could've easily lost his high position. After Jesus' crucifixion, Nicodemus helped give Jesus a proper burial (John 19:39)—which is the last time he is mentioned in scripture.

God put Nicodemus in his position for a reason. His humility and open heart toward Jesus made him wise in his words and actions. God put you where you are for a reason too. Ask Him for opportunities to speak out and act on His behalf, for His glory.

Lord, give me the wisdom to use my
position for You. Guide me and direct me.

1 Samuel 30–31 / John 8:12–47 / Psalm 84:1–4

Light of Life

Then Jesus spoke again to them, saying, "I am the
light of the world. He who follows Me shall not
walk in darkness but shall have the light of life."

JOHN 8:12 SKJV

Flip a switch, and light fills a dark room. Say a command to your virtual home assistant, and a lamp turns on. Or tread near a motion-activated floodlight, and you'll be blinking in the brightness. Unlike our ancestors, we have so many ways to illuminate darkness. We often take light for granted—until a tripped breaker or a power outage leaves us searching for matches and candles.

In John 8, Jesus is preaching in the area of the Temple where candles were lit to symbolize the pillar of fire that led the people of Israel through the wilderness on their journey to the promised land. The fire represented God's presence, protection, and guidance (Exodus 13:21–22). Here in the Temple, Jesus is once again telling His followers that He is God when He says He is "the light of the world." The Messiah offers God's presence, protection, and guidance to everyone who believes in Him.

Since darkness and sin entered the world in the Garden of Eden, humans have sought a source of light that won't flicker or fade. That source is Jesus. If you have accepted Jesus as your Savior, that light lives inside you—and nothing can extinguish that.

Thank You, Jesus, for being the true light of my life.

2 Samuel 1–2 / John 8:48–9:12 / Psalm 84:5–12

What Caused This?

Walking down the street, Jesus saw a man blind from birth.
His disciples asked, "Rabbi, who sinned: this man or his parents,
causing him to be born blind?" Jesus said, "You're asking the
wrong question. You're looking for someone to blame. There is no
such cause-effect here. Look instead for what God can do."

JOHN 9:1–3 MSG

We teach children cause and effect as soon as they can understand consequences. Touch a hot stovetop and it will burn you. Eat too much candy and your tummy will hurt. Cross your eyes and they will stay like that (this one might not be true).

Many people in ancient Jewish culture believed that bad things happened because of some big, possibly hidden, sin. Here in John 9, Jesus points out this false assumption and instead teaches the disciples His perspective. Rather than looking at the suffering in the situation, Jesus said, look at how God is working through it.

Why do bad things happen to good people and why do good things happen to bad people? We live in a fallen world, and causes don't always result in the effect we expect—the innocent sometimes suffer. We see in scripture that Jesus is less concerned with the whys and more concerned with easing suffering and making people whole again—all the while giving God the glory. We should be concerned with the same.

Lord, when bad things happen, please give me Your perspective.
Give me peace even when I don't know the "why."

2 Samuel 3–4 / John 9:13–34 / Psalm 85:1–7

I Know This

*So for the second time they called in the man who
had been blind and told him, "God should get the glory
for this, because we know this man Jesus is a sinner."
"I don't know whether he is a sinner," the man replied.
"But I know this: I was blind, and now I can see!"*

JOHN 9:24–25 NLT

The man who had been born blind was probably tired of the Pharisees' questions by this point. The religious leaders had already interrogated him once, then questioned his parents, and now they were drilling him again. The Pharisees wanted desperately to charge Jesus with a crime—the more heinous the better.

But the man wouldn't respond to their baiting by speaking against his healer. Jesus had performed a miracle in his life, and even though he didn't understand why or how it happened, he wasn't afraid to tell the truth of his experience: he was born blind, but now he could see!

Follow the example of this man in telling others about Jesus. Sharing your faith doesn't have to be complicated, and you don't have to be an expert in theology, doctrine, or have lengthy passages of scriptures memorized. All it takes is simply talking about the difference Jesus makes in your life. The Holy Spirit will use your shared story to plant seeds in the hearts of the hearers.

*Jesus, because I know You, I am changed for the better!
Please give me the opportunity to tell others that story.*

2 Samuel 5:1–7:17 / John 9:35–10:10 / Psalm 85:8–13

The Lord Did It!

David went to Baal-perazim and defeated the
Philistines there. "The LORD did it!" David exclaimed.
"He burst through my enemies like a raging flood!"

2 SAMUEL 5:20 NLT

David was a powerful man. A king to a nation of people. A mighty warrior. A wise and benevolent leader. With his impressive list of accomplishments and victories, he should've been one of history's great egotists.

Instead, we repeatedly see David humble himself, ask God for direction, faithfully obey the Lord, and then give God glory for success. David relied on God for his strength (1 Samuel 30:6), acknowledged his mistakes (Psalm 51:3), and was willing to change to become more like God (Psalm 51:10). Whether it was David's defeat of Goliath, escape from his enemies, or victory in battle, rather than pumping his fists and proclaiming, "Look what I did!" he'd shout, "Look what God did!" All of these things and more are what led the prophet Samuel to describe David as "a man after [God's] own heart" (1 Samuel 13:14 NLT).

Today, look for opportunities to shout God's glory. That starts with a thankful heart for all He has done in the past, what He's doing now, and what He will do in the future. When you're celebrating a success, "The Lord did it!" can be the first words out of your mouth.

Lord, I claim Your victory in every area of
my life. You did it and You will do it!

2 Samuel 7:18–10:19 / John 10:11–30 / Psalm 86:1–10

The Perfect Shepherd

"I am the Good Shepherd. The Good Shepherd puts the sheep before himself, sacrifices himself if necessary. A hired man is not a real shepherd. The sheep mean nothing to him. He sees a wolf come and runs for it, leaving the sheep to be ravaged and scattered by the wolf. He's only in it for the money. The sheep don't matter to him."

JOHN 10:11–13 MSG

In Bible times, farmers in small villages often combined their sheep into large, communal flocks. Then they'd split the cost by hiring one caretaker to tend their animals. But even the most vigilant hired hand lacked the commitment of an owner shepherd. If a wolf or bear or lion attacked, a for-hire shepherd would often run for his life rather than defend and protect the sheep.

Here in John 10, Jesus describes Himself as the Good Shepherd—the perfect Shepherd, really. We are His sheep, and we are precious and important to Him. He protects us from our greatest enemy, the devil, a predator that "prowls around like a roaring lion, looking for someone to devour" (1 Peter 5:8 NLT). Jesus proved His commitment as our Good Shepherd when He willingly followed God's perfect plan by dying on the cross in our place, preserving and protecting us, and offering forgiveness and salvation.

The Good Shepherd is leading you in love today. Rest in His care and trust Him to protect you.

Jesus, You are my great protector. I trust You!

2 Samuel 11:1–12:25 / John 10:31–11:16 / Psalm 86:11–17

A Delay in the Plan

Jesus loved Martha and [Mary] and Lazarus,
but oddly, when he heard that Lazarus was sick,
he stayed on where he was for two more days.
JOHN 11:5–6 MSG

Lazarus, Mary, and Martha were close friends and followers of Jesus. So when Jesus and His disciples heard the news that Lazarus was sick, people assumed He would either hurry to Bethany to heal Lazarus or maybe even restore his health from afar.

Yet Jesus didn't rush to His friends to fix the problem. In fact, Jesus began His journey to their home only *after* Lazarus had died. His delay wasn't because He didn't love them, but instead He had a specific plan and purpose—one that would display God's power and show His followers just how deeply He cares for hurting people.

Have you ever felt like God's timing is a mystery? Sometimes God's will—His best plan for you—is painful in the moment. Jesus told His followers in John 16:33 (NLT), "Here on earth you will have many trials and sorrows. But take heart, because I have overcome the world." Hope in Jesus doesn't shield you from life's hard things, but God can use difficult times for good—making you more compassionate for others who are hurting—and your faith can grow stronger through challenges.

Jesus, when I question Your timing, remind me of
the story of Lazarus. You are working all things
together for my good and God's glory!

He Understands

*Then when Mary had come where Jesus was and saw Him,
she fell down at His feet, saying to Him, "Lord, if You had
been here, my brother would not have died." Therefore when
Jesus saw her weeping, and the Jews who came with her also
weeping, He groaned in the spirit and was troubled.*

JOHN 11:32–33 SKJV

When Jesus saw how deeply Mary was hurting after the death of her brother, Lazarus, He also wept openly (v. 35), His spirit deeply troubled by her loss. This isn't the first emotion we see from the Messiah in this story. He has already shown feelings of frustration and anger, sorrow and compassion—often expressing the same deep emotions as the people around Him.

Fully God yet fully human, Jesus experienced all the same feelings you do today, and He cares so much for you that He weeps with you in your sorrow. He comforts you in your disappointment, celebrates with you in your victory, and laughs with you in your joy.

God created our emotions to be part of us. We aren't robots or artificial intelligent beings that react with programmed responses. You don't need to be ashamed or afraid to reveal your true, raw, unfiltered thoughts and emotions to Jesus. He understands how you feel because He has felt that way too.

*Jesus, when I'm overwhelmed by emotion, please
be with me. Give me wisdom to navigate the storm,
and bring me back to peace in Your arms.*

Not Okay

My soul is deeply troubled, and my heart can't bear the weight
of this sorrow. I feel so close to death. I'm like the poor and
helpless who die alone, left for dead, as good as the unknowable
sea of souls lying under our feet, forsaken by Him and cut off
from His hand, abandoned among the dead who rest in their
graves. And You have sent me to be forgotten with them, in the
lowest pits of the earth, in the darkest canyons of the ocean.

PSALM 88:3–6 VOICE

The writer of Psalm 88 is in a state of despair, and this is one of the few psalms that feels utterly hopeless from beginning to end—the writer offers no change in perspective or hope for the future to get any better. If you open scripture looking for encouragement, you won't find much to cling to in Psalm 88.

So why is this psalm included in the Bible? One reason is to show us that we don't have to always be positive. It's okay to not be okay. Difficult times, disappointments, grief, and failure take time to heal. But even in the psalm writer's deepening despair, he trusts God enough to talk to Him about his dark feelings. This teaches us to bring everything—every struggle and every despairing feeling—to God. He is faithful to hear us and comfort us and build us back up and even grow stronger in our faith.

Father, when I'm not okay, please be near.

2 Samuel 15:13–16:23 / John 12:20–43 / Psalm 88:10–18

The Spiritual Zone

*A considerable number from the ranks of the leaders
did believe. But because of the Pharisees, they didn't come
out in the open with it. They were afraid of getting kicked
out of the meeting place. When push came to shove they
cared more for human approval than for God's glory.*

JOHN 12:42–43 MSG

Their fear was real. Anyone openly confessing Jesus as the Messiah would be kicked out of the synagogue (John 9:22). Thus, many kept their faith in Jesus to themselves. Only a few, such as Nicodemus and Joseph of Arimathea, came out into the open. Yet even they didn't express their faith publicly until Jesus had died on the cross.

Jesus wants us to be rooted in Him. To study His Word, pray to, and praise Him. At the same time, He wants us to build our lives up from Him. That means openly confessing He's our Lord. We're not born to seek our fellow human's approval but to seek His.

Perhaps there are some areas in your life where you keep your faith hidden. You'd rather not confess you're a Christian for fear of what others will say or how they may treat you. If so, ask God for the strength to step out of your comfort zone and into the strength, light, and power of the spiritual zone where Christ awaits, giving you the confidence and courage to please and proclaim Him alone.

*Help me, Lord, to step out of my comfort
zone and into the spiritual zone!*

2 Samuel 17:1–18:18 / John 12:44–13:20 / Psalm 89:1–6

God's Plan

*Then Absalom and all the men of Israel said, "Hushai's advice
is better than Ahithophel's." For the LORD had determined
to defeat the counsel of Ahithophel, which really was the
better plan, so that he could bring disaster on Absalom!*

2 SAMUEL 17:14 NLT

King David's son Absalom was determined to completely oust his
father from the throne. The young man had already taken up residence in Jerusalem and had his father on the run. Now he was looking for a way to defeat him in battle, hoping, most likely, to kill the
king altogether. So Absalom asked his counselor, Ahithophel, for
advice, advice that God would use to bring an end to Absalom's
rebellion and ultimately his life.

God has a plan. A better plan. For your life and the lives of all
those around you. Thus, you need never worry about nor fear anyone
or anything, for it is the Lord who determines all outcomes, rewarding His faithful followers and bringing the plans of the unfaithful
to ruin.

Remember, as you remain faithful and loving to God, He remains
faithful and loving to you. And all His plans for you are good ones.
Better than you could ever imagine.

*"I will sing of the LORD's unfailing love forever!
Young and old will hear of your faithfulness. Your
unfailing love will last forever. Your faithfulness is as
enduring as the heavens" [Psalm 89:1–2 NLT].*

2 Samuel 18:19–19:39 / John 13:21–38 / Psalm 89:7–13

Love

*So I give you a new command: Love each other deeply and fully.
Remember the ways that I have loved you, and demonstrate
your love for others in those same ways. Everyone will know
you as My followers if you demonstrate your love to others.*

JOHN 13:34–35 VOICE

This command Jesus gives His followers is not a new one. For God had already made clear to His people that they were to love their neighbors as themselves (Leviticus 19:18). The difference in the command Jesus relates to His disciples in this passage is that His followers are to love *as He loved*. That Jesus' love for us is to be our motivating power in loving others.

And how did Jesus love? By showing compassion to others. By reaching out to those no others wanted to touch—or wanted to touch them. By treating the least desirable as His dearest companions. By putting others above and before Himself. By dying so that others could live.

This love of Jesus is not to be a surface love or a love only expressed when we deem others worthy or good. It's to be a love that is above all others and is to come directly from the heart.

Consider areas in which you can demonstrate your love for others as Jesus demonstrated His love for you. Then watch a garden of love begin to blossom all around you.

Help me, Lord, to be a conduit of Your all-encompassing love.

2 Samuel 19:40–21:22 / John 14:1–17 / Psalm 89:14–18

Keep on Believing

*Don't get lost in despair; believe in God, and keep on believing
in Me. My Father's home is designed to accommodate all of you. . . .
I am going to make arrangements for your arrival. I will be there to
greet you personally and welcome you home, where we will be together.*

JOHN 14:1–3 VOICE

In this topsy-turvy world, it's easy to get so overwhelmed by the constant bombardment of bad news that you find yourself lost in despair. But Jesus warns you of this. He tells you to continue believing in God and in Him.

To help us stay rooted in Him, Jesus tells us that there's a home for us in heaven, one that will hold every one of us. And that He's gone ahead to not only make arrangements for our stay but to personally greet us when we arrive!

Afraid you don't know the way? No worries. Jesus is "the path, the truth, and the energy of life" (John 14:6 VOICE). All you have to do is follow Him. To accept the truth that He is in God and God is in Him. To understand that with Him, nothing is impossible. To know that anything we ask in His will and name will be given to us. To understand that God resides within us.

Today, don't get lost in despair. Instead, keep on believing in Jesus. And live as He lived.

*Thank You, Jesus, for showing me the way,
the truth, and the life I have in You.*

2 Samuel 22:1–23:7 / John 14:18–15:27 / Psalm 89:19–29

Never Let Go

*Peace I leave with you; My [own] peace I now give and bequeath
to you. Not as the world gives do I give to you. Do not let your
hearts be troubled, neither let them be afraid. [Stop allowing
yourselves to be agitated and disturbed; and do not permit yourselves
to be fearful and intimidated and cowardly and unsettled.]*

JOHN 14:27 AMPC

Jesus tells us not to allow ourselves to be agitated, disturbed, fearful,
intimidated, cowardly, and unsettled. Instead, we're to home in on
the peace He has gifted us. The peace that we, as believers, gain from
having the Holy Trinity ever abiding within us.

One way to stay rooted in Jesus and grow up in His peace is
to remember who God is and what He does for us. Perhaps even
writing a song or prayer of praise like David did. In 2 Samuel 22,
David thanked and praised God, describing Him as his rock, fortress,
deliverer, refuge, salvation, and stronghold. When in distress, he called
out to God and God answered, saving him from his enemies. God
continually reached down and pulled David out of deep water. He
circled David with strength.

When fear and fretting rise, don't give them a foothold. Instead,
tap into God's Word. Remind yourself who He is. Remember you
have the Spirit within you. Take hold of Jesus' peace and never let go.

*I'm hanging on to You and Your peace,
Lord, never to be parted from either!*

2 Samuel 23:8–24:25 / John 16:1–22 / Psalm 89:30–37

Always within Reach

It is profitable (good, expedient, advantageous) for you that I go away. Because if I do not go away, the Comforter (Counselor, Helper, Advocate, Intercessor, Strengthener, Standby) will not come to you [into close fellowship with you]; but if I go away, I will send Him to you.

JOHN 16:7 AMPC

Jesus has equipped you with the Holy Spirit. That Spirit comforts you, easing your heart when bruised or broken. He also advises you. You simply need to ask for wisdom—and then listen to His voice. The Spirit will also help you out of sticky situations and prompt you as to which path to take.

This same helper also serves as your advocate. He's the member of your team who'll speak up for you. He's your intercessor, interpreting your groans and sighs and sending the words you wish you could form up to the ear of the Father.

The Spirit is also the one who'll give you the strength you need to do what seems impossible or improbable. And He's always on standby, just waiting for you to turn to Him, to ask Him for help, to listen to His voice, to heed His wisdom, to give you the power you need in the nick of time.

Spirit, may I be in constant awareness of Your presence within, a helper always on standby, always within reach.

1 Kings 1 / John 16:23–17:5 / Psalm 89:38–52

Perfect Peace

I have told you these things, so that in Me you may have [perfect] peace and confidence. In the world you have tribulation and trials and distress and frustration; but be of good cheer [take courage; be confident, certain, undaunted]! For I have overcome the world. [I have deprived it of power to harm you and have conquered it for you.]

JOHN 16:33 AMPC

Jesus has made it as plain as could be. He has told you many things in His Word so that you could have perfect peace and confidence in your life with Him regardless of what's going on around you. By contrast, the world will bring you nothing but trouble, trials, distress, and frustration, especially if you live your life trying to please people instead of God.

Yet, although we are foreigners here in this world, we can still be joyful. We can be brave, confident, assured, and unfazed by what's happening around us. Why? Because Jesus has made the world powerless to harm us. In fact, He has conquered it.

The art of believing is to keep the Word in your mind. To keep your eyes on Jesus. To keep your ears open to the prompting of the Holy Three. To follow the greatest commandments—to love God and others as yourself. That's how you can keep the perfect peace of Jesus in your heart and mind.

Thank You, Lord, for that perfect peace only You— my Word, Way, Light, and Love—can provide!

1 Kings 2 / John 17:6–26 / Psalm 90:1–12

A Foreigner by Faith

*I'm not asking that you take them out of the world but
that you guard them from the Evil One. They are no more
defined by the world than I am defined by the world.*

JOHN 17:15–16 MSG

The disciples may have thought that the best way to avoid danger and trouble would be to be taken out of this world with Jesus. But that's not how God would have it. Each believer has work to do here, a purpose, a task only she can perform. Thus, Jesus asks not for His followers to be taken *out* of this world but that God would guard them from the Evil One while they are *in* the world, until their task is finished.

Jesus also makes it clear that His followers are not to be defined by this world, just as He isn't. The same thing applies to believers today. We're not to strive for material things, for riches, for fame. Instead, we're to live our lives by the Word of God, look to Him as our guard and guide, seek our pathway based on His direction. We've been chosen to live outside of this world, like Abraham who "by faith. . .stayed as a foreigner in the land of promise" (Hebrews 11:9 HCSB).

Today, take stock of who you are and how you are to live, grounded in Christ in the land of promise.

Lord, help me be a stranger to this world as I follow You.

1 Kings 3–4 / John 18:1–27 / Psalm 90:13–17

Focusing on the Father

*"I told you I am He," Jesus replied. "So if you're looking for
Me, let these men go." This was to fulfill the words He had
said: "I have not lost one of those You have given Me."*

JOHN 18:8–9 HCSB

Judas came into the garden with his entourage to witness Jesus'
arrest. Yet Jesus—even as He was being confronted with a military
force, knowing He would soon be killed, He, the one who "knew
all things" (John 18:4 VOICE)—had only one intention. To keep His
disciples—those who would spread His Word—safe from harm, not
just spiritually but physically.

After Jesus had identified Himself and told the soldiers to let
His followers go, "Simon Peter, who had a sword, drew it, struck the
high priest's slave, and cut off his right ear. (The slave's name was
Malchus.) At that, Jesus said to Peter, 'Sheathe your sword! Am I not
to drink the cup the Father has given Me?'" (John 18:10–11 HCSB).
Even though it's Judas the betrayer who stands before our Savior in
this scene, Jesus is not focused on the evil His one-time disciple is
leveling but on the task His Father set before Him.

May we see before us in all situations not the Judases that betray
us but the Father who stands with us, leads us, keeps us, and stays
faithful to us. To the end of days.

*Lord, may I always see You before me,
leading, loving, and looking after me.*

1 Kings 5–6 / John 18:28–19:5 / Psalm 91:1–10

Covered by God's Wings

*He who takes refuge in the shelter of the Most High will be safe
in the shadow of the Almighty. He will say to the Eternal, "My
shelter, my mighty fortress, my God, I place all my trust in You."
. . . Like a bird protecting its young, God will cover you with His
feathers, will protect you under His great wings; His faithfulness
will form a shield around you, a rock-solid wall to protect you.*

PSALM 91:1–2, 4 VOICE

In whom or what are you taking refuge? If it's in the people and things
of this world, chances are you'll be shaken up, stressed out, and bereft
of joy. God provides a better way.

When you take refuge in the Lord, sheltering in His presence,
trusting in Him alone for e-v-e-r-y-t-h-i-n-g, you will find the peace
and protection your soul longs for. By placing your entire being in
God's hands, you will be covered by God's wings. His faithfulness to
you will be like a shield that can never be penetrated. No evil will find
you. Your stress will melt away. Your anxiety will find no purchase.
For nothing, no power in heaven or on earth, can defeat that of God
Almighty.

Take this promise to heart and mind as you slip away into God's
presence and rest in His peace.

*In You, Lord, I take shelter, trusting You with all my heart,
soul, spirit, and mind. Cover me with Your wings.*

1 Kings 7 / John 19:6–25 / Psalm 91:11–16

Clinging to God

"If you'll hold on to me for dear life," says GOD, *"I'll get*
you out of any trouble. I'll give you the best of care
if you'll only get to know and trust me. Call me and
I'll answer, be at your side in bad times."
PSALM 91:14–15 MSG

Infants cling to their mothers, holding on for dear life. For they know that in her arms they are safe. Nurtured. Provided for. Comforted.

God wants you to know Him just like an infant knows her mother. He wants you to trust Him; to understand that He is your safe place; to realize that at one cry from your lips, He will come running; to remember that He'll be at your side in good times and bad.

To know God as a child does her mother, seek out Jesus. He's the one who can help you understand your Father, the one who has commanded "his angels to protect you wherever you go. . .[to] hold you up with their hands so you won't even hurt your foot on a stone" (Psalm 91:11–12 NLT).

Trust God in all things. Cling to Him, holding on with all your might, just as an infant wraps its arms around its mother's neck. See the Lord, your provider and protector, as your safe place. Build your life up from there.

Lord, my safe place, help me to trust You
more, to cling to You like no other.

1 Kings 8:1–53 / John 19:26–42 / Psalm 92:1–9

Giving Thanks

How good it is to give thanks to the Eternal and to praise Your name with song, O Most High; to speak of Your unfailing love in the morning and rehearse Your faithfulness as night begins to fall. . . . Because You, O Eternal One, thrill me with the things You have done, I will sing with joy in light of Your deeds.

PSALM 92:1–2, 4 VOICE

Thousands of years ago, the psalmist recommended thanking God, praising Him in song. He encouraged talking about God's forever love when you awaken and then thinking about all the ways He has been faithful when evening comes.

Today people are just beginning to realize and emphasize the mental and physical benefits that come from expressing gratitude. When you are feeling thankful, say the experts, you'll sleep better, be in a better mood, and build up your immune system. When expressing gratitude, depression, anxiety, and pain will either disappear completely or lessen significantly.

So why not begin this practice today? When you arise in the morning, praise God, giving Him thanks for His forever love. Then at night, write down at least five things you are thankful to God for. And reap the benefits of doing so, not just mentally and physically but spiritually!

Today, Lord, I will sing of Your love. And as night falls, I will thank You for being so faithful to me, for the things You've done, for the God You are!

1 Kings 8:54–10:13 / John 20:1–18 / Psalm 92:10–15

He Calls Your Name

"Dear woman, why are you crying?" Jesus asked her.
"Who are you looking for?" She thought he was the gardener.
"Sir," she said, "if you have taken him away, tell me where you
have put him, and I will go and get him." "Mary!" Jesus said.

JOHN 20:15–16 NLT

One of the ways we can build up our faith in Jesus is by trusting in God's goodness, even during those hard times. Times when we aren't sure what He's doing and when we feel lost, alone, and abandoned.

That's how Mary must have felt when she came to visit Jesus at the tomb and couldn't find the body of her master and friend. Even when Jesus asked her why she was crying and who she was looking for, Mary didn't recognize Him as her Savior but thought He was the gardener. Yet then, as soon as Jesus spoke her name, she realized who He was and was overtaken with joy.

When the hard times and tears come, trust in God's goodness. Know that He is there with you. Understand that because of Jesus, you will never be lost, alone, or abandoned. For He is here. Listen. He's calling your name.

Thank You, Lord, for always being here with me.
When troubles come, may I see You through my tears.
May I trust in Your goodness and hear You calling my name.

1 Kings 10:14–11:43 / John 20:19–31 / Psalm 93

Peace Be with You

*Eight days later the disciples were together again, and this time
Thomas was with them. The doors were locked; but suddenly,
as before, Jesus was standing among them. "Peace be with you,"
he said. . . . Then Jesus told [Thomas], "You believe because you
have seen me. Blessed are those who believe without seeing me."*

JOHN 20:26, 29 NLT

All the disciples—except for Thomas—were in a room, hiding behind
locked doors, fearful of the Jewish leaders. In the evening on the first
day of Jesus' resurrection, He suddenly appeared in the upper room
and stood among His followers. The first words out of His mouth were
"Peace be with you" (John 20:19 NLT). He then showed the disciples
the holes in His hands and feet and repeated the words, "Peace be
with you" (John 20:21 NLT). He breathed on them, telling them to
receive the Holy Spirit.

Eight days later, Thomas was in the room with the disciples.
Jesus again appeared out of nowhere and greeted His followers with
peace. He then showed Thomas the holes in His hands and feet. Then
Thomas believed. Because he'd seen Jesus.

Yet Jesus says, blessed are you, woman, who believes without ever
having seen Him. For you not only gain the Holy Spirit to lead and
guide you but the peace Jesus, appearing seemingly out of nowhere,
keeps bringing into the room.

Today, grow up and into Jesus' peace.

*Thank You, Lord, for Your blessing of the
Spirit and Your ever-flowing peace.*

1 Kings 12:1–13:10 / John 21 / Psalm 94:1–11

153 Fish

So Simon Peter went aboard and dragged the net to the shore.
There were 153 large fish, and yet the net hadn't torn.
JOHN 21:11 NLT

After Jesus had appeared twice to the disciples in the upper room, Simon Peter told his fellow followers he was going to go fishing. Others decided to join him. They fished all night but had caught nothing.

Now Jesus enters the scene. He stands on the shore, looking at His followers upon the sea. But they didn't know it was Him. Jesus calls out, "You don't have any fish, do you?" (John 21:5 HCSB). They yell back, "No." The man on the shore says, "Cast the net on the right side of the boat. . .and you'll find some" (John 21:6 HCSB).

The disciples followed Jesus' directions, and suddenly their net was so full of fish they had trouble hauling it into the boat. That's when the disciple Jesus loved best realized the man on the shore was Jesus.

When you are at a loss, feeling defeated, Jesus will appear. As you recognize and tune in to Him, becoming willing to follow His direction, you will reap your reward.

Jesus, I open my eyes to Your presence. Tell me
what You would have me do. Help me be patient
as I wait for Your Word to lead me.

1 Kings 13:11–14:31 / Acts 1:1–11 / Psalm 94:12–23

Held Up by Love

When I said, "My foot is slipping!" Your unfailing love,
O Eternal One, held me up. When anxiety overtakes me
and worries are many, Your comfort lightens my soul. . . .
The Eternal has been my citadel; my God, a sure safe haven.

PSALM 94:18–19, 22 VOICE

Life can be like performing a highwire act. As you're trying to balance everything you feel you must do or are expected to do or have scheduled to do, things can get a little shaky. Soon you begin to feel as if your foot is slipping, and before you know it, you're free-falling.

The Word reminds you to cry out to God in those moments. To let Him know that you feel as if your foot is slipping, that your balance will soon be thrown off, and that you're not sure how secure the safety net is below you. When you do, God and His unfailing love will rush in to hold you up. His presence will give you the comfort and security that can be satisfied no other way.

God is always there for you, just waiting to catch you, to help you regain your balance, to give you the rest you need, to shield you with His strength and fill you with His peace. What a rock! What a fortress! What a God!

Lord, remind me that You are closer than a breath,
no further than a prayer. Thank You for holding me up,
for lightening my soul, for being my safe haven!

1 Kings 15:1–16:20 / Acts 1:12–26 / Psalm 95

Bow Down

*Come, let us worship Him. Everyone bow down; kneel before
the Eternal who made us. For He is our God and we are
His people, the flock of His pasture, His sheep protected and
nurtured by His hand. Today, if He speaks, hear His voice.*
PSALM 95:6–7 VOICE

The Lord requires you, His follower, "to live justly and to love kindness
and to walk with your True God *in all humility*" Micah 6:8 (VOICE,
emphasis added). That means that when you worship Him, you're
to demonstrate that He alone is Lord by bowing down, kneeling, or
lowering your head. Humbling yourself before God when you praise
Him helps you to have the right heart attitude. To remember you're
not the shepherd but the sheep. He leads, you follow.

Another part of living a life humbly is to not just listen for God's
voice. But to pause when you hear it. To step out of this world and
into His with all your mind, heart, soul, and spirit. And then respond
to what He tells you to do or how He wants you to be.

You're still a work in progress. But thank God today that He's
in your life. Worship Him in all humility. Ask your Good Shepherd
what He would have you do. Then do it.

*My beloved Good Shepherd, I come before You,
bowed in Your presence. Speak. Your servant is
listening, pausing with You in this moment.*

1 Kings 16:21–18:19 / Acts 2:1–21 / Psalm 96:1–8

A Reward Awaits

"Don't be afraid! Go ahead and do just what you've said, but make a little bread for me first. Then use what's left to prepare a meal for yourself and your son. For this is what the LORD, the God of Israel, says: There will always be flour and olive oil left in your containers until the time when the LORD sends rain and the crops grow again!"

1 KINGS 17:13–14 NLT

In the middle of a drought, God sent Elijah to Zarephath for He'd instructed a widow living there to feed His prophet. So off Elijah went. When he arrived at the city gate, he saw a widow gathering wood. Elijah called out to her, asking her to bring him some water and then a piece of bread.

The widow said she had nothing baked, only a handful of flour in a jar and a bit of oil in a jug. She had been gathering some sticks to cook the last meal she and her son would eat.

Elijah told her to make her bread and give it to him. Then to use what was left over to make a meal for herself and her son. God promised she'd have enough flour and oil left until the rains came and crops grew again.

Trusting in God's word, the widow exchanged her uncertainty for His certainty and was rewarded with plenty of provision while the drought continued.

Trusting in You and Your Word, Lord, I exchange my uncertainty for certainty and am rewarded.

1 Kings 18:20–19:21 / Acts 2:22–41 / Psalm 96:9–13

A Voice on the Breeze

This was not a divine wind, for the Eternal was not within this wind. After the wind passed through, an earthquake shook the earth. This was not a divine quake, for the Eternal was not within this earthquake. After the earthquake was over, there was a fire. This was not a divine fire, for the Eternal was not within this fire. After the fire died out, there was nothing but the sound of a calm breeze. And through this breeze a gentle, quiet voice entered into Elijah's ears.

1 KINGS 19:11–13 VOICE

Forces of nature can sometimes speak to our moods. There are times we may feel as if we are being thrown about by a fierce wind. But then it passes. The next thing we know, we feel shaken. Yet a calm follows, and all seems well once more. Next comes a fire, but eventually that too dies out. Then, after being blown about, shook up, and overheated, we come to a place of stillness. Of silence. A calm breeze flows within and without. And in that place, in that peaceful quiet, we hear the voice of God.

When you feel bruised and battered, shaken and forsaken, alone and unloved, frightened and forlorn, God will send His angels to minister to you. He'll provide you with the direction you need and the strength to follow it. And then He'll speak in that still, gentle voice that rides upon the wind and enters into your spirit.

Lord, I am here in the quiet. Speak. I'm listening.

Continually Committed

The community continually committed themselves to learning what the apostles taught them, gathering for fellowship, breaking bread, and praying. . . . There was an intense sense of togetherness among all who believed; they shared all their material possessions in trust.

ACTS 2:42, 44 VOICE

Regardless of the danger the early church was in, the community of believers began to root their lives in Christ. They *continually committed* themselves to learning the apostles' teachings. Hour after hour, day after day, week after week, believers chose to make God a priority. To learn about Jesus was uppermost in their minds.

Yet they didn't stop there. They *continually committed* to gathering together even while the outside world was trying to pull them apart, to destroy them and their message. They *continually committed* to fellowshipping, eating and drinking and living together. And they *continually committed* to praying, letting God know their requests and hear their praises, spending time in His presence.

That's how you build your life in Christ. Continually committing to your study of the Word, communicating with God, and spending time in community with fellow believers, making God a part of your very being, existence, life.

Lord, help me be continually committed to You, learning about You, praying to You, and loving others through You.

Seeking Wisdom

I am with you. I will do what you do. My troops will be your troops;
my horses will be your horses. But first, ask the Eternal for His
wisdom and guidance in this matter. . . . I need counsel. Is there
a prophet of the Eternal present whom we can ask for advice?

1 KINGS 22:4–5, 7 VOICE

Evil king Ahab of Israel wanted good king Jehoshaphat of Judah
to join him in waging war against Ramoth-gilead. Jehoshaphat was
willing to help, yet he had one caveat. He first wanted to talk to God
about the matter. To seek His wisdom and guidance as to whether
this was a good idea.

What a novel concept this may be for some of us. To seek God's
wisdom through His Word and prayer *before* making any kind of move
in any direction. *Then* to take God's advice above that of any person
or institution or gut feeling. To follow and obey what He advises.

Seeking God's wisdom—and following it—may mean going
against the wishes of those closest to us. Yet who's closer than God?
If we're rooted in Him, committed to taking His wisdom above all
others, He'll give us the strength, the plan, the perseverance to do
what we're called to do. He will give us the victory that comes with
our living in obedience to Him.

Lord, I come to You for wisdom and for the strength to do Your will.

1 Kings 22:29–2 Kings 1:18 / Acts 4:23–5:11 / Psalm 98

Refill, Please!

*They finished their prayer, and immediately the whole
place where they had gathered began to shake. All the
disciples were filled with the Holy Spirit, and they began
speaking God's message with courageous confidence.*

ACTS 4:31 VOICE

The apostles Peter and John had recently been arrested for telling others about Jesus. They had to speak before the council of Jewish leaders, who told them to keep quiet about Him. Immediately after their release, Peter and John went back to the fold of fellow believers, told their story, and shared the warning they'd received.

The entire community of believers responded to this news by lifting their voices to God in prayer, ending with asking God to "take note of their intimidations intended to silence us. Grant us, Your servants, the courageous confidence we need to go ahead and proclaim Your message while You reach out Your hand to heal people, enabling us to perform signs and wonders through the name of. . .Jesus" (Acts 4:29–30 VOICE). God answered their prayer by shaking up the place where they'd gathered and refilling them with the Holy Spirit.

When you feel you have no more to give, when you need strength, help, and courage, make prayer your first choice. Then you'll receive the much-needed refilling required to keep on keeping on.

*I need You, Lord, now more than ever. Fill me with Your Spirit,
with the strength, power, help, and courage to carry on.*

2 Kings 2–3 / Acts 5:12–28 / Psalm 99

Dare to Hope and Believe

The Chief Priest and those on his side. . .arrested the apostles and put them in the town jail. But during the night an angel of God opened the jailhouse door and led them out. He said, "Go to the Temple and take your stand. Tell the people everything there is to say about this Life."

ACTS 5:17–20 MSG

The apostles, who continued to teach about Jesus after their arrest and were also performing miracles among the sick and bedeviled, were arrested once again. But God had other ideas. He sent an angel to open the prison door and lead the apostles out. The heavenly being also relayed a message from God, telling them to continue spreading the word about Jesus and His life. The apostles, "promptly obedient . . .entered the Temple at daybreak and went on with their teaching" (Acts 5:20 MSG).

When you see no way out of a troublesome situation, when you are imprisoned by doubt, dismay, discouragement, and despair, dare to hope, to believe that God will make a way where there seems to be no way; that He will open doors that have kept you in the dungeon; that He will send His aid in the form of an angel and help you take a stand.

You know where I'm at, Lord, what doors need to be opened, what demons suppressed. I dare to hope, to believe, that You can and will do the impossible within, for, and through me.

2 Kings 4 / Acts 5:29–6:15 / Psalm 100

All Will Be Well

Don't worry; all will be well.
2 KINGS 4:23 VOICE

A rich yet childless woman of Shunem had befriended Elisha. She would invite him into her home for a meal whenever she saw him pass by. Later, after discussing it first with her husband, they built a small room onto their house, a place where the prophet could stay when he was in town.

Grateful for this kind woman's generosity, Elisha predicted she would have a child, a son, within a year. And his words became a reality. Yet one day this woman of Shunem's son fell ill. He'd been in the fields with his father and complained of a headache. He was carried home to his mother and died in her lap.

The woman of Shunem carried the boy up to Elisha's room and laid him on the man of God's bed. Then she determined to look for Elisha. Before she left the house, her husband, unaware of their child's death, asked her where she was headed. She explained she was going to look for Elisha. When asked why, she simply answered, "Don't worry; all will be well."

This is the attitude of faith that should be on our lips. Like this woman, we need not worry. For we live with the certainty that no matter what happens in our lives, *all will be well.*

Lord, because You're beside me, within me, protecting and watching over me, I know I need not worry. With You, all is and will be well.

2 Kings 5:1–6:23 / Acts 7:1–16 / Psalm 101

Open to Heavenly Realities

Elisha: Have no fear. We have more on our side than they do.
(praying) O Eternal One, I ask You to allow my servant to
see heavenly realities. The Eternal awakened Elisha's servant
so that he could see. This is what he saw: the mountain was
covered with horses and chariots of fire surrounding Elisha.

2 KINGS 6:16–17 VOICE

The king of Aram was warring against Israel. Yet before his troops even reached various battlefields, they were thwarted. The prophet Elisha had somehow been able to "see" where the Arameans were heading and would inform the king of Israel of their whereabouts, giving the Jews an advantage every time.

To rid himself of this prophet, the king of Aram sent his armies to capture Elisha in Dothan. One morning, Elisha's servant woke up and went outside only to find a great army encircling the city. Panicked, he ran back inside to ask Elisha what they were going to do. That's when Elisha prayed to God to open the servant's eyes so he could see "heavenly realities."

There will be times in our lives when there's fighting around us and fear within. That's when prayer is most needed. Pray for God to help you see heavenly realities, to remind you that you need not fear, for there's more power on our side than that of the enemy.

When fear comes upon me, Lord, I pray You
would open my eyes to Your heavenly realities.

2 Kings 6:24–8:15 / Acts 7:17–36 / Psalm 102:1–7

God's Way

*The Lord had caused the Aramean army to hear the clatter
of speeding chariots and the galloping of horses and the
sounds of a great army approaching. . . . So they panicked
and ran into the night, abandoning their tents, horses,
donkeys, and everything else, as they fled for their lives.*

2 KINGS 7:6–7 NLT

Things were dire for the people of Samaria. They were suffering a great famine because the Aramean army was besieging them. The king of Israel, witnessing the devastation and starvation among his people, said to Elisha, "All this misery is from the LORD! Why should I wait for the LORD any longer?" (2 Kings 6:33 NLT). Speaking for God, Elisha told the king that tomorrow things would be different. Prices would lower and people would be able to afford food.

That night, God caused the enemy to hear the approach of a great army. Panicked, all the men ran off into the night, fleeing for their lives, leaving all their clothes, equipment, and food behind.

Somehow, God makes a way so that all turns out right. Your job is to continue to ground yourself in Jesus. To simply believe, knowing your reward awaits.

*Thank You, Lord, for making a way when
there seems to be no way. May Your miracles,
Your Word, Your power help me keep the faith.*

2 Kings 8:16–9:37 / Acts 7:37–53 / Psalm 102:8–17

An Unlimited God

*"Since My throne is heaven and since My footstool is earth—
what kind of structure can you build to contain Me? What
man-made space could provide Me a resting place?" asks the
Eternal One. "Didn't I make all things with My own hand?"*

ACTS 7:49–50 VOICE

God's presence is not contained in a manmade temple. Nor is it contained in a church building. It is in all and of all. Nothing can contain the Lord who made all and fills every place He inhabits with His glory.

The only thing that puts limits on God is the human mind. Yet God has already told us, "My intentions are not always yours, and I do not go about things as you do. My thoughts and My ways are above and beyond you, just as heaven is far from your reach here on earth" (Isaiah 55:8–9 VOICE).

Put no limits on God's power, His mercy, His forgiveness, and His blessings. Take to heart the fact, the *truth* that He will find a solution to all seemingly impossible situations. That He can and will heal the heart that's crushed, the spirit that's broken, the soul that's withered. He can and will help move forward the feet that seem rooted to the spot and the will that appears to be frozen.

Friend, God is all around you. Don't limit Him. Instead, expand your faith in Him.

*Lord, help me realize You are unlimited in all
things and all ways. I leave all in Your hands.*

An Unchanging God

*In the beginning, You laid the foundation of the earth and set the
skies above us with Your own hands. But while they will someday
pass away, You remain forever; when they wear out like old clothes,
You will roll them up and change them into something new, and
they will pass away. But You are the same, You will never change.*

PSALM 102:25–27 VOICE

Change is all around us. As glaciers melt and the seas rise, the
landscapes and shorelines of continents and islands are altered. As
volcanoes continue to erupt, islands appear where there were none
before. As the earth quakes, land masses shift.

Just as the natural landscapes around us change, so do we ourselves.
We are born as helpless infants, unable to care for and provide for
ourselves. As the years continue, we learn to crawl, stand, walk, and
run. We learn the alphabet, how to read and write, as well as perform
arithmetic. We may go off to college or learn a trade. Some of us then
have families of our own, and the cycle begins all over again.

Yet, although we and the landscape around us may change, God
is and will always remain the same. He's the one constant throughout
our lives, throughout all eternity. In that fact, that truth, take comfort
and be at peace.

*Thank You for the assurance, Lord, that You,
the unchanging God, are with me through all eternity.*

2 Kings 12–13 / Acts 8:9–40 / Psalm 103:1–9

Days of Praise

O my soul, come, praise the Eternal with all that is in me—body, emotions, mind, and will—every part of who I am—praise His holy name. O my soul, come, praise the Eternal; sing a song from a grateful heart; sing and never forget all the good He has done.

PSALM 103:1–2 VOICE

It's good for us to thank God for all He has done and continues to do through us. We're meant and built to praise the Lord with all our being, to find those things for which we can be grateful to Him, just as David does in today's psalm.

Our God continues to forgive us our offenses. He releases us from the punishment of our wrongdoing. He heals our diseases, reaches down into the pits of darkness to deliver us from death. The Lord pours upon us His love that never fails and His compassion that never ends.

When our heart is withered and our soul weary, He fills us with good things to more than satisfy us. He gives us strength, restoring our youth. He rights all the wrongs done against us so we don't have to.

Every day, thank God for what He has done and promises to do in, with, for, and through you. Do so with all your heart, mind, and soul.

*Lord of love, thank You for Your compassion,
forgiveness, and forever love! Use me as You will.*

2 Kings 14–15 / Acts 9:1–16 / Psalm 103:10–14

Walking the Way

*All this time Saul was breathing down the necks of the Master's
disciples, out for the kill. He went to the Chief Priest and got
arrest warrants to take to the meeting places in Damascus so that
if he found anyone there belonging to the Way, whether men or
women, he could arrest them and bring them to Jerusalem.*

ACTS 9:1–2 MSG

Saul was out for the kill. He wanted to arrest, persecute, and destroy
all those who were walking Jesus' Way. Loaded down with arrest
warrants, he set off for Damascus. There he was blinded by a flash
of light. Falling to the ground, Saul heard a voice saying, "Saul, Saul,
why are you out to get me?" (Acts 9:4 MSG).

Saul asks a question in return: "Who are you, Master?" (Acts
9:5 MSG).

In response, he hears, "I am Jesus, the One you're hunting down"
(Acts 9:5 MSG).

Notice how Jesus identifies Himself with those who suffer for
His sake. When you hurt, He hurts. When you cry, He cries. When
evil is done against you, it's done against your Lord. Such is the
compassion Jesus continues to have for all those who walk His Way.
Such is His protection of those He loves and nurtures.

May this truth give you comfort, strength, and assurance,
reminding you that you never walk alone when you walk the Way.

*Thank You, Lord, for Your love, compassion, and comfort.
In You may I continue to walk no matter what comes my way.*

2 Kings 16–17 / Acts 9:17–31 / Psalm 103:15–22

Running Shoes

*The unfailing love of the Eternal is always and eternal for those
who reverently run after Him. He extends His justice on and
on to future generations, to those who will keep His bond of
love and remember to walk in the guidance of His commands.*

PSALM 103:17–18 VOICE

Many of us, after we've accepted Christ, eventually reach a point where we quit pursuing Him. We get comfortable. We settle in for the long haul. We grow passive—our formerly-on-fire faith cooling to lukewarm. Our once-energetic run toward the Savior slows to a leisurely stroll.

To keep the fire of faith alive, it's imperative that we take the advice of Psalm 103 and "reverently run after Him." Why should we "run"? For *so many* reasons: (1) To know Christ better tomorrow than we do today. We still have so much to learn from Him! (2) Because we belong to Him. He is our Father; we are His daughters. (3) And to keep our focus on more of Him and less of the world.

When we faithfully pursue Christ, we benefit from all His blessings, including His eternal love, His justice, His grace, and His provision, just to name a few. Are you ready? Lace up your running shoes—and get moving!

*God, I'm sorry for getting too comfortable in my faith.
Help me to ignite a fire in my soul today. I'm getting
my running shoes ready right now!*

2 Kings 18:1–19:7 / Acts 9:32–10:16 / Psalm 104:1–9

"All-In"

Hezekiah trusted in the LORD, the God of Israel. There was no one like him among all the kings of Judah, either before him or after him. He held fast to the LORD and did not stop following him; he kept the commands the LORD had given Moses. And the LORD was with him; he was successful in whatever he undertook.

2 KINGS 18:5–7 NIV

Two people who are fully committed to each other are open and honest. They are generous with their time and attention. When there's a problem, they stay and resolve it rather than run away. Their relationship is enduring—they're "all-in" today, tomorrow. . .*no matter what*!

Hezekiah was all-in when it came to his relationship with God. He trusted; he held tightly to the Lord; he never stopped following; and he kept God's commands. His deep loyalty to God was evident in all he did; and because of his "all-in" faith, he was a wildly successful man. The Bible says, "There was no one like him among all the kings of Judah" and "he was successful in whatever he undertook." Who wouldn't want to be like Hezekiah?

How's your commitment to Jesus? If you have something keeping you from fully devoting yourself to Him, examine your heart. Let Him know you want to be "all-in" today!

Father God, I want to be all-in! Help me remove any obstacles that stand in the way of my wholehearted commitment to You.

2 Kings 19:8–20:21 / Acts 10:17–33 / Psalm 104:10–23

"You Alone"

"You alone are God of all the kingdoms of the earth. You alone
created the heavens and the earth. . . . It is true, Lord, that
the kings of Assyria have destroyed all these nations. And they
have thrown the gods of these nations into the fire and burned
them. . . . They were not gods at all—only idols of wood and
stone shaped by human hands. . . . Rescue us. . .then all the
kingdoms of the earth will know that you alone. . .are God."

2 Kings 19:15, 17–19 nlt

Hezekiah repeats the two-word phrase *"You alone"* in his prayer to the
Almighty. He is acknowledging that no one else—and no *thing*—is
worthy of the title Ruler and Creator of everything on earth and in
heaven. Only God!

As Christ followers, we should trust that no human beings or
manmade gods—regardless of their position or popularity—can do
what God can do. People will inevitably fail us. They won't keep their
promises. They'll disappoint, confuse, and hurt us. The same goes for
any *thing* we idolize: Bank accounts. Houses. Phones. Cars. Careers.
Those "things" can be lost in a moment, leaving us feeling alone and
empty—unless we know Jesus.

Because *with Him*, we have all we'll ever need—the one and
only promise keeper, rescuer, friend, Creator, all-powerful King of
everything!

Lord, in You alone I trust and find my hope.

2 Kings 21:1–22:20 / Acts 10:34–11:18 / Psalm 104: 24–30

You Matter

Peter fairly exploded with his good news: . . . "God plays no favorites! It makes no difference who you are or where you're from—if you want God and are ready to do as he says, the door is open. The Message he sent to the children of Israel—that through Jesus Christ everything is being put together again—well, he's doing it everywhere."

ACTS 10:34–36 MSG

Have you ever been treated unfairly or as if you were "less than"? Perhaps you were slighted because of your last name, or you grew up on the wrong side of the tracks. Maybe a coworker gossiped behind your back because of your past. Whatever the situation, you surely felt discouraged, deserted, brokenhearted.

The sad truth is human beings will let us down; they'll hurt us in one way or another. But it's time to lift our heads and embrace the "good news" that Peter shared in Acts 10: "God plays no favorites!" When it comes to His love, His grace, His acceptance, His rescue, His faithfulness. . .God doesn't care whether we live in a six-thousand-square-foot mansion or a tiny, dilapidated house in the woods. He doesn't care if we're a "somebody" or a "nobody" when it comes to cultural standards. His door is always open to us.

In God's view, you are a *somebody*! Praise Him!

Lord, You are so good, so kind, so fair. Thank You for showing me that I am loved and I matter to You!

2 Kings 23 / Acts 11:19–12:17 / Psalm 104:31–35

Faith on Fire

*Oh, let me sing to GOD all my life long, sing hymns to my
God as long as I live! Oh, let my song please him; I'm so
pleased to be singing to GOD. . . . O my soul, bless God!*
PSALM 104:33–35 MSG

The writer of this psalm is on fire for the Lord! You can sense it in
his words as he expresses his utter delight in God. And this is key:
his delight isn't just for a moment—but *all his life. . .as long as he lives*!
No doubt about it, this guy is exceedingly passionate about God.

How does *your* passion for God rate? If it's at a 10, keep it up!
But if it's in a season of decline, consider:

- Are you fully surrendered to God? If you're unsure, ask
  yourself: *Am I living for myself or for the Lord?*
- Are you focused on the here and now—or on eternity?
- Are you feeding your faith with regular time in the Word,
  prayer, and fellowship with other Christ followers?
- Have you asked God to help you discover your purpose?

Make a commitment to fully surrender, focus on heaven, feed your
faith, and discover (and tap into!) your purpose, then see what happens.
Your faith and passion for Jesus will be ignited in no time at all!

*God, thank You for helping me stoke the fires of my faith.
I want to delight in You all the days of my life!*

The Power of Story

Offer thanks to the Eternal. . . . Tell. . .about the things He has done. Sing songs of praise to Him; tell stories of all His miracles. . . . May the hearts of the people who seek the Eternal celebrate and experience great joy. Seek the Eternal and His power; look to His face constantly. Remember the wonderful things He has done, His miracles and the wise decisions He has made.

PSALM 105:1–5 VOICE

Books and songs are powerful storytelling tools. The words on a page and the lyrics of a song can inspire, teach, entertain, challenge, evoke emotion, and more. Perhaps awareness of the "power" of story is why the psalmist encouraged the people to "sing songs of praise," to "tell stories of all His miracles," to "remember the wonderful things [God] has done."

Every time we share a story of transformation, express gratitude for a blessing, sing a song of praise, or simply remember God's goodness, we are not only strengthening our own devotion to God, but we are also drawing others into His light. With each story shared, we are helping others see God as He really is. . .Father, provider, Redeemer, and friend.

Dear one, embrace every opportunity to share your faith story, and help others understand the true reason for your hope, your joy, your thankful heart!

Lord, when I think of Your goodness, my faith grows more resilient. Thank You for the power of story, so I can inspire others!

Do You Believe?

*"Through Jesus the forgiveness of sins is proclaimed to you.
Through him everyone who believes is set free from every sin,
a justification you were not able to obtain under the law of Moses.
Take care that what the prophets have said does not happen to you:
"'Look, you scoffers, wonder and perish, for I am going to do something
in your days that you would never believe, even if someone told you.'"*

ACTS 13:38–41 NIV

In Acts 13, we read the first-ever recorded sermon of the apostle Paul. The heart of his message may have been a bit of a shock to the people listening. After all, they had been living by the Ten Commandments. They believed that was the best way to honor God.

But Paul poked a hole in their belief system that day with this truth: humans, left to their own devices, will never be good enough to get into heaven. *But God* made a way through Jesus. Through the cross, the weight of our sins is removed from us and placed on Him. When we accept His gift, God's love is freely poured out—on you and me. God accepts us, imperfections and all, because Jesus paid the price for our sins.

While it's difficult for our finite minds to comprehend, we have a choice to make. *Will you say yes to Jesus?*

God, thank You for the precious gift of Jesus. I believe!

1 Chronicles 3:1–5:10 / Acts 13:44–14:10 / Psalm 105:16–28

Noticeable Results

Paul and Barnabas. . .preached with such power that a great number of both Jews and Greeks became believers. Some of the Jews. . .spurned God's message and poisoned the minds of the Gentiles against Paul and Barnabas. But the apostles stayed there a long time, preaching boldly about the grace of the Lord. And the Lord proved their message was true by giving them power to do miraculous signs and wonders.

ACTS 14:1–3 NLT

Do you have the kind of faith that gets noticeable results? Paul and Barnabas sure did! The powerful preachers were bold with their words. These men not only had a resilient faith, but they were courageous too!

When face-to-face with doubters and deniers, their words were such that both Jews and non-Jews—"a great number," in fact—were convinced these men were telling the truth about God's saving grace. Though there were some who rejected the men and their message, Paul and Barnabas were not discouraged. They stayed and continued preaching—and the Lord took notice! God further proved the truth of their message "by giving them power to do miraculous signs and wonders."

Do you share Jesus in such a way that even the Lord can't help but notice your resilience?

Father God, thank You for the reminder that a resilient faith can capture the attention of those who have yet to meet You. When I share You with the world, give me the right words so others will believe too.

Rise

Unbelieving Jews came. . .and incited the crowds. . . .
[They] turned on Paul, stoned him, dragged him out of the city
. . .thinking he was dead. As the disciples gathered around him,
he suddenly rose to his feet and returned to the city. The next
day he and Barnabas left for Derbe. After they proclaimed the
good news there. . .they returned to some of the cities they had
recently visited. . . . In each place, they brought strength to the
disciples, encouraging them to remain true to the faith.

ACTS 14:19–22 VOICE

Imagine. . . One minute, you're sharing the gospel; the next, you're getting pummeled with stones. The angry mobs grow increasingly violent. They beat you, drag you through the streets, and leave you for dead. Would you get up, dust yourself off, and limp away to safety? Would you stop sharing Jesus altogether? Or would you choose instead to *rise*?

Paul "rose to his feet" after his terrifying encounter. He knew God's plan was *still* good and that he was an integral part of it. And so, Paul tapped his inner resilience and continued his journey. Paul's persistence challenged and encouraged the disciples and gave them the strength they needed to "remain true to the faith" as well.

When faced with opposition, may we, like Paul, choose to rise.

Heavenly Father, when I am beaten down and discouraged, please help me muster up the resilience and courage I need to keep going.

God Remembers His Promise to You

God spread a cloud to keep them cool through the day and a fire to light their way through the night; they prayed and he brought quail, filled them with the bread of heaven; he opened the rock and water poured out. . . . All because he remembered his Covenant, his promise to Abraham, his servant.

PSALM 105:39–42 MSG

Not once while the Israelites were wandering in the wilderness did God fail to provide for them. That's not to say they didn't endure hardship or frustration—they most certainly did! Forty years of wilderness travel doesn't come without some colossal challenges! However, God met their *every need*. When they were growing weary from the heat of the day, God sent clouds to help keep them cool. When it was too dark to see, God provided fire to light the way. When they were hungry, God sent quail and manna from heaven. When they were thirsty, He made water flow from a rock.

When you're floundering in your faith and facing some mighty big mountains, remember all the ways God has provided for His people. God remembers you, and He'll keep every promise He's ever made to you too. Steep your soul in His goodness. Allow His never-ending love and care to bolster your faith!

God, I am so very thankful You never forget the promises You've made to me. You have never failed to provide for me—and You never will.

1 Chronicles 9:10–11:9 / Acts 15:19–41 / Psalm 106:1–12

Nevertheless

Like our ancestors, we have sinned; we have done wicked things.
When our ancestors were leaving Egypt, they did not consider
Your marvelous acts. They forgot Your overwhelming kindness
to them and instead rebelled at the Red Sea. Nevertheless, God
saved them for the honor of His name so He could show His
power to the world. He gave the order, and the waters of the
Red Sea dried up, and He led the people across the sea floor.
PSALM 106:6–9 VOICE

Nevertheless means "nonetheless; notwithstanding; however; in spite of that" (dictionary.com). Consider this for a minute.

We women are busy. We work. We run errands. We do chores. We play. Repeat! We're consumed by a never-ending cycle of *doing*. And in our busyness, we tend to forget God. It's not that we no longer love Him. Not that we quit believing in Him. Not that we no longer trust Him. But rather, we *overlook* Him. He gets lost in the shuffle. . .and until we face a crisis, we live like we really don't need Him. We take His goodness for granted—especially when life is easygoing. Truthfully, we're not all that different from the Israelites who "did not consider [God's] marvelous acts," who "forgot [His] overwhelming kindness" to them and then rebelled at the Red Sea.

But just like God saved the Israelites despite their terrible behavior, He saves you and me. *Nevertheless*. Doesn't that make your soul sing?

Nevertheless, Lord, You love me. You saved me. Thank You!

Open-Heart Faith

*We went. . .to the river, where we expected to find a place of prayer.
We sat down and began to speak to the women. . . . One of those
listening was a woman from the city of Thyatira named Lydia, a
dealer in purple cloth. She was a worshiper of God. The Lord opened
her heart to respond to Paul's message. When she and the members
of her household were baptized, she invited us to her home.*

ACTS 16:13–15 NIV

What is the state of your heart? Is it cocooned off, closed tight, hard, unavailable? Or is it wide open, ready to love and be loved, soft, and readily available to the heavenly Father and to others?

Lydia, a savvy businesswoman in her day, sat near the river listening to Paul and his friends. She had a heart that was soft and pliable—a heart that the Lord opened so she would respond to Paul's message. She got baptized, along with other people from her household, and then she invited the Lord's disciples into her home. Once she received Jesus into her heart, she immediately acted on her faith. Showing love. Showing hospitality. Showing kindness.

Do you have the same kind of openhearted, Lydia-like faith? Is your heart visible not only to God—but to the world?

*Heavenly Father, would You please check the state
of my faith? If my heart is closed off, open it
so my authentic faith shines through.*

Ask God

*When the Philistines heard that David had been anointed
king over all Israel, they mobilized all their forces to capture
him. . . . David asked God, "Should I go out to fight the
Philistines? Will you hand them over to me?" The LORD
replied, "Yes, go ahead. I will hand them over to you."*

1 CHRONICLES 14:8, 10 NLT

How many decisions do you make in a day? Have you ever really
thought about it? Odds are, probably not. We typically make decisions
without much forethought:

Soup or salad?

The blue jacket or the red?

Caramel macchiato or white raspberry mocha?

Most of our decisions don't result in life-altering consequences.
However, from time to time, we must make some difficult choices that
do make a lasting impact—either on our lives or the lives of others:

Move the family across the country or stay put?

Purchase a new car or try to get a few more miles out of the old one?

Splurge on a vacation or save the money for an unexpected expense?

When there is a big decision to be made, consult the heavenly
Father first. Ask Him what He would have you do. And then quiet
your heart and mind and listen for His voice. His answer is *always*
the right one.

> *Before I make any big decisions, Lord, remind me to
> consult You first—no matter what my heart wants
> in the moment. Your way is always best.*

Eternal Blessing

"I have been bold enough to pray to you because you have revealed to your servant that you will build a house for him—a dynasty of kings! For you are God, O LORD. And you have promised these good things to your servant. And now, it has pleased you to bless the house of your servant, so that it will continue forever before you. For when you grant a blessing. . .it is an eternal blessing!"

1 CHRONICLES 17:25–27 NLT

Throughout our lives, most of us become accustomed to disappointment and rejection. And so, rather than counting on people to come through for us, we expect the opposite—and then we're not sorely disappointed.

But thankfully, we serve a very good God. David celebrated the goodness of God's character in 1 Chronicles 16. Notice David's choice of words that expresses 100 percent certainty: "you *have*," "you *will*," "you *are*," "it *is*." He didn't use wishful words like *maybe, hopefully,* and *possibly* when talking about his God. David had no doubt that God would fulfill every single promise He had made and that God wouldn't let him down—not ever!

Today, spend some time thinking about the many ways God has come through for you. Then, like David, work on building the kind of resilient faith that allows you to pray bold prayers to the one who will never let you down.

Blessings-giver, I don't come to You with wishful thinking—I know You will come through for me.

Get Busy Living

*"The God who made the world and everything in it. . .doesn't
. . .need the human race to run errands for him, as if he couldn't
take care of himself. . . . Starting from scratch, he made the entire
human race and made the earth hospitable, with plenty of time
and space for living so we could seek after God, and not just grope
around in the dark but actually find him. He doesn't play hide-
and-seek with us. . . . He's near. . . . 'We're the God-created.'"*

ACTS 17:24–29 MSG

"We're the God-created." If that's true, then God is greater, more
powerful, more in control than we are. If He made the world and
everything in it, He certainly doesn't need us to step in and help run
the show.

When we submit entirely to God and acknowledge Him as the
master Creator, the owner of everything in the world—*including us*—
then we can be free to get busy living our lives just as He intended:
seeking Him, finding Him, living and moving in Him. We can let
go of our daily little (and big!) worries and cares, giving them all to
Him because He can handle them.

And as we learn to let go, God will reward us with a faith more
resilient, more lovely, more fulfilling than we could ever imagine.

*You are God, and I am not. I'm sorry for trying to control
what's rightfully Yours, Father. I wholly submit to You.*

The Best Advice

"May the LORD be with you and give you success as you follow
his directions in building the Temple of the LORD your God.
And may the LORD give you wisdom and understanding, that
you may obey the Law of the LORD your God as you rule over
Israel. For you will be successful if you carefully obey the decrees
and regulations that the LORD gave to Israel through Moses.
Be strong and courageous; do not be afraid or lose heart!"

1 CHRONICLES 22:11–13 NLT

Here in 1 Chronicles 22, David gives advice to his son Solomon, who was tasked with the important job of building the Temple. Like any caring parent, David offers support and encouragement to his son while instructing him on the best path to success:

1. Follow God's direction. BE OBEDIENT!
2. Be strong and courageous. BE GUTSY!

David knew that if Solomon ignored God's guidance, he would fail. David also knew if Solomon was weak or afraid, he would likely give up and quit before the Temple was finished.

David's long-ago wisdom can benefit us even today. If you're fearful and struggling to complete a task the Lord has laid on your heart, take David's advice and push ahead. Don't look back. With the Lord on your side, you can do anything He has called you to do.

Father God, thank You for Your Word that speaks wisdom into
my life. It offers the best advice for living life as You intended.

Saved!

*Some people were locked up in dark prisons. . . . They were
captives bound by iron chains and misery. . . . In their distress,
they called out to the Eternal; He saved them from their misery.
He rescued them from the darkness, delivered them from the
deepest gloom of death; He shattered their iron chains.*

PSALM 107:10, 13–14 VOICE

A dark prison sounds like a terrible place. Surely, it's damp and cold.
It probably reeks of fear and despair. And while we'd never willingly
choose to spend any amount of time locked up in prison, many of us
spend too much time in miserable chains of our own making. It's not
that we make a conscious choice to stay there; we just get stuck and
can't locate the "hidden" key to our spiritual and emotional freedom.

If you're in that stuck place today, call out to Jesus. He alone
holds the key to your freedom—it's been within your reach all along.
When you choose Jesus, when you ask Him to come to your rescue,
you'll encounter a clear path to light, freedom, hope, and His never-
ending love.

No matter your desperate situation, God is gracious. Any time
you're held captive by sin and shame, the heavenly Father will forgive,
He will rescue. He will free you from whatever binds you.

> *Lord Jesus, my rescuer, my hope, shatter the chains
> that are keeping me stuck. Bring me back to
> a resilient faith and hope in You!*

Sunshine and Rainbows

Out at sea you saw GOD in action. . . . With a word he called up the wind—an ocean storm, towering waves! You shot high in the sky, then the bottom dropped out; your hearts were stuck in your throats. . . . Then you called out to God in your desperate condition; he got you out in the nick of time. He quieted the wind down to a whisper, put a muzzle on all the big waves. . . .He led you safely back to harbor.

PSALM 107:23–27, 29–30 MSG

God never promised us a nothing-but-sunshine-and-rainbows kind of life. In fact, His Word says we *will* experience many difficult times (John 16:33 NLT). But in the same breath, God also offers assurance and hope: "But take heart, because I have overcome the world."

While we will, at some point, encounter the not-so-sunny side of life—fear, uncertainty, grief, pain—we don't have to stay there, drowning in our feelings. Why? Because we serve a God who is in control, who loves, rescues, and protects. Even when it seems like all is lost, if we call out to Him, He will save us in the nick of time.

When your sunny skies cloud over, when lightning strikes and thunder booms, remember almighty God will *always* rescue you!

Father God, when life is hard and my emotions get the best of me, help me to remember Your promises of protection and hope.

Nothing Less

*"Get to know well your father's God; serve him with a whole heart
and eager mind, for GOD examines every heart and sees through
every motive. If you seek him, he'll make sure you find him, but
if you abandon him, he'll leave you for good. . . . GOD has chosen
you to build his holy house. Be brave, determined! And do it!"*

1 CHRONICLES 28:9–10 MSG

David is talking to his son Solomon, expressing his wishes that
Solomon chase after God and serve Him with everything he has.
Nothing less will do! Why? Because David knows that the very best
kind of life *always* includes God as the focus.

So often, we give God 80 percent or, if we're being honest (painful
as that might be), sometimes much, much less. And while we try to
kid ourselves that we're doing the best we can, deep down we know
it's not true. We have more to give, including "a whole heart and
eager mind."

If we are truly seeking God, He will be available to us. He'll make
sure we find Him. And, as David understood very well, God knows
our hearts! He knows our motives! So today, check your heart. Are
you on the path to knowing God—*really* knowing Him?

*God, You know my heart, inside and out. I wouldn't
want it any other way. Help me give You my all.
Nothing less will do when it comes to serving You!*

So Much More!

*Solomon replied, . . . "Give me the wisdom and knowledge
to lead. . .for who could possibly govern this great people of
yours?" God said. . ."Because your greatest desire is to help your
people, and. . .you asked for wisdom and knowledge. . .I will
certainly give you the wisdom and knowledge you requested.
But I will also give you wealth, riches, and fame such as no
other king has had before you or will ever have in the future!"*

2 Chronicles 1:8, 10–12 nlt

God basically handed Solomon a blank check and instructed him
to fill in the amount. Solomon could have anything he wanted—
anything!—and God would provide it. Yet Solomon didn't ask for
lots of money or fame or a long life. He didn't ask for vengeance on
his enemies. Solomon requested only wisdom and knowledge so he
could be a good ruler. His answer exposed his true heart—Solomon
genuinely cared about the well-being of his people.

How would you respond if God asked, "What do you want?
. . . I will give it to you!" (1 Chronicles 1:7 nlt). Would your answer
please God's heart?

God blessed Solomon with not only wisdom and knowledge—
but so much more! And, like Solomon, when we delight God, He
will bless us beyond anything we could ever imagine!

*Heavenly Father, increase my faith so my selfish ways become a
thing of the past. I want to delight Your heart—today and always.*

"That's OK"

I served the Lord with humility and tears, patiently enduring...
many trials.... I told everyone...we must turn toward God and
have faith in our Lord Jesus.... My future is uncertain.... But
that's OK.... The only value I place on my life is that I may finish
my race, that I may fulfill the ministry that Jesus our King has
given me, that I may gladly tell the good news of God's grace.
ACTS 20:19–24 VOICE

If anyone ever displayed a resilient faith, it was Paul. He faced more trials than most, and yet he endured. He understood that if he was going to serve God well, he also had to serve people. And so, he traveled near and far, sharing the gospel message. Paul knew, due to the nature of his work (many despised him and his message), that his future was uncertain. But he didn't let fear deter him.

Human nature nudges us to pack up and quit when things get tough. But Paul understood his purpose. Instead of saying, "I quit!" he said, "But that's OK."

Paul set a remarkable example of what it truly means to follow Christ. When our days on earth end, what matters is that we finished our race well. That we fulfilled Christ's purpose for our lives, sharing "the good news of God's grace."

God, be with me as I run my race. I want to finish well!

Bold Prayers

Can it be that God will actually move into our neighborhood?
Why, the cosmos itself isn't large enough to give you breathing room,
let alone this Temple I've built. Even so, I'm bold to ask: Pay attention
to these my prayers. . .O GOD, my God. . . . Keep your eyes open to
this Temple day and night. . . . And listen to the prayers that I pray
in this place. And listen to your people Israel when they pray at this
place. Listen from your home in heaven and when you hear, forgive.

2 CHRONICLES 6:18–21 MSG

Solomon's prayer was gutsy! But before demonstrating his boldness, he first acknowledged the greatness of God. He admitted that no building, not even the far-reaching universe, could contain the presence of God. Then, immediately after, he got down to business, telling God to hear the people's prayers from the Temple and to forgive them.

Solomon's approach wasn't soft and timid but assertive. Notice his choice of words:

"Pay attention."
"Keep your eyes open."
"Listen."

If you didn't know better, you might think Solomon was telling God exactly what He should do rather than deferring to Him. Crazy, right? But understand this: our God is mighty; He is powerful; He is big enough to handle our bold prayers. Pray a courageous, super-direct prayer today, and see for yourself!

God, thank You for the reminder that You are
big enough to handle my bold prayers.

If. . .Then

*"If my people, who are called by my name, will humble
themselves and pray and seek my face and turn from
their wicked ways, then I will hear from heaven, and I
will forgive their sin and will heal their land."*

2 CHRONICLES 7:14 NIV

God's love isn't conditional. There are no requirements we must meet
to earn it.

He never says:

"If you learn to control your anger, then I'll love you more."

"If you try harder, then you'll have a better chance of getting
into heaven."

"If you stop sinning. . .then you'll be worth saving."

He simply loves us, no matter what—whether we're at our worst
or our very best.

However, God does sometimes place conditions on His blessings
and promises. Here in 2 Chronicles 7, Solomon's prayer was answered
with a promise—but to receive it, the people had to meet certain
terms: be humble, seek God's face, turn from their sins. . . If the people
obeyed, God would hear their prayers, forgive them, and heal their land.

Today, thank the heavenly Father for His unconditional love.
Then remember who He is—the one who controls everything, the
one who holds you in His hands, the promise keeper. Be humble and
open to receiving all the wonderful blessings He has in store for you.

*Lord, no matter what, You call me worthy of
Your love. Help me to live obedient to Your Word
so I receive all Your wonderful blessings.*

2 Chronicles 9:29–12:16 / Acts 21:33–22:16 / Psalm 110:1–3

Your Story

[Ananias] said, "Brother Saul, regain your sight!" I could immediately see again. . . . Then he said, "You have been chosen by the God of our ancestors to know His will, to see the Righteous One, and to hear the voice of God. You will tell the story of what you have seen and heard to the whole world. . . . Don't delay. Get up, be ceremonially cleansed through baptism, and have your sins washed away, as you call on His name in prayer."

ACTS 22:13–16 VOICE

Saul (now Paul) had an incredible story to tell! His faith transformation was nothing short of astounding. His life, once marked by a deep-seated hatred for and mistreatment of Christ followers, was now characterized by an intense love of God and passion for sharing the gospel.

Sure, Paul could have chosen to share the finer points of the law with the crowd he was addressing, which might have had some impact. But instead, he chose to tell his personal story of Christian-hater-turned-Christ-follower. Oh, how a personal redemption story grabs the attention of listeners. There's nothing quite like a story to connect souls to a life-changing message.

Friend, what's *your* story? (You have one, you know.) *Every* Christ follower has been saved by the blood of Jesus—and that doesn't happen without a very powerful story!

*Heavenly Father, thank You for choosing me,
for saving me, for giving me a story to share.*

2 Chronicles 13–15 / Acts 22:17–23:11 / Psalm 110:4–7

As He Promised

Remember. . .that the True God is on our side and is leading us. His priests will blow the signal trumpets to alert Him that you are here to fight us, and He will rescue us from our enemies as He promised.

2 CHRONICLES 13:12 VOICE

Every day it's becoming clearer that the world is in a tug-of-war battle with almighty God. And the world is determined to win.

- People lie, cheat, and steal to get what they want.
- Men and women in powerful positions take advantage of the poor, the young, the weak.
- Everywhere you look, false messages are being sold as truth—and people are wholeheartedly buying into the propaganda.
- People live and act according to their feelings.
- Human life is devalued.

You may be wondering, *When will the madness stop?* and worrying, *Will evil ultimately win?* Certainly, when you look around, it seems like "good" is on the losing side of the battle.

Yet God is on the side of good. He is in charge and will ultimately lead His people to victory.

When the world leaves you weary and weighed down with worry, remember who's on your side. He, who acknowledged that our lives would never be trouble-free, said, "But take heart! I have overcome the world" (John 16:33 NIV). God (and good!) *always* wins!

Father God, the state of the world troubles me. Ease my anxiety-ridden soul with promises from Your Word. I trust You to win the battle!

2 Chronicles 16–17 / Acts 23:12–24:21 / Psalm 111

Hallelujah!

Hallelujah! I give thanks to GOD with everything I've got. . . . GOD's
works are so great, worth a lifetime of study—endless enjoyment!
Splendor and beauty mark his craft; his generosity never gives out.
His miracles are his memorial—this GOD of Grace, this GOD of Love.

PSALM 111:1–4 MSG

Why do we praise God? Have you ever thought about it?

Yes, we praise Him *because* He's God. But there's more to it than
that!

He is good. His works (all He does) are great.

His creation is beautiful. (Just look around—a fiery sunset, a
field of wildflowers in bloom, snow-capped mountains, a white-sand
beach—there's no denying it!)

He is generous—in fact, His generosity never stops. He keeps on
giving and giving some more.

He is a God of miracles—both big and small!

He is grace.

He is love.

Our God just keeps on keeping on with His never-ending
goodness. And what's so special about it all is that He doesn't have a
checklist in hand, crossing off the boxes to make sure we're worthy.
No! His goodness is just who He is—regardless of our behavior,
regardless of our own goodness. And if that doesn't deserve all our
praise, what does?

Today give thanks to the heavenly Creator with everything
you've got!

Today, and all my days to come, I will shout a holy "Hallelujah!" God,
You are worthy of my praise. Thank You for Your unending goodness!

2 Chronicles 18–19 / Acts 24:22–25:12 / Psalm 112

The Joyful Difference

Praise the LORD! How joyful are those who fear the LORD and delight in obeying his commands. . . . Those who are righteous will be long remembered. They do not fear bad news; they confidently trust the LORD to care for them. They are confident and fearless and can face their foes triumphantly. They share freely and give generously to those in need. Their good deeds will be remembered forever.

PSALM 112:1, 6–9 NLT

Take note: Followers of Jesus stand out from the crowd. While they may blend in in some ways, there's a noticeable difference in their emotions, their interactions with others, their reactions to situations.

People "in the crowd" today are on edge. They are quick to react in anger or fear or disgust. They are irrational in their thinking and behaviors. In contrast, Christ followers are cool, calm, and collected. When they get bad news, instead of reacting in panic, they reach out to Jesus, confident He is on their side. They trust Him wholeheartedly! When face-to-face with an enemy, they don't cower in fear. They are generous with their time and treasures. In a nutshell, followers of Jesus are. . .*different*!

How about you, friend? Does your life radiate the joy of Jesus?

Lord, I want to celebrate my "joyful difference." Thank You for giving me a happy heart, for making me confident, fearless, generous. I am so glad I'm Yours!

2 Chronicles 20–21 / Acts 25:13–27 / Psalm 113

He Speaks

*"This is what the LORD says: Do not be afraid! Don't be discouraged
by this mighty army, for the battle is not yours, but God's. Tomorrow,
march out against them. You will find them coming up through the
ascent of Ziz. . . . But you will not even need to fight. Take your
positions; then stand still and watch the LORD's victory. He is with
you, O people of Judah and Jerusalem. Do not be afraid or discouraged.
Go out against them tomorrow, for the LORD is with you!"*

2 CHRONICLES 20:15–17 NLT

When was the last time you heard God speak? When did you last really,
truly listen for His voice? Maybe you've never really listened at all.

Whenever you're down and discouraged, alone or fearful,
frustrated or anxious, know and trust that God is bigger than all
of it. He will fight every battle you'll ever face. And when God is
fighting your battles, victory is guaranteed! So, when He says, "Do
not be afraid! Don't be discouraged," really listen! Allow His words to
make their way from your mind to your heart. Sit with them awhile
as you steep your soul in His love and care for you.

Daughter of the King, if you haven't heard God's voice in some
time, quiet your heart. Be still and listen. The Lord will speak!

*God, I'm listening! What wisdom and
encouragement do You have for me today?*

2 Chronicles 22–23 / Acts 26 / Psalm 114

Handpicked!

*"[Saul] said, 'Who are you, Master?' The voice answered, 'I am Jesus.
. . . I've handpicked you. . . . I'm sending you off to open the eyes of the
outsiders so they can see the difference between dark and light, and
choose light, see the difference between Satan and God, and choose
God. I'm sending you off to present my offer of sins forgiven.'"*

ACTS 26:15–18 MSG

From time to time, we struggle with feelings of not being good enough, not pretty enough, not smart enough. . .just not enough. And, if we're being completely honest, we've also had moments where we felt like God must be sorely disappointed in us—that perhaps we're not worthy of His calling. And yet. . .

God used the worst of sinners to represent Him and His saving power to the world! He "handpicked" the terrible, horrible, no-good Saul to do His kingdom work. And Saul had hated Christ followers so much that he had them arrested, beaten, and murdered! But God works in ways we often don't understand. He uses imperfect people to do His perfect work. And He is a pro at transforming lives and hearts—as evidenced by the life of Saul (who was later renamed Paul).

Anytime you feel less than enough, remember Saul's story. You're *always* enough for the heavenly Father!

*Lord, when I get stuck in my not-enoughness, remind me that
You chose me and will keep choosing me. Thank You!*

Alive!

Our God is in heaven doing whatever he wants to do.
Their gods are metal and wood, handmade in a basement shop:
carved mouths that can't talk, painted eyes that can't see, tin ears
that can't hear, molded noses that can't smell, hands that can't grasp,
feet that can't walk or run, throats that never utter a sound. Those
who make them have become. . .just like the gods they trust.

PSALM 115:3–8 MSG

Who would you rather serve? The one true living God or a lifeless, manmade god? Seems like a no-brainer, doesn't it? However, throughout history, humans have set their sights on all kinds of idols—including the sun, the moon, and a golden calf (Deuteronomy 4:15–20)!

When it comes to choosing who we will serve, there's no comparison, friend! Because God is alive! And when we put our trust in Him, we become more alive too! It's through our relationship with Him that we find our purpose. And when we discover our purpose, we have indescribable joy! But without Him in our lives, we inevitably turn to false gods that are nothing more than "metal and wood." When our focus is on anything other than God, we become just like those idols—aimless, unfeeling, lifeless—not living our best life, that's for sure!

Are you interested in becoming "more alive" today? Say *yes*. Choose to serve the living God!

Father God, I want more life! More love! More joy!

2 Chronicles 25:17–27:9 / Acts 27:21–28:6 / Psalm 115:11–18

Still Good

May the Eternal prosper your family, growing both you and your descendants. May the blessings of the Eternal, maker of heaven and earth, be on you. The heavens above belong to the Eternal, and yet earth in all of its beauty has been given to humanity by Him.

PSALM 115:14–16 VOICE

Perhaps you're struggling today, and your worries press heavy on your shoulders. In our grossly imperfect world, there are numerous hardships we will face. If not today, then tomorrow.

Loved ones get sick.

Our children stray from their faith.

Relationships become strained—or severed.

Finances grow tighter by the week.

Our home needs pricey repairs.

We are let go from our jobs.

Whatever might be causing you grief, anxiety, fear, stress, worry, or a combination of all of these, breathe deep. In. . .and out. Soothe your troubled soul with the living, breathing Word of God. Remember the Almighty's promises to you: He will bless and prosper you. In fact, the Creator of the universe has given you the "earth in all of its beauty"! It's a gift for your enjoyment!

When life is hard, your Creator is still good. Still loving. Still overflowing with mercy and grace. Though our circumstances will change, He never does. He's the same yesterday, today, forever (Hebrews 13:8).

Father God, my heart is heavy, and I need You. Please take my burdens. Alleviate my worries and fears. Remind me of Your goodness and blessings that surround me even now.

It Just Takes Time

*I love the Eternal; for not only does He hear my voice,
my pleas for mercy, but He leaned down when I
was in trouble and brought His ear close to me.
So as long as I have breath, I will call on Him.*

PSALM 116:1–2 VOICE

Faith takes time to grow. The psalmist may have a deep understanding of the power in crying out to God for help, but chances are it took time for that truth to take root in his heart. Some may assume that a strong, sustaining faith comes naturally once you accept Jesus as Savior. But while its beginnings may be evident, we all need the Holy Spirit to grow our faith with strong roots. And friend, that just takes time and intentionality.

If you're not quite there yet, take heart! The goal is to do the things that deepen your confidence and conviction in the Lord. Let each day bring you one step closer to fully trusting that God is ready, willing, and able to intervene in your life, even in those messy situations and difficult circumstances. And as you grow closer to the Lord, watch as your faith becomes strong and resilient, certain of His love and convinced of His devotion.

*Lord, I want You to be the only one I cry out to for help.
Let Your Holy Spirit grow my faith deeper every day.*

2 Chronicles 29:20–30:27 / Romans 1:1–17 / Psalm 116:6–19

The Value of Togetherness

I find myself constantly praying for you and hoping it's in God's will for me to be with you soon. I desperately want to see you so that I can share some gift of the Spirit to strengthen you. Plus I know that when we come together something beautiful will happen as we are encouraged by each other's faith.

ROMANS 1:10–12 VOICE

Paul understands how community helps to strengthen faith. He sees the value in prayer, asking God to be with others. He recognizes the importance of being together and sharing stories of the Lord's goodness because it strengthens those who speak and hear them. And Paul knows the power of unity and how spending time as a collective brings much needed encouragement to stand strong and be resilient. It's so important to stay connected rather than be isolated.

Are you part of a community of believers? Do you bring hope and support to those around you while finding reassurance from them too? If so, thank God for them! If not, ask Him for friends and family who will help you grow in your faith. Togetherness is a beautiful gift from the one who cherishes it Himself, and it's available to every believer who seeks it.

Lord, thank You for community and the value of encouraging one another in the faith. Help me grow resiliency through togetherness.

2 Chronicles 31–32 / Romans 1:18–32 / Psalm 117

The Ways of the Unrighteous

They have become filled with every kind of wickedness, evil, greed and depravity. They are full of envy, murder, strife, deceit and malice. They are gossips, slanderers, God-haters, insolent, arrogant and boastful; they invent ways of doing evil; they disobey their parents; they have no understanding, no fidelity, no love, no mercy.

ROMANS 1:29–31 NIV

This portion of scripture is talking about the unrighteous. It's a sobering description of those who are not walking in God's will. They are not thriving in His ways. Their faith is not growing and deepening, becoming stronger each day. Instead, they are choosing to live in ways that will most certainly bring His wrath. And that's not God's hope for them.

If you want to follow the Lord through your words and actions, be mindful of your choices. Ask yourself if you are in step with the world, subscribing to its advice to doing things that are in direct opposition to God. Or if you are spending time in the Word and in prayer, learning how to live righteously. Decide today to let your ways be a delightful offering to the Lord.

Lord, help me choose to live in ways that bless and glorify You, knowing they will also be ways that benefit me each day. I want to live in righteousness.

God Is Your Champion

*The Eternal is on my side, a champion for my cause;
so when I look at those who hate me, victory will be in
sight. It is better to put your faith in the Eternal for your
security than to trust in people. It is better to put your
faith in Him for your security than to trust in princes.*

PSALM 118:7–9 VOICE

What a privilege to know God is our champion. No matter what you may be going through right now, He is your security. Are you watching your marriage fall apart? Have you lost someone very dear to death? Is this another month of battling infertility? Are you tired of being single? Is there a sense of hopelessness about finding a cure? Is your workplace a hostile environment? Have you discovered an epic betrayal? Are your finances a mess? Remember that God is your champion.

There is no solution this world can offer that comes close to what the Lord promises. He's a safe place. And when you're struggling to find joy and peace, He is your hope. Cry out to Him today, friend. Surrender your worrisome heart and let Him build you up in miraculous ways.

Lord, I confess the times I've looked to the world for help rather than embracing the truth that You're my champion. Continually remind me that You are my security when life feels shaky.

2 Chronicles 34:8–35:19 / Romans 3:1–26 / Psalm 118:19–23

Good News

But now for the good news: God's restorative justice has entered the world, independent of the law. Both the law and the prophets told us this day would come. This redeeming justice comes through the faithfulness of Jesus, the Anointed One, the Liberating King, who makes salvation a reality for all who believe—without the slightest partiality.

ROMANS 3:21–22 VOICE

When Jesus stepped out of heaven and into the world, it changed everything. That act of love on the cross is what made salvation a reality for those who choose to believe in Him. It gave us an eternal option of heaven rather than hell. It bridged the gap left by sin, washing us clean through His spilled blood. Jesus became the ultimate sacrifice, replacing the law with grace. He brought restoration and redemption to the lost. And the deeper we dig into all that faith affords us, the more resilient we become.

Let this good news saturate your heart today. Let it drive you into a more robust relationship with the Lord. Dig into the Word and read about His promises and precautions. Find peace and hope in parched places. And let your roots find security in God's love and faithfulness because they will help you weather every storm until you see Him face-to-face.

Lord, thank You for the gift of Jesus!

Embracing the Hard Truths

*The LORD, the God of their ancestors, repeatedly sent his prophets
to warn them, for he had compassion on his people and his Temple.
But the people mocked these messengers of God and despised
their words. They scoffed at the prophets until the LORD's anger
could no longer be restrained and nothing could be done.*

2 CHRONICLES 36:15–16 NLT

One of the best ways we grow deep in our faith is to heed the Word of God. He divinely inspired humans to write the Bible so we could learn about who He is, what He has done, and what He promises to each believer. Every word in its pages is God-breathed, making it a trusted authority in every way. It's how He reveals Himself to us.

If your desire is to have hardy faith to take you through the ups and downs of life, cling to God's Word with gusto. Let it be what holds you steady and gives you strength. Rather than picking and choosing, trust the Bible to be your ultimate guide to navigating your daily journey. Embrace the hard truths and walk them out with grit. Then watch as your faith becomes strong and durable for whatever comes your way.

*Lord, I love Your Word! In it I can find help and hope for these
mountain tops and valleys alike. Let it always be my guide.*

Ezra 1–3 / Romans 5 / Psalm 119:1–8

Pathway to Happiness

*Happy are the people who walk with integrity, who live according
to the teachings of the Eternal. Happy are the people who keep His
decrees, who pursue Him wholeheartedly. These are people who
do nothing wrong; they do what it takes to follow His ways.*

PSALM 119:1–3 VOICE

According to today's scripture, there is a clear pathway to happiness
for believers. Did you catch it? Happiness comes from choosing a life
of integrity. It happens by living according to God's will and ways.
When you follow His commands, happiness is a result. Pursuing the
Lord with passion, being intentional to do what is right, and making
the decision to be obedient brings happiness too. Simply put, believers
find happiness from an increasingly significant relationship with God.

The Christian walk should be one where joy prevails. We should
seek Him most because we know the blessings doing so brings to our
heart, like happiness, comfort, security, and wisdom. Choosing to focus
on the Lord and living righteously is how faith grows deep roots and
keeps us strong during hard times. And it's how we can stay positive
and expectant regardless of what comes our way.

*Lord, I want happiness through You alone, not by anything
the world offers. At every turn, let me choose to walk in Your
ways because I know it's for my good and Your glory.*

Ezra 4–5 / Romans 6:1–7:6 / Psalm 119:9–16

The Privilege to Pursue

I have pursued You with my whole heart; do not let me stray
from Your commands. Deep within me I have hidden Your
word so that I will never sin against You. You are blessed,
O Eternal One; instruct me in what You require.

PSALM 119:10–12 VOICE

Pursuing God is a privilege. It's an honor to be in a relationship with the Father—the one who created the heavens and earth. Our greatest desire should be to connect with the Lord in meaningful ways every day, deepening our dependence on His goodness. And as we invest our time and heart in following Him, it will produce in us a real and robust faith.

How do you walk this out? How can you pursue God with passion? Make an intentional effort to spend time in the Word regularly. Meditate on scripture, asking God for revelation on how to incorporate His commands into your life. Learn what righteousness looks like and let it inform your decisions. Be prayerful throughout the day, inviting God to be a part of what you're navigating. These practices will allow your faith to grow hearty roots to weather any storm life may bring.

Lord, give me the strength and desire to pursue You
with my whole heart. Let Your Word sink deep into
my DNA. Create in me a resilient faith.

Ezra 6:1–7:26 / Romans 7:7–25 / Psalm 119:17–32

God's Hand Is in It

*This Ezra was a scribe who was well versed in the Law of Moses, which
the LORD, the God of Israel, had given to the people of Israel. He came
up to Jerusalem from Babylon, and the king gave him everything he
asked for, because the gracious hand of the LORD his God was on him.*

EZRA 7:6 NLT

God's hand was all over this situation. Not only had He raised up
Ezra as a scribe, skilled in the Law of Moses, but He would use Ezra's
knowledge to restore righteousness to God's children in Jerusalem. At
the same time, God prompted the heart of King Artaxerxes to favor
every one of Ezra's requests to return to Israel.

The takeaway from today's scripture is a reassurance that we aren't
left to navigate life by ourselves. We don't have to cross our fingers
and hope all will work out. It's not left to chance. Instead, we can have
hardy faith because there is assurance that God is always at work. Be
it behind the scenes or right in front of our eyes, He is intimately
involved every day. Knowing this powerful truth will strengthen our
faith in mighty ways.

*Lord, thank You for having Your holy hands in the details
of my life. Let that knowledge be what increases my faith,
keeping it steadfast no matter what I am facing.*

Ezra 7:27–9:4 / Romans 8:1–27 / Psalm 119:33–40

An Animated Life

If you live your life animated by the flesh—namely, your fallen, corrupt nature—then your mind is focused on the matters of the flesh. But if you live your life animated by the Spirit—namely, God's indwelling presence—then your focus is on the work of the Spirit. A mind focused on the flesh is doomed to death, but a mind focused on the Spirit will find full life and complete peace.
ROMANS 8:5–6 VOICE

Friend, what stirs you? Do you find excitement in what the world can offer, or are you awakened by all that faith affords a believer? The truth is that we are focused on one or the other. And every day, we are faced with a decision. We will either look to the flesh to fill our wants and meet our needs, or we will choose to rely on our faith to pull us through. Which option animates your heart?

If your desire is to have resilient faith, then focus on growing your relationship with God. Study His Word. Meditate on the promises found in its pages. Pray without ceasing. Take worldly thoughts captive. Choose to be content with a grateful heart. And as you do, you'll find your life animated by a steadfast faith, immovable and unwavering, no matter what.

Lord, help me focus on a life dedicated to following You.

Ezra 9:5–10:44 / Romans 8:28–39 / Psalm 119:41–64

No Doubt

*For I am persuaded beyond doubt (am sure) that neither death
nor life, nor angels nor principalities, nor things impending
and threatening nor things to come, nor powers, nor height nor
depth, nor anything else in all creation will be able to separate
us from the love of God which is in Christ Jesus our Lord.*

ROMANS 8:38–39 AMPC

Why can you have resilient and immovable faith in God? Because
there is nothing that will separate you from Him. The Lord's love is
unshakable. His trustworthiness in your life is resolute. His heart for
you is constantly good. And today's passage of scripture is a dose of
power-packed truth meant to stabilize insecurities that try to shut
you down and weaken your resolve.

Paul says he no longer doubts God's love. He is certain his
shortcomings won't cause the Lord to turn His back in frustration
or disgust. He understands the Lord is after progression and not
perfection. That belief allowed Paul—and allows us—to live in freedom,
trusting God is dependable without fail. Knowing that we don't have
to perform to be accepted, that we can be secure in God's love, that
we are valued, allows our faith to grow deeper and stronger.

*Lord, what a relief to know there is nothing that can separate me
from You. My job is to love and serve You, even if imperfectly.*

Nehemiah 1:1–3:16 / Romans 9:1–18 / Psalm 119:65–72

Committed to Living His Way

Train me in good common sense; I'm thoroughly committed to living your way. Before I learned to answer you, I wandered all over the place, but now I'm in step with your Word. You are good, and the source of good; train me in your goodness.

PSALM 119:66–68 MSG

Like the psalmist, we should be fully committed to living each day according to God's will. We should make it a priority to learn and walk out His ways through the choices we make. Yet unless we are digging deep in the Bible regularly, we won't know the Lord's hopes and expectations. We'll wander aimlessly and without purpose.

When we embrace our faith with fervor, we'll go from surviving to thriving. We'll find divine direction in His Word. Our roots will sink down deep into the Lord's soil and our lives will grow upward from there. The Bible is our roadmap for righteous living that benefits us, blesses others, and glorifies God. It's our guide as believers. And as we surrender our fleshy desires for His faith-filled doctrine and seek the Lord's guidance in our decisions, we'll become strong and resilient in Him.

Lord, train me in Your ways so it becomes my default way of living. I want to be in step with Your Word every day and in every situation.

Nehemiah 3:17–5:13 / Romans 9:19–33 / Psalm 119:73–80

Don't Stop the Work

*When our enemies heard that we knew of their plans and that
God had frustrated them, we all returned to our work on the
wall. But from then on, only half my men worked while the other
half stood guard with spears, shields, bows, and coats of mail. The
leaders stationed themselves behind the people of Judah who were
building the wall. The laborers carried on their work with one
hand supporting their load and one hand holding a weapon.*

NEHEMIAH 4:15–17 NLT

Today's scripture reinforces the truth that when we do God's work, the
enemy will come against our efforts. Yet notice that as the Israelites
were rebuilding the wall in Jerusalem, they had tools in one hand
and weapons in the other. The work didn't stop. Progress happened
even though there was fear and worry.

Let this be how we respond to spiritual warfare in our own
lives. God's Word, time in prayer, moments of worship, and sweet
community are weapons in the hands of believers. When we wield
them with precision, they will allow our faith to grow and deepen.
We'll become resilient, able to stay focused on doing God's work.

*Lord, let me be as determined as the Israelites working
on the wall. May nothing stop me from doing
Your work. Make me brave and bold!*

Nehemiah 5:14–7:73 / Romans 10:1–13 / Psalm 119:81–88

How Faith Grows

So if you believe deep in your heart that God raised Jesus from the pit of death and if you voice your allegiance by confessing the truth that "Jesus is Lord," then you will be saved! Belief begins in the heart and leads to a life that's right with God; confession departs from our lips and brings eternal salvation.

ROMANS 10:9–10 VOICE

It was God's love and Jesus' death that made eternity in heaven an option for sinners. But it's our belief and confession that activate the gift of salvation. Scripture is clear there is a necessary response from us. This is how faith is planted in our heart, ready to be watered and fertilized for maximum growth.

From there, the Holy Spirit begins to mature our faith in miraculous ways. Through prayer, we learn to share our worries and fears. Through reading His Word, we learn to trust Him for hope. Through trials and testing, we learn to lean on God for help. Through community, we learn to support each other's journey. This is how we develop strong roots that are deep and stabilizing. And with time, this is how we become bold believers.

Lord, thank You for the gift of salvation. Thank You for calling me into Your family. Help me grow resilient roots of faith.

Nehemiah 8:1–9:5 / Romans 10:14–11:24 / Psalm 119:89–104

The Power of God's Word

I watch my step, avoiding the ditches and ruts of evil so I can spend
all my time keeping your Word. I never make detours from the route
you laid out; you gave me such good directions. Your words are so
choice, so tasty; I prefer them to the best home cooking. With your
instruction, I understand life; that's why I hate false propaganda.

PSALM 119:101–104 MSG

If we're lacking the direction provided in God's Word, we're simply lost as believers. To think we can live in ways that glorify the Lord without saturating ourselves with His instruction is absurd. For how will we know His commands? How will we stand firm on His promises? How will we know how to walk out His will? How will we benefit from the experiences of those who have gone before us? Unless we commit to spending time in the Bible, we'll wander aimlessly.

The only way to develop a faith that is healthy and hearty is spending intentional time in the Word, where God uses every passage to reveal Himself. Each page brings wisdom and guidance. This complete God-breathed book is here to help believers understand how to live from a place of victory. So, friend, don't overlook the value of the Bible in your daily walk. Steep yourself in its timeless truths and powerful promises.

Lord, give me a deep desire for Your Word.
Let it feed my soul and direct my path each day.

Nehemiah 9:6–10:27 / Romans 11:25–12:8 / Psalm 119:105–120

Embracing the Word

Your word is a lamp for my steps; it lights the path
before me. . . . You are my hiding place and my
shield of protection; I hope in Your word.
PSALM 119:105, 114 VOICE

The value of God's Word isn't a new concept. There are countless passages of scripture pointing to this truth. Yes, God makes it clear that the Good Book is something He wants us to know and believe without doubt. And if He mentioned this idea once, we'd need to pay attention. But because God reminds us repeatedly of this truth, we need to recognize the Word's extreme importance, His desire for us to grab on to it with passion and purpose, to allow it to help us grow and deepen our faith.

Think about a time a verse penetrated your heart or a character's story gave you hope. Remember a desperate moment where the Word settled your spirit and encouraged you. Have you found peace in its pages? Have you found wisdom in its writings? Has the Word given you a deeper respect for God, a better appreciation for Jesus, or a clearer understanding of the Holy Spirit? Treat the Bible as what it is: an extremely valuable gift, a precious love letter, from our beloved Father to us.

Lord, I am grateful for the Bible and how it helps me
find hope and direction. Let it become clearer and
dearer to my heart with each passing day.

Nehemiah 10:28–12:26 / Romans 12:9–13:7 / Psalm 119:121–128

God-Enabled Love

Love others well, and don't hide behind a mask; love authentically.
Despise evil; pursue what is good as if your life depends on it.
Live in true devotion to one another, loving each other as sisters
and brothers. Be first to honor others by putting them first.

ROMANS 12:9–10 VOICE

We are commanded to love others with honor, authenticity, and devotion. We're to think of their needs before we think of our own. And unless we depend on God to infuse us with the ability to love, such a task will be almost impossible to do. . .at least for the long haul.

Do you ask the Lord for help? Each day, do you pray for the power to love those around you? Are you trusting Him for compassion at the right times and in the right ways? Do you ask for a servant's heart? Are your eyes and ears open to ways you can be God's hands and feet?

Something supernatural happens to a believer's faith when she relies on God. That faith deepens. It solidifies. It produces confidence. And it empowers her to do things she simply can't on her own.

Lord, the command to love others in such ways is a
tall order and something I cannot walk out on my own.
Please make me bold so I'm able to bless those around me.

Nehemiah 12:27–13:31 / Romans 13:8–14:12 / Psalm 119:129–136

Softening the Rough Edges

Guide my steps in the ways of Your word, and do not let any sin
control me. Rescue me from the torment of my human oppressors
so that I may live according Your decrees. Let Your face shine
upon Your servant, and help me to learn what You require.

Psalm 119:133–135 voice

We're all victims of the human condition. No one escapes it. Even when we try to be good and do good, our flesh often wins out and we sin. Be it selfishness, anger, lewdness, wanting to dominate, or a myriad of other ugly responses to people and life, we need God to soften the rough edges. He is the only one who can guide us into living in righteous—right with Him—ways.

Do you know what God expects from you? Are you inviting Him into the places that need liberation? Have you asked the Lord to create in you a strong, sustaining faith?

You don't have to walk this journey alone, trying to figure out how to please God. Trust Him to grow your faith into something robust. As you study His Word, pray daily, learn of His promises, and seek Him in all things, your heart will long for more and your eyes will stay trained on Him for guidance.

Lord, I know sin is a big deal, and I confess it often
gets the best of me. Help me stay focused on You,
knowing You're always the answer.

An Infused Life

*I pray that God, the source of all hope, will infuse your lives with
an abundance of joy and peace in the midst of your faith so that
your hope will overflow through the power of the Holy Spirit.*
ROMANS 15:13 VOICE

We all need God to infuse us with hope, joy, and peace from time to time. This life isn't a cakewalk, right? Relationships bring unmatched stress at inopportune times. Financial burdens weigh us down with anxiety. Grief pulls us under, making it hard to catch our breath. And we're bombarded with division, hatred, and doom every time we watch the news. All these things can leave us discouraged and disheartened, overwhelmed and depleted, unable to thrive in the fruits of our faith.

Yet as we cry out to God in troubled times, He will infuse us in abundance. We will receive an overflowing of His goodness through the work of the Holy Spirit. Each time we ask and God answers, our faith is strengthened because we have proof that He sees us. We know He is always for us. And hope, joy, and peace rise up in plenty.

*Lord, I'm feeling crushed by the heaviness of life.
Meet me right here and infuse me with Your goodness.*

Esther 2:19–5:14 / Romans 15:14–21 / Psalm 119:153–168

Impressed upon Your Heart

*"If you keep quiet at a time like this, deliverance and relief
for the Jews will arise from some other place, but you and
your relatives will die. Who knows if perhaps you were made
queen for just such a time as this?" Then Esther sent this reply
to Mordecai: "Go and gather together all the Jews of Susa and
fast for me. Do not eat or drink for three days, night or day.
My maids and I will do the same. And then, though it is against
the law, I will go in to see the king. If I must die, I must die."*

ESTHER 4:14–16 NLT

Esther was resolved. She understood both the heaviness of her call and
the weight of its consequences. And while the Bible doesn't directly
reveal this, we can safely assume Esther had a robust and resilient
faith. Why? Because she saw the bigger picture and faced her fears
to do what God had impressed upon her heart. He used her to save
His people.

When you put faith first, you'll feel the leading of the Holy Spirit
too. It may be a gut feeling or an overwhelming drive. You may be
compelled to stand up or step out. There may be a burst of courage
or compassion. Regardless, your call will align with God's will and
ways. What's the Lord impressing on you today?

Lord, give me ears and eyes to follow You.

Knowing God

Put your hand out and steady me since I've chosen to live by your
counsel. I'm homesick, GOD, for your salvation; I love it when you
show yourself! Invigorate my soul so I can praise you well, use
your decrees to put iron in my soul. And should I wander off like
a lost sheep—seek me! I'll recognize the sound of your voice.

PSALM 119:173–176 MSG

The psalmist knows what God can do to steady his anxious heart. Undoubtedly, he has watched God's goodness manifest in meaningful ways. He's probably navigated hard seasons that required divine intervention. Perhaps he has clung to God's promises by following the teachings found in the Word. Maybe he's even found peace and comfort for his soul by flexing his faith muscle through prayer. That the psalmist knows God's perfect peace so keenly points to an intentional relationship with the Lord.

Friend, resilient faith grows over time. It takes consistency to connect your heart to God's.

The greatest privilege we have as believers is to know Him. And as we invest our days meditating on scripture, talking with Him daily, taking wrong thoughts captive, and following the Spirit's leading, we, as did the psalmist, will experience the Lord in powerful ways too.

Lord, I want to know You better. I want to experience the fruit that
comes from resilient faith. Show me how. Come ever so close.

Esther 9–10 / Romans 16 / Psalm 120–122

Keeping Clear of Bad Influences

I am pleading with all of you, brothers and sisters, to keep up your guard against anyone who is causing conflicts and enticing others with teachings contrary to what you have already learned. If there are people like that in your churches, stay away from them. These kinds of people are not truly serving our Lord Jesus the Anointed; they have devoted their lives to satisfying their own appetites.

ROMANS 16:17–18 VOICE

What a clear warning for us to watch out for those who are a bad influence. For we become like those we hang out with. And if we connect with the wrong kind of community, it can dull our faith, often without us even realizing it.

Ask yourself: Are your friends believers who pursue the Lord daily? Do you surround yourself with people who continually point you to the Lord? Do they encourage you to stand strong in faith when faced with tough seasons in life? Are they quick to remind you of God's goodness? Do they boldly challenge your stinkin' thinkin'? Will they pray with and for you? If this doesn't describe your tribe, scripture says to stay away from this kind of crowd. Instead, find friends (and be a friend to those) who chase after the Lord every day.

Lord, I desire to be in a community where You're the firm foundation for us all. Help me find it.

Job 1–3 / 1 Corinthians 1:1–25 / Psalm 123

Hard Things Will Happen

There was a man in the land of Uz whose name was Job; and that man was blameless and upright, and one who [reverently] feared God and abstained from and shunned evil [because it was wrong].

JOB 1:1 AMPC

Imagine being known as blameless and upright in God's eyes. No doubt Job was an honorable man in every way. But that didn't stop hard things from happening. God allowed him to be tested by fire, intense and severe. Take time this week to read his encouraging story from beginning to end.

While we see Job struggling through difficult periods, there are some important takeaways. First, he kept an open communication with God, even asking Him very challenging and honest questions at times. And second, his enduring faith was eventually rewarded by the Lord. For Scripture says the second half of his life was better than the first!

Friend, let these nuggets of truth refresh your faith today. Know that even when your circumstances feel completely overwhelming, God is there with you. Talk to Him candidly. Let the Lord know your deepest pains and worries. Then cling to your faith, asking Him to strengthen you, to help you be as steadfast as Job.

Lord, remind me that You're with me in good times and bad. Strengthen my resilience to stay faithful amid both.

The Only Good Boasting

It is because of him that you are in Christ Jesus, who has become for us wisdom from God—that is, our righteousness, holiness and redemption. Therefore, as it is written: "Let the one who boasts boast in the Lord."

1 CORINTHIANS 1:30–31 NIV

Boasting is a bad habit, one that keeps our eyes focused inward. Rather than cultivate a servant's heart, we nurture a selfish one. We amplify our efforts and accomplishments rather than embracing humility. It's not that we can't share good things with others. Rather it's the motive behind that sharing.

Paul tells us in today's scripture that the only boasting we should do is around God's ability to glorify Himself in our weakness. It's boasting *of* the Lord. It's sharing with others what He has done for us, what He is currently doing in us, and talking about the promises we are watching for as we live in expectation of His goodness. This kind of faith-filled attitude and perspective produces resiliency within because we understand that God is God, and we are not. We realize that it's *His* power that allows us to experience the reality of being rescued and made right (1 Corinthians 1:18 VOICE). If we are going to boast, let's boast in the Lord.

Lord, keep my eyes and ears trained on who You are and what You promise to do. Let that be what I boast about to others rather than singing my own praises.

Sowing and Reaping

*Those who walk the fields to sow, casting their seed in tears, will
one day tread those same long rows, amazed by what's appeared.
Those who weep as they walk and plant with sighs will return
singing with joy, when they bring home the harvest.*
PSALM 126:5–6 VOICE

Friend, let these verses encourage your heart today. They contain a
beautiful and powerful promise that our resilient faith will be rewarded.
They are a much-needed reminder that as we remain steadfast in our
belief that God is working in our situation, our resolve will pay off in
the end. These verses tell us that we and every tear we shed are seen
by God; that we and every prayer we pray are heard by Him. They
allow us to stay hopeful.

What seeds are you planting today, trusting the right harvest will
grow from them? Are you ready to be married, or is your marriage
heading in the wrong direction? Do you want children, or is one walking a destructive path? Do you need financial relief or divine
intervention because of a medical condition? Keep asking! Pray with
expectation! Hold on to hope! The Lord is listening and watching,
and your steadfastness matters to Him.

*Lord, give me the endurance to keep moving forward as I
cry out to You for help. Let my resolve to trust You bring
treasured and timely answers. For I know You are good!*

Even When We Can't Understand

How many counts do You have against me? How many sins must I account for? Spell out the nature of Your indictment against my rebellious ways. Why do You hide Your face from me; why is my name now "nemesis" to You?

JOB 13:23–24 VOICE

The Word says Job was a righteous man, which means his faith was strong and secure. And while he struggled when Satan came against him—and boy did the Accuser wreak havoc in Job's life—ultimately, his trust in God endured.

While encouragement can be found throughout Job's story, there is one particular part that's an inspiration for believers today. Rather than adopt a victim mentality or abandon his faith altogether, this righteous man took his hard questions directly to God. He remained in a relationship with the Lord.

We will find ourselves in deep, dark valleys from time to time. We will suffer great loss, even when we purpose to follow God's commands. Our lives will be upended and interrupted. Yet those trying times can and should drive us closer to the Lord. We can ask the hard questions, like Job. Our faith may shake. But our resiliency will keep us trusting, even as we struggle to understand.

Lord, help me remember You are good all the time, especially in the dark valleys.

Being a Source of Hope

*All the things from you sound the same. You are all terrible as
comforters! Have we reached the end of your windy words, or
are you sick with something that compels you to argue with me?
If we were to trade places, I could rattle on as you do. I could
compose eloquent speeches as you do and shake my head smugly
at you and your problems. But I believe I would use my words
to encourage you; my lips would move only to offer you relief.*

JOB 16:2–5 VOICE

When we're experiencing heartache, our friends' best efforts, like those of Job's companions, don't always help and instead only add to our frustration.

Sometimes we just need to be comforted by our friends. We don't need them to solve our problems or fix what's broken. We don't need big, flowery words to calm us down. We won't be reassured by platitudes that feel void of substance. So often what we *do* need is someone who chooses her words wisely and is simply present. We need reminders to persevere.

When the roles are reversed, may we be the kind of friend who seeks God's guidance on how to best help and comfort another who's hurting. Before we spout human remedies, let's dig deep in prayer and give the Lord room to lead us, to tell us what role we're to play in a friend's restoration and how we can be a source of hope.

Lord, show me how to bring comfort.

Job 17–20 / 1 Corinthians 6 / Psalm 131

Calm, Quiet, and Contented

Of one thing I am certain: my soul has become calm, quiet, and contented in You. Like a weaned child resting upon his mother, I am quiet. My soul is like this weaned child.
PSALM 131:2 VOICE

This is what resilient faith looks like. It's learning to rest in the Lord no matter what circumstances are threatening to crush you. It's choosing to be quiet and wait on the Lord rather than letting your emotions spiral out of control. It's deciding to stand firm and trust His plan when your heart is restless. This takes great intentionality. And while we may not always find ourselves calm and contented when storms hit, it's where we'll eventually land because we have come before God, seeking His help to get there.

So today, ask the Lord to quiet your soul. Spend time reading the Word where you can find hope and peace. Listen to worship music that helps you focus on God's goodness. Surround yourself with faith-filled friends and family who'll speak truth. Take pesky thoughts captive. And cling to the Lord, the only one who can truly calm your soul.

Lord, You are fully aware of the situations that have me stirred up and stressed out. Quiet my soul as I come to You for comfort. Help me be certain of Your goodness when life feels too big.

Dependent Promises

The LORD swore an oath to David, a promise He will not
abandon: "I will set one of your descendants on your throne.
If your sons keep My covenant and My decrees that I will
teach them, their sons will also sit on your throne forever."

PSALM 132:11–12 HCSB

When God makes a promise, we can rest assured it will come to pass. We may not know when or how, especially if it seems unimaginable, but God won't let us down. He won't forget or go back on His word.

Yet there are promises dependent on our faith and actions, just as there were with David and his sons. Our obedience is often a precursor to God fulfilling a vow.

Remember the Lord isn't looking for perfection. He knows all too well our human limitations. He is, however, looking for our progress. And every time we purpose to follow God's leading, He takes note.

So friend, dig in deep with God. Don't let a setback cause a breakup. Don't walk away or decide you're unworthy. Time in God's Word will help you stay committed to His path. Prayer will settle His ways in your heart.

Lord, I know Your love and goodness are not conditional. But I
also know Your promises won't be realized until my heart is ready.
Thank You for preparing me through my obedience to You.

Resilient Woman of Faith

*Come, bless GOD, all you servants of GOD! You priests of GOD,
posted to the nightwatch in GOD's shrine, lift your praising
hands to the Holy Place, and bless GOD. In turn, may GOD
of Zion bless you—GOD who made heaven and earth!*

PSALM 134:1–3 MSG

What enables us to bless God and praise Him with passion and
purpose? What allows us to lift our hands in gratitude and celebrate
His goodness? It's a heart that's seen God move in mighty and
meaningful ways. It's a believer who has journeyed through a tough
season under His care and come out hopeful. It's a faith that's learned
to stand strong and trust when inclined to give up. It's someone who
is saturated in the Word and committed to a robust prayer life. You
see, friend, once you've experienced the richness of the Lord, you can't
help but become a resilient woman of faith.

Think about all the times you've watched God do the impossible in
your life. Consider His unwavering love and compassionate responses.
Meditate on His praiseworthy ways and unmatched kindness.
Remember God's generosity. Then lift your hands in thanksgiving.

*Lord, I see all You've done and who You are. What
a wondrous Father and provider and healer. I love
You so. May I bless and praise You every day.*

Idols

The nations have idols of silver and gold, crafted by human hands!
They shaped mouths for them, but they cannot speak; they carved
eyes into them, but they cannot see; they placed ears on them, but
they cannot hear; they cannot breathe, not even a puff of air from
their mouths! The artisans who made them are just like them,
and so are all who mistakenly trust in them, no exceptions.

PSALM 135:15–18 VOICE

Today's verses talk about the worthlessness of idols. They are manmade items that are incapable of having a relationship. They hold no power. They cannot heal, rescue, or empower. And they pale in comparison to what God can do in the lives of believers. Yet many of us choose idols over Him without even realizing it.

What are your idols? Think about where you spend the most time. Who or what do you trust in hard times? The answers to these questions will often tell the tale.

But, friend, know this: God wants to be your hero. He wants to be your destination when you're facing challenges or sharing celebrations. And when you choose to worship and praise Him over everything else in your life, your faith will deepen. You'll find hope, becoming resilient as you wait for His answers. Your focus will change from the creation to the Creator.

Lord, I want You above all else.

Job 31–33 / 1 Corinthians 9:1–18 / Psalm 136:1–9

Repeat and Repeat Again

Give thanks to the LORD, for he is good!
His faithful love endures forever.
PSALM 136:1 NLT

Did you memorize multiplication tables in elementary school? Remember learning the states and their capitals? Maybe you spent hours on the US presidents, the planets, or spelling words. Whether you used flash cards, mnemonic devices, songs, or chants, you repeated these things again and again until they were imprinted on your brain. So permanent is this knowledge that to this day you may be able to recite it!

Throughout Psalm 136, the phrase "His faithful love endures forever" is repeated twenty-six times. Bible scholars say that worshippers may have spoken or sung these words in unison as a sort of responsive reading—and the repetition helped engrave these important truths on their hearts and minds: God is good and His faithful love endures forever. God will never run out of love because God *is* love (1 John 4:8).

What truths do you need to repeat to yourself today? Here are a few suggestions: God keeps His promises (2 Corinthians 1:20). God is all-powerful (Matthew 19:26). God loved you when you were still a sinner (Romans 5:8). Nothing can separate you from God's love (Romans 8:39). God rejoices over you (Zephaniah 3:17). Jesus is the same yesterday and today and forever (Hebrews 13:8).

Father, I am rejoicing in and repeating the truths of
scripture today. Thank You for Your Word that offers
such encouragement and peace to my soul.

Job 34–36 / 1 Corinthians 9:19–10:13 / Psalm 136:10–26

Common Ground

Even though I am a free man with no master, I have become
a slave to all people to bring many to Christ. . . . When I am
with those who are weak, I share their weakness, for I want
to bring the weak to Christ. Yes, I try to find common ground
with everyone, doing everything I can to save some.

1 Corinthians 9:19, 22 NLT

The man named Saul was anything but complacent. He poured his efforts into studying to become a Pharisee and was zealous for God and His law. He passionately believed that Christianity was a dangerous threat to his Jewish heritage, so he did all he could to eliminate Christians and the church. But then Saul met Jesus on the road to Damascus. The Messiah changed his heart and his name to Paul, and his passion became winning souls to Christ.

Paul found true freedom in Jesus, but he didn't use that freedom to simply do whatever he wanted. Instead, Paul used his freedom to take Christ's love to people where they were and became like them—in their weaknesses, struggles, and imperfections.

Who in your life needs to experience the love of Jesus? Common ground is the best place to start. That doesn't mean you need to be fake or put on a mask. It means being authentic and caring and seeing others as Jesus sees them—as beloved children of God.

Father, please help me find common ground with
those who need to experience Your love.

Incomprehensible God

*"Listen carefully to the thunder of God's voice as it rolls
from his mouth. . . . He does not restrain it when he
speaks. God's voice is glorious in the thunder. We can't
even imagine the greatness of his power."*

JOB 37:2, 4–5 NLT

The Bible is full of insight into the nature and characteristics of God. We can spend time searching scriptures and praying to gain new understanding of our Creator, Savior, Father, and friend.

Yes, our God is accessible and near. He sent His Son to live as one of us. And He's given the gift of the Holy Spirit to live inside each follower of Christ. But despite all these things, one theme throughout the wisdom books of the Old Testament (Job, Psalms, Proverbs, Ecclesiastes, and Song of Solomon) is that God is incomprehensible.

This may sound frustrating, but you can take comfort in that you don't have to have all the answers. He is in charge of keeping the world spinning from the beginning to the end of time—and you are not. Ecclesiastes 3:11 speaks of the beauty of God's plan, His timing, and the fact that we won't fully understand it all. Because He is God and we are not.

*God, I praise You for the greatness of Your power.
You are the one who holds all things together. You are
so wondrous that I can spend an eternity getting to
know You more. You are a beautiful mystery!*

An Important Announcement

Every time you eat this bread and drink this cup, you are announcing the Lord's death until he comes again.

1 CORINTHIANS 11:26 NLT

Wear a t-shirt from your college and you're showing others you're an alumna, or pull on a hoodie of your favorite classic rock band and you're announcing you're a fan. A sticker on your bumper with a simple "26.2" tells the world you're a marathon runner, and rings worn on the third finger of your left hand shows the world you're married.

Today when we celebrate the Lord's Supper, or Communion, in our churches, we are announcing something even more important. When we crunch a little cracker that represents Jesus' broken body and drink a sip of juice representing His spilled blood, we're announcing, reminding, and remembering the sacrifice He made on the cross. This practice renews our commitment to the new covenant that Jesus established through His death, burial, and resurrection. We remember and celebrate the fact we are no longer under the burden of the Old Testament laws but now live in the freedom of God's grace and love.

"Come, eat, drink. . .announce and remember," Jesus beckons us to join Him around the table as a family of believers, His church.

Jesus, I will never be ashamed of the sacrifice You made. I will joyfully eat and drink with You around the Communion table and announce to the world that you mean everything to me!

Ecclesiastes 1:1–3:15 / 1 Corinthians 12:1–26 / Psalm 139:1–6

Church Harmony

*God has put the body together such that extra honor and care
are given to those parts that have less dignity. This makes for
harmony among the members, so that all the members care
for each other. If one part suffers, all the parts suffer with
it, and if one part is honored, all the parts are glad.*

1 CORINTHIANS 12:24–26 NLT

Whether it's from a lack of sleep, poor diet, sickness, or something else, when your body isn't working the way it should, everything can feel out of kilter. But when your body is working in harmony—when you've given it proper nutrition, mental relaxation, rest, and exercise—every part can benefit.

It's the same in the body of Christ. A church that lives and serves in harmony is a well-functioning body where each person is valued and valuable because of who they are—a beloved child of God. But not every part of the body of Christ is the same, and no part is perfect. That's why it's so important that we are all guided by and unified in our faith in Jesus.

Do you see any members of your church family who needs encouragement, help, or care? Ask God to open your heart to the needs of others. You can help the body of Christ live a full, healthy, harmonious life.

*Jesus, show me how to build up my church family. I want
to be part of a healthy body that gives all glory to You!*

The Most Excellent Way

*Are we all apostles? Are we all prophets? Are we all teachers?
Do we all have the power to do miracles? Do we all have the gift of
healing? Do we all have the ability to speak in unknown languages?
Do we all have the ability to interpret unknown languages? Of
course not! So you should earnestly desire the most helpful gifts.
But now let me show you a way of life that is best of all.*

1 CORINTHIANS 12:29–31 NLT

Earlier in 1 Corinthians 12, Paul made it clear that one spiritual gift is not better than another. Here he urges us to use our gifts to serve others so the church can strengthen, grow, and represent Christ in the world in effective and powerful ways.

As with so many things in our spiritual journey, using our gifts well is a heart matter. It doesn't matter what spiritual gift you have, Paul writes, what matters is that you use that gift in love. How? If you have the gift of service, help someone who needs it but would never ask for it. If you are a giver, give generously (and anonymously when you can), and joyfully expect nothing in return. If you have the gift to understand scripture, use that wisdom to build up someone who needs encouragement. And if you love showing hospitality, invite someone who feels like an outsider. Do all things in love (1 Corinthians 16:14).

Jesus, show me how to love like You do.

Anxious Thoughts

Search me, O God, and know my heart; test me and know
my anxious thoughts. Point out anything in me that offends
you, and lead me along the path of everlasting life.
PSALM 139:23–24 NLT

You may call it worry or anxiety or fear or nervousness, but each of us will face these feelings from time to time. While our emotions may not accurately represent reality, our feelings and reactions to things like disappointment, failure, sickness, and disasters are still valid and can affect everyday life. Worry and anxious thoughts can make us feel alone—like no one understands—and have the potential to steal our joy. Sometimes these issues might get bad enough that we need extra help from a professional—and there's no shame in that.

Whether anxious thoughts are a mild inconvenience or a debilitating problem, God is with us and He cares about what we're feeling (1 Peter 5:7). He repeatedly asks us to give Him our burdens including worry and anxiety and fear and nervousness (Psalm 55:22). Our heavenly Father—the greatest of all comforters (2 Corinthians 1:3–4)—will strengthen us, help us worry less, and rely more on Him (Isaiah 41:10).

Lord, when I cannot calm the storm that's inside my head,
I will talk to You first and give You my burdens. Let me feel Your
powerful presence. I know You will supply all my needs from Your
glorious riches. I trust You, Father, with my heart and mind.

You First, Lord

Today I am who I am because of God's grace, and I have made
sure that the grace He offered me has not been wasted. I have
worked harder, longer, and smarter than all the rest; but I
realize it is not me—it is God's grace with me that has made the
difference. In the end, it doesn't matter whether it was I or the
other witnesses who brought you the message. What matters is that
we keep preaching and that you have faith in this message.

1 CORINTHIANS 15:10–11 VOICE

Saul's passion for Jewish law (and stamping out Christianity) was only
matched and exceeded by the converted Paul's passion for preaching
the message of salvation. Paul's work led him on multiple missionary
trips across the Roman empire to take the good news of Jesus to the
Gentiles. He faced persecution, prosecution, incarceration, shipwreck,
relational rifts, and the list goes on—yet his desire for reaching one
more lost soul continued until his death.

Paul taught us that when we're sold on the gospel, it's the message
we will care about—rather than the messenger. Throughout the New
Testament we see Paul's deep humility. He didn't care whether it was
his sermon or another's preaching that led someone to find Jesus and
eternal life. The point was that new faith grew because God's grace
is powerful.

Jesus, use me to share the gospel, but I humbly
ask that others see You first and me second.

Going on a Fox Hunt

*"Catch the foxes, the little foxes that ruin the
vines. For our vines have tender grapes."*
Song of Solomon 2:15 skjv

God created humans to be in relationships, first with Him and
then with others. Adam and Eve were the first married couple, but
as the earth became populated, opportunities for other types of
relationships grew. Parent–child, siblings, in-laws, extended family,
friends, coworkers, acquaintances, and the list goes on. Oftentimes
it's our close, intimate relationships that require the most attention
and work. For example, a marriage takes sacrifice and daily effort to
nurture a dynamic, healthy relationship, while a coworker relationship
can be perfectly fine without nearly the same amount of work.

Here in today's verse, "little foxes" represent the small, irritating
problems that may seem like no big deal but left unchecked can wreak
havoc in any relationship. "Little foxes" can build up over time and cause
massive problems. Little foxes of hurt feelings, misunderstandings,
noncommunication—even small doses of these can lead to resentment,
unmet expectations, bitterness, and eventually a rift in the strongest
relationships.

Today, go on a fox hunt. Consider your most important relationship
and see if there are any pesky issues that threaten it. If you find one
(or more), don't ignore them. With God's help, you can banish the
little foxes from the vineyard of your relationship.

*Father, please bless my relationships and give
me Your wisdom to help them flourish.*

Song of Solomon 5–8 / 1 Corinthians 15:35–58 / Psalm 141

Splendid Bodies

There are heavenly bodies and earthly bodies, but the splendor
of the heavenly bodies is different from that of the earthly ones.
There is a splendor of the sun, another of the moon, and another
of the stars; for one star differs from another star in splendor.

1 CORINTHIANS 15:40–41 HCSB

In 1 Corinthians 15, Paul writes about the resurrected bodies believers will receive in heaven. While you can and should look forward to your resurrected body, 1 Corinthians 15:40–41 is a reminder that your earthly body was created by God and has its own type of beauty. God knit you together in your mother's womb and knows you intimately from the inside out (Psalm 139:13–14).

If all you see in the mirror is a body full of flaws, you're not alone. But consider, just for a moment, the fact that the beauty, splendor, and glory of all of God's creation includes your current body. Not a perfected, thinner, fitter version of your body—as it is right now, this very moment. The wonder of the blood coursing through your veins, the features handed down through your family tree, the hands that take care of the tasks of the day, and the arms that encircle the people you love—all these and more make up the gorgeous, magnificent, elegant, grand creation of you—God's cherished daughter that He made in His image (Genesis 1:27).

God, thank You for making me so wonderfully well.

Isaiah 1–2 / 1 Corinthians 16 / Psalm 142

Pep Talk

Keep your eyes open, hold tight to your convictions,
give it all you've got, be resolute, and love without stopping.
1 CORINTHIANS 16:13–14 MSG

Outside of our parents and close family members, coaches are often the individuals who have the biggest impact on our young lives. Coaches (and teachers and directors) set the course, vision, and goals for a team, but they also influence each person in unique ways. Perhaps you can still recall a few words of wisdom, a pep talk, a life lesson, specific encouragement, or a piece of advice you received from a coach.

The apostle Paul was a spiritual coach for the Corinthian church. Paul knew these people well; he had started the church and spent more than eighteen months in Corinth during his second missionary journey (Acts 18:1–18). In this letter, Paul addressed divisions and disorder within the church and gave practical advice for questions they asked him. At the heart of his letter, Paul explained how to live out the gospel in a dark world.

These two verses from 1 Corinthians 16 are part of Paul's sign-off from the letter. This is Paul's bullet point pep talk to his friends, coaching and teaching and wanting the best for them in all things. His excellent advice here applies to us even today: work hard and love harder.

Lord, thank You for the spiritual coaches You've
placed in my life. Help me encourage others in
the same way—always pointing to You.

Isaiah 3–5 / 2 Corinthians 1:1–11 / Psalm 143:1–6

Comfort

Blessed be God, even the Father of our Lord Jesus Christ,
the Father of mercies and the God of all comfort,
who comforts us in all our tribulation, that we may be able
to comfort those who are in any trouble, by the comfort
with which we ourselves are comforted by God.

2 CORINTHIANS 1:3–4 SKJV

What comes to mind when you read the word *comfort*? Maybe it's a hot bowl of soup with a warm buttered roll. Or maybe it's a soft pair of sweatpants. Perhaps it's the warmth of a loving embrace or a snuggle with a furry friend. All these things—and more—can provide a sense of rest, relief, and renewal.

Here in 2 Corinthians 1:3–4, Paul describes your Father as the God of all comfort. That doesn't mean that God will always take away your pain immediately. But within this scripture lies the promise that God will be your comfort in any challenge by providing strength, encouragement, support, peace, and hope. God's comfort can help you know Him better as you learn to trust Him more. Life's greatest challenges often result in life's greatest growth.

Today, ask God for opportunities to bless others who are struggling through similar trials that you've been through. You can be the hands, feet, open heart, and listening ears of the God of all comfort.

Father, thank You for providing exactly what I need
to not just endure but to flourish in any situation.

Isaiah 6–8 / 2 Corinthians 1:12–2:4 / Psalm 143:7–12

Renewal

*Let me hear of your unfailing love each morning, for I am
trusting you. Show me where to walk, for I give myself to
you. . . . Teach me to do your will, for you are my God. May
your gracious Spirit lead me forward on a firm footing.*

PSALM 143:8, 10 NLT

A vow-renewal ceremony can be a beautiful example of a husband and wife reaffirming the love they share while revisiting the promises they made to each other on their wedding day. Whether the vow renewal takes place after five years or five decades, it's a chance to pause from everyday life and remind themselves of the importance of their marriage covenant. It offers revival, replenishment, refreshment, and revitalization in their relationship.

Here in Psalm 143, David asks God to renew and reaffirm His love for him. David's faith in God was strong, but this passage reminds us that *everyone* struggles sometimes. Yet here we see that even when David doesn't feel God's love, he trusts that God's love remains—because God's love is constant and steadfast (Psalm 86:15).

Today, if you're feeling unsure, insecure, on shaky ground, or if you are doubting what you're doing, where you're going, or what your purpose is, ask God to remind you of His steadfast, unwavering love. He is faithful to renew your heart with His care and compassion and lead you forward confidently.

*Lord, when my faith is fickle, thank You for being a
constant source of renewal, strength, and love.*

Isaiah 9–10 / 2 Corinthians 2:5–17 / Psalm 144

Dark to Light

Nevertheless, that time of darkness and despair
will not go on forever. . . . For those who live in
a land of deep darkness, a light will shine.
ISAIAH 9:1–2 NLT

After the Israelites repeatedly disobeyed God, we see just how dire their situation would get in Isaiah 8:21–22 (NLT) where it says, "They will rage and curse their king and their God. They will look up to heaven and down at the earth, but wherever they look, there will be trouble and anguish and dark despair. They will be thrown out into the darkness."

Yes, things looked grim, but that wasn't the end of Judah's story. Isaiah 9 describes a child who would come to extinguish the darkness, the Messiah, the promised Savior, Jesus. "I am the light of the world," He said in John 8:12 (NIV). "Whoever follows me will never walk in darkness, but will have the light of life."

Light makes darkness disappear. Light keeps us from stumbling, wandering and aimless. Light offers protection and warmth and growth and healing. God is passionately committed to His plan of salvation through Jesus Christ, and you are part of that plan. If you have accepted that gift of grace, rejoice! If you are still working through the gift of grace, don't delay—step into the light of Jesus today!

Jesus, I will live every day in the light of Your love. Please shine brightly in my heart so I can share that light with others.

Isaiah 11–13 / 2 Corinthians 3 / Psalm 145

Shine Bright

Since this new way gives us such confidence, we can be very bold. We are not like Moses, who put a veil over his face so the people of Israel would not see the glory, even though it was destined to fade away. . . . But whenever someone turns to the Lord, the veil is taken away. For the Lord is the Spirit, and wherever the Spirit of the Lord is, there is freedom.

2 CORINTHIANS 3:12–13, 16–17 NLT

When Moses came down from the mountaintop with the Ten Commandments, his face radiated light from being in God's presence (Exodus 34:29–35). His brother Aaron and the other Israelites were spooked by his appearance, so Moses covered his face with a veil until the glow eventually faded away. Moses' shining face illustrated the new covenant and the veil symbolized the old covenant—Aaron and the Israelites couldn't understand it because God hadn't yet revealed His plan of salvation to the world.

When you accept Jesus as your Savior, He removes the veil from your heart. You have the promise of eternal life and the freedom to live in Christ's grace—no longer bound to the strict rules of Old Testament law. Without the veil, you have access to be face-to-face with God—just as Moses was—and can reflect God's glory and light to a dark and troubled world.

Jesus, thank You for removing the veil between us. I will shine Your light every day!

Isaiah 14–16 / 2 Corinthians 4 / Psalm 146

Helper God

*Blessed are those whose help is the God of Jacob, whose hope is in
the LORD their God. He is the Maker of heaven and earth, the sea,
and everything in them—he remains faithful forever. He upholds the
cause of the oppressed and gives food to the hungry. The LORD sets
prisoners free, the LORD gives sight to the blind. . . . The LORD watches
over the foreigner and sustains the fatherless and the widow.*

PSALM 146:5–9 NIV

Fred Rogers, best known for his TV show *Mister Rogers' Neighborhood*,
is quoted as saying, "When I was a boy and I would see scary things
in the news, my mother would say to me, 'Look for the helpers. You
will always find people who are helping.'"

Helpers come in many forms, and often all it takes is a willing
heart to lend a hand, to meet a need, to ease someone's burden.
When we support someone else, we are joining together with God
in something He loves to do—help. Yes, He's the Almighty, Creator,
powerful Lord—and He's also our helper God, who keeps His
promises to give aid in any circumstance. When the oppressed cry
out for justice, He will settle the score. When starvation looms, He
provides nourishment. When hearts are broken, He offers comfort
and healing. He sets captives free and opens blind eyes to see. And
He helps the most vulnerable—outsiders, widows, and orphans.

Father, thank You for being the helper I need today.

Isaiah 17–19 / 2 Corinthians 5 / Psalm 147:1–11

Fair Trade

*For God made Christ, who never sinned, to be
the offering for our sin, so that we could be
made right with God through Christ.*

2 CORINTHIANS 5:21 NLT

Even the youngest kid knows that trades only work when both parties exchange goods of equal value. A hair tie for a bicycle with streamers on the handlebars? No deal. A homemade chocolate chip cookie for a celery stalk? Not on your life.

Unlike most playground trades, the lopsided nature of the trade God offers us seems altogether too good to be true: In exchange for our sin, He gives us His righteousness. Jesus takes the blame for sin on the cross, and He gives us a new life where we are redeemed, justified, and forgiven. Our Savior got a death sentence and was buried in a tomb, and we receive hope and joy and peace and purpose, immeasurable love, and eternal life. It is a trade that is too good—but it's also *true*!

The world is full of trades that try to outwit and take advantage of the other party, but God isn't in that business. What He offers is a standing deal, a promise of salvation that will exist until Jesus comes back to earth. Who in your life needs to know about this trade? It's time to tell them about God's plan that is so, so good.

*You are so kind to me, Lord. You were willing
to sacrifice Your only Son. . .for ME!*

The Time Is Now

As God's partners, we beg you not to accept this marvelous gift
of God's kindness and then ignore it. For God says, "At just the
right time, I heard you. On the day of salvation, I helped you."
Indeed, the "right time" is now. Today is the day of salvation.

2 CORINTHIANS 6:1–2 NLT

Want to buy a house? A wise person will take the time to save a down payment and research the market before purchasing. A chef aiming for a perfect soufflé knows to stick to an exact technique and bake time or she'll end up with a deflated dessert. Many Pulitzer Prize–winning photos result from the perfect timing of the camera's shutter. And couples who struggle with infertility know the importance of timing. The Bible, in Ecclesiastes 3, reminds us that God's plan includes timing for *everything*. . .timing that requires faith.

While there are many parts of life that take waiting and patience, there's one action that Paul urges us not to put off: accepting God's gift of salvation.

If you're already a believer, you may think this scripture has nothing for you. But the truth is that *today* is the day to dig deeper into God's grace. *Now* is the moment to meet with God in prayer. Don't ignore the opportunity you have to strengthen your faith, gain insight into God's wisdom, and embrace God's love. It's always the right time.

Father, I will not waste this moment. I am here with You.

Isaiah 24:1–26:19 / 2 Corinthians 7 / Psalm 148

The Creation Concert

Let all things join together in a concert of praise to the name of the
Eternal, for He gave the command and they were created. He put
them in their places to stay forever—He declared it so, and it is final.
PSALM 148:5–6 VOICE

Music performed by a live orchestra is a multisensory experience. You
get to *see* an array of instruments of varying shapes and sizes—from
the tiny piccolo to the enormous timpani. You *hear* the unique sounds
that come from each instrument. And you get to *feel* the swell of the
symphony as individuals work together to create beautiful melodies
and harmonies.

Psalm 148 uses the picture of a symphony or a great choir to
describe how all of creation offers up a song of praise to its Creator.
God, on the day of creation "spoke, and it came to be; he commanded,
and it stood firm" (Psalm 33:9 NIV). God's steadfast care of everything
He created reaches from the stars in the heavens to the depths of the
sea. Each part of God's creation is part of the whole, and it sings a
song that proclaims the majesty and beauty of the Creator.

As God's cherished masterpiece, you are part of that concert of
praise. How will you raise your voice to join in today?

I will shout Your praises today, God! I gladly sing
to You because You are good and Your love and
faithfulness continue forever (Psalm 100).

Praise Him!

Let them praise His name with dancing and make music to Him with tambourine and lyre. For Yahweh takes pleasure in His people; He adorns the humble with salvation. Let the godly celebrate in triumphal glory; let them shout for joy on their beds.

PSALM 149:3–5 HCSB

Scripture repeatedly tells us to praise the Lord, but there's not just one way to do it. Dancing, singing, or playing instruments are a few suggestions here in Psalm 149, but what if you're not rhythmically or musically gifted?

"Make a joyful noise to the LORD," Psalm 98:4 (SKJV) says, ". . . make a loud noise and rejoice." Joy and gusto seem to be the name of the praise game here. Nothing is said about praise needing to sound pleasant or melodic or beautiful. If you are able, shout a praise to God—however it comes out. If you can only whisper, do it with all your heart. If you can beat on a drum in thanksgiving for all He's done, pound with all your might! If you enjoy dancing, it can be a powerful way to worship. But even if you can't physically shake a leg, you can praise from any posture—standing, sitting, kneeling, or lying flat—in any way that brings you joy.

The point is, whatever your ability or inability, joyfully praise Him for His goodness, His mightiness, and for who He is!

Let every fiber in my being praise the Lord!

Solomon's Legacy

*"I, Solomon, David's son and Israel's king, pass on to you these
proverbs—a treasury of wisdom. . . . These proverbs teach
the naive how to become clever; they instruct the young
in how to grow in knowledge and live with discretion."*

PROVERBS 1:1, 4 VOICE

Solomon, a son of King David, was Israel's third king. He reigned for forty years during Israel's golden age and is known for his vast wealth, his seven hundred wives (and three hundred concubines), and, most notably, his God-given wisdom.

In 1 Kings 3:5–14, God appeared to Solomon in a dream and offered to give him whatever he asked for. Solomon (wisely) asked God for wisdom. God was pleased with Solomon's request, and He not only made Solomon wise but also gave him great riches, power, and a peaceful reign. Solomon went on to build the first Temple in Jerusalem (1 Kings 6) and write and compile most of Proverbs, Song of Solomon, and even a few psalms.

Solomon left a legacy of wisdom that we still learn from today. Each of us has opportunities to share Bible wisdom with others—especially our children. Whether you're a mother or a grandmother or an aunt or have other kids in your life, ask God to help you plant seeds of His wisdom in their hearts from the pages of Proverbs. He is faithful to grow their faith and wisdom throughout their lives, just as He did for Solomon.

Lord, thank You for the practical gift of Proverbs.

Isaiah 31–33 / 2 Corinthians 10 / Proverbs 1:10–22

Rebel Thoughts

*We are human, but we don't wage war as humans do. We use
God's mighty weapons, not worldly weapons, to knock down the
strongholds of human reasoning and to destroy false arguments. . . .
We capture their rebellious thoughts and teach them to obey Christ.*

2 CORINTHIANS 10:3–5 NLT

While we often describe sin as the act of doing something wrong,
the strongholds Paul talks about in 2 Corinthians 10 are the sins
that take place in our minds. It's easy to downplay the significance of
our thoughts, but what we think about ourselves is truly where we
are most vulnerable. . .especially as women.

The "false arguments" Paul mentions are different for everyone,
but in practical terms they are any thoughts that don't line up with
God's truth. When we tell ourselves we're worthless, God says we are
treasured (1 Peter 2:9). When we feel like a failure, God says we are
more than victorious through Him (Romans 8:37). When we feel
hopeless and powerless, God will uphold and strengthen us (Jeremiah
29:11; Isaiah 40:31). When we feel overwhelmed and anxious, God
offers to take our burdens and replace them with peace (1 Peter 5:7;
John 14:27).

Take inventory of your thoughts today. Which ones are rebelliously
beating you up from the inside out? Seek out the truth in the Bible,
and you can begin the process of teaching your rebel thoughts to
obey Jesus.

Lord, replace my wrong thoughts with Your holy thoughts.

Get a Grip

*So, with confidence and hope in this message, strengthen those
with feeble hands, shore up the weak-kneed and weary. Tell those
who worry, the anxious and fearful, "Take strength; have courage!
There's nothing to fear. Look, here—your God! Right here is your
God! The balance is shifting; God will right all wrongs. None other
than God will give you success. He is coming to make you safe."*

ISAIAH 35:3–4 VOICE

Are you a champion of hauling your groceries from vehicle to kitchen
in one trip? Whether you use plastic or reusable bags, one-trip success
is usually less about how strong your arms are and more on your ability
to get a grip on all the bag handles. This applies to difficult times in
life too. When we've got the firm grip on the situation—when we
share God's perspective on what's going on—then it's easier to endure
any circumstance and encourage others at the same time. "Take a
new grip with your tired hands and strengthen your weak knees,"
Paul challenged his readers in Hebrews 12:12–13 (NLT). "Mark out
a straight path for your feet so that those who are weak and lame will
not fall but become strong."

Whatever you're facing today, take a deep breath, ask God to help
you get a grip on the situation, and move forward in courage. God is
here and there's nothing to fear.

*Father, when I am anxious and struggling, give me
Your perspective. I know You are with me.*

Isaiah 37–38 / 2 Corinthians 12:1–10 / Proverbs 1:27–33

Pray First

"O LORD of Heaven's Armies. . .you alone are God of all the
kingdoms of the earth. You alone created the heavens and the earth.
Bend down, O LORD, and listen! Open your eyes, O LORD, and see!
Listen to Sennacherib's words of defiance against the living God."
ISAIAH 37:16–17 NLT

King Hezekiah had just received a letter from Sennacherib, the king of Assyria. Sennacherib's threatening message promised that the army of Judah and their God would also be no match for him. For generations, Assyria had wreaked havoc in the region, murdering, plundering, taking captives, defiling holy sites, and wiping entire people groups off the face of the earth. Sennacherib's letter could've sent Hezekiah into panic or despair, but instead Hezekiah prayed.

Hundreds of years before the New Testament was written, Hezekiah followed scripture's command in Philippians 4:6 (NLT): "Don't worry about anything; instead, pray about everything."

What resulted from Hezekiah's prayer? In Isaiah 37:21–35, God says that because Hezekiah prayed, He would rescue Judah and Jerusalem from the Assyrians—and give Sennacherib a taste of his own medicine.

When you're facing impossible circumstances, instead of panicking or despairing, *pray*. God is waiting to hear from you and to grant you peace (Philippians 4:7), and He will do the impossible when you trust Him enough to ask.

Lord, thank You for hearing me when I pray.
I will first come to You, no matter what. You are
my Father who wants to hear everything from me!

God with Us

*"Prepare the way for the LORD; make straight in the desert a highway
for our God. Every valley shall be raised up, every mountain and
hill made low; the rough ground shall become level, the rugged
places a plain. And the glory of the LORD will be revealed."*

ISAIAH 40:3–5 NIV

In Isaiah 40, the prophet is announcing God's preparation to send His Son to the world—and nothing would stand in the way. Here God promises He will move heaven and earth to go to His people. He will fill the valleys and flatten the mountains and hills. He'll straighten the curves and make the rough road smooth—all so Jesus could come to earth and be *Immanuel*, God with us.

For the Old Testament reader, this concept of God coming to humans would seem backward. Because for them to be near to God, they had to travel to the tabernacle or to the Temple in Jerusalem to present offerings and go through Jewish ritual. But the coming glory of the Lord, the new covenant of Jesus Christ, meant that God (in the form of the Holy Spirit) lives in the heart of each believer. Today, celebrate the gift of the nearness of God. Thank Him for His promise to never leave you or abandon you (Hebrews 13:5).

*Father, thank You for being such a personal God.
I don't have to travel or go through rituals and
sacrifice to be near to You. You seek me out, Lord!*

You Are Chosen

*"But as for you, Israel my servant, Jacob my chosen one, . . .
I have chosen you and will not throw you away. Don't be
afraid, for I am with you. Don't be discouraged, for I
am your God. I will strengthen you and help you. I will
hold you up with my victorious right hand."*

ISAIAH 41:8–10 NLT

God picked the Israelites to be His chosen people because He wanted to—not because they deserved it. If you claim Jesus as your Lord and Savior, the same is true for you. God chose you—not because you deserve it, but because He wanted to and He loves you that much.

Here in Isaiah 41, God uses powerful language to remind us of His promises. "I have chosen you" emphasizes God's commitment to us. Like the people of Israel, maybe you've gone through times when you felt separated from God, exiled from His presence. "I. . .will not throw you away," He told them then, and He says the same to you today. God does not and will not reject you.

If you're facing some uncertainty today, rest in these promises. Lift your head and resist discouragement. Put your hope in your Father God, who is with you and for you. He is faithful to not just pull you through but give you victory!

*I praise You, God, for the security, safety, and reassurance
of Your presence. Thank You for choosing me.*

Discipline vs. Punishment

*My child, don't reject the LORD's discipline, and don't be upset
when he corrects you. For the LORD corrects those he loves,
just as a father corrects a child in whom he delights.*

PROVERBS 3:11–12 NLT

For most people, the words *discipline* and *punishment* may mean essentially the same thing. But while discipline and punishment may seem similar, each has a very different motivation. Punishment imposes pain so that wrongs won't be repeated. But discipline imposes training for a better future.

When God disciplines His children, it's not about inflicting pain. Instead, God's discipline is rooted in His love and concern for our growth and character and maturity. The apostle Paul explained in Hebrews 12:11 (NLT), "No discipline is enjoyable while it is happening—it's painful! But afterward there will be a peaceful harvest or right living for those who are trained in this way." Receiving God's discipline isn't a pleasurable experience, but it *can* make sense—especially in hindsight.

If God is putting you through some discipline training now, remember His goodness and great love for you. Humble yourself and repent of whatever sin prompted the discipline. Focus on growing in faith, and be willing to learn all that He wants you to.

*Lord, even when I mess up, I know You aren't angry with
me. Thank You for being my kind Father. Help me to learn
everything I can from You so I can become more like Christ.*

Isaiah 44:21–46:13 / Galatians 3:1–18 / Proverbs 3:13–26

Evidence All Around

For the LORD. . .made the world to be lived in, not to be a
place of empty chaos. "I am the LORD," he says, "and there is
no other. I publicly proclaim bold promises. I do not whisper
obscurities in some dark corner. I would not have told the
people of Israel to seek me if I could not be found. I, the LORD,
speak only what is true and declare only what is right."

ISAIAH 45:18–19 NLT

Ancient pagans saw the world as a place of empty chaos, and many people today view it the same way. But God's provision and love are all around us—in the beauty of His creation, in the kindness one person shows to another, or in the logic embedded in His design of the heavens, earth, and every living thing.

God's promises are public, and He is easy to find. He doesn't hide behind a locked door or at the end of a maze. Hebrews 4:14–16 (NLT) says that through Jesus Christ—who acts as our High Priest—we can "come boldly to the throne of our gracious God. There we will receive his mercy, and we will find grace to help us when we need it most."

When you struggle with doubt, look for evidence of God's promises all around. We have a God of truth and righteousness in whom we can rely.

God, when the world seems to spin in chaos,
I will point others to You.

Isaiah 47:1–49:13 / Galatians 3:19–29 / Proverbs 3:27–35

Pay Attention

"If only you had paid attention to my commands,
your peace would have been like a river,
your well-being like the waves of the sea."
ISAIAH 48:18 NIV

Here in Isaiah 48, God reminds His chosen people that each moment they spend in disobedience is a moment they are robbed of His peace. If you are a parent, you may have said something similar to your child: "If you had just paid attention, you wouldn't be in this predicament...."

It's important to realize that God, even more than an earthly parent, sees the big picture. His plan *is* the big picture. His commands aren't meant to control us or be a burden. Instead, they're like guardrails or traffic signals that keep us headed in the right direction (and not careening off a cliff). New drivers quickly learn the first rule of the road: pay attention.

Even when we don't pay attention, even when we disobey, God is still there with us. And as our loving Father, He will teach us, offering corrective discipline to direct us. A wise woman will learn from Israel's rebellion and stubbornness and will quickly humble herself and obey. When she does so, God is faithful to restore her to peace, well-being, and righteousness.

Lord, I admit I don't always pay attention, and my selfishness
keeps me from following Your Word. Forgive me and guide
me back onto the path You have prepared for me.

Isaiah 49:14–51:23 / Galatians 4:1–11 / Proverbs 4:1–19

Never Forgotten

*Yet Jerusalem says, "The LORD has deserted us; the Lord
has forgotten us." "Never! Can a mother forget her nursing
child? Can she feel no love for the child she has borne?
But even if that were possible, I would not forget you!
See, I have written your name on the palms of my hands."*

ISAIAH 49:14–16 NLT

Of all your body parts, your hands are the most visible to you. Even as you read this devotion, it's likely you can see your hands as you hold the book. As you take care of children, as you type out a text, as you cook and craft and clean and complete any number of tasks, your hands are in your line of vision.

Here in Isaiah 49, God tells His chosen people (that includes you!) even though they feel abandoned by Him, He will *never* forget them. You are constantly in His thoughts and on His heart like a mother who is enchanted by her baby. He will not forget you, and if somehow He did forget you (which He won't), your name is permanently engraved on His hands as a reminder—His hands that work all things together for your good (Romans 8:28), that sustain you (Psalm 63:8; Isaiah 41:10), rescue you from danger (Psalm 138:7), and hold you safe and secure forever (John 10:28).

You are known, dear one. You are cherished. You are loved by a God who will *never* forget you.

Thank You, Father, for always remembering me!

Isaiah 52–54 / Galatians 4:12–31 / Proverbs 4:20–27

Don't Be Anxious

*There's no need to be anxious—the Eternal One goes before and
behind you. The God of Israel paves the way with assurance
and strength. He watches your back. . . . Even if the mountains
heave up from their anchors, and the hills quiver and shake,
I will not desert you. You can rely on My enduring love.*

ISAIAH 52:12; 54:10 VOICE

The Word is full of God's good promises, promises you can sink your
heart and mind into, promises that will give you peace, hope, security,
and staying power for life in this world.

Hopefully, you already have a good idea of who you are in Jesus.
Now you need to take that information, that truth, forward a bit
and use it as you live your life. Each and every day, God would have
you remember that there is really no need to be anxious about what
happens in this world. Because wherever you are and wherever you
go, God will be with you. He will be scouting out the terrain ahead
and looking back to see what may be coming up from behind, ready
to defend you at a moment's notice.

If the world seems to be falling apart or the fabric of your life
begins to unravel, rest assured that God is with you. He always will
be. He will not in any way abandon you but love you more than you
could ever know.

*In You alone, Lord, I find the peace, confidence,
and strength to carry on—with You.*

Growing in the Word

*"The rain and snow come down from the heavens and stay on the
ground to water the earth. They cause the grain to grow, producing
seed for the farmer and bread for the hungry. It is the same with my
word. I send it out, and it always produces fruit. It will accomplish
all I want it to, and it will prosper everywhere I send it."*

ISAIAH 55:10–11 NLT

God's Word has an amazing effect on all it touches, including you.
When Jesus enters your life, His presence waters your stony and dirt-
packed heart, making it more malleable for Him to plant the seed of
His Word. You grow up on it, allowing it to feed you, nourish you,
give you all the light you need to produce the fruit He would have
you bear in your life and in the lives of others.

God's Word does not return to Him without accomplishing the
results He intends—on you, the earth itself, His church, and the world
at large. So stretch yourself toward Him. Reach out for His Word.
Allow it to feed and water you deep within. Then you will become
the woman God had created you to be from the beginning of time.

*Grow me up in Your Word, Lord. Feed me upon
Your promises so that I will produce the fruit You
would have me bring forth into this world.*

Spiritual Sowing

Make no mistake: God can't be mocked. What you give is
what you get. What you sow, you harvest. Those who sow
seeds into their flesh will only harvest destruction from
their sinful nature. But those who sow seeds into the
Spirit shall harvest everlasting life from the Spirit.
GALATIANS 6:7–8 VOICE

The message is very clear. What you sow, you will reap. If you sow discord, that's what you will harvest. Same with hatred, selfishness, cruelty, anger, etc.

This message has been relayed to God's people before. In today's reading in Isaiah 58, God sends the message that to please Him we are not to simply go through the motions of wearing sackcloth and ashes as we fast. Instead, we are to free those who are wrongly imprisoned, lighten the burden of those who work for us, free the oppressed, feed the hungry, clothe the naked, and make ourselves available to family members who need our help. Then God will be there when we call, help us when we're in trouble, brighten the darkness around us, and guide, feed, and strengthen us.

Today, in this moment, consider what you've been sowing. Then think about what you've been reaping. Finally, pray, asking God to help you make changes where needed.

Lord, help me to sow seeds in the Spirit,
following Your desires for me in this world.

The Focus of His Love

The Father of our Master, Jesus Christ. . .takes us to the high
places of blessing in him. Long before he laid down earth's
foundations, he had us in mind, had settled on us as the focus of
his love, to be made whole and holy by his love. Long, long ago
he decided to adopt us into his family through Jesus Christ.

EPHESIANS 1:3–5 MSG

In his letter to the Ephesian church, the apostle Paul reminds us of what God has done for us. This is something we should remember not only every waking moment but especially during times when we feel weakened by the world.

Today, in your quiet time with the Lord, remember that God is the Father of our Master, Jesus. That He takes us to the heavenly places, to the unseen and eternal world, and into His presence. That is where we can find restoration and refreshment in His blessings—the strength, energy, and power we need to keep on keeping on.

Friend, remember that even before He created the world, God had you in mind. He had already decided to make you the focus of His love. And by that love you are made holy and perfect, forever His lovely daughter. Rise up in this blessing, this power, this family of God.

Thank You, Lord, for loving me before time or the world began.

Isaiah 63:1–65:16 / Ephesians 2 / Proverbs 6:6–19

Gifted with Grace

*It's by God's grace that you have been saved. You receive it
through faith. It was not our plan or our effort. It is God's gift. . . .
You didn't earn it. . .so don't go around bragging that you must
have done something amazing. For we are the product of His
hand, heaven's poetry etched on lives, created in the Anointed,
Jesus, to accomplish the good works God arranged long ago.*

EPHESIANS 2:8–10 VOICE

God's grace. Truly there's no better gift. For it's given by God with
zero effort on your part. You simply receive it, automatically, through
your faith.

Yet the story doesn't end there. For you've been made by God
and are deemed by Him to be a masterpiece, especially and uniquely
recreated in Christ Jesus. His aim is for you to do what He's already
arranged for you to do—good works. That means you're to take those
paths He has already prepared for you to walk in, living the life He's
prepared you to live. Loving God with all your heart, soul, mind,
and strength. Loving others as you love yourself. Caring for others.
Allowing God's love and light to shine upon you, within you, and
through you, spilling out onto others surrounded by darkness.

God has created you and gifted you with grace so you could live
a life of love. Who can you love today?

*Lord, thank You for Your gift of amazing grace.
Make me a conduit of Your love.*

Beyond Imagination

*God can do anything, you know—far more than you could
ever imagine or guess or request in your wildest dreams!
He does it not by pushing us around but by working
within us, his Spirit deeply and gently within us.*

EPHESIANS 3:20 MSG

Paul, the author of Ephesians, writes out a prayer for his readers, asking that God strengthen His people with the power of His Spirit; that through faith Jesus would abide in their hearts; that in the rich soil of His love, their roots would grow deep, "and keep [them] strong" (Ephesians 3:17). All so that His people would understand the amazingly infinite love of Christ.

Paul also makes clear that the power God comes to life when His Spirit works within us, deeply and gently, quietly and profoundly, so we can do what we have been created to do. Things we never imagined possible are possible with God. He, the Creator, comforter, protector, and provider can do more than we could ask or dream. For He is the same God who divided the Red Sea, stopped the sun, turned back shadows, and so much more.

Today meditate on God's Spirit working deeply and gently within you. Commune with the all-powerful Lord. Feel His love and light. Then open your eyes and walk in His way.

*Here I am, Lord. Help me to feel Your Spirit
working within me. Fill me with Your light and love.
Lead me in the way You would have me go.*

Jeremiah 1–2 / Ephesians 4:17–32 / Proverbs 6:27–35

The True You

Throw off your old sinful nature and your former way of life, which is corrupted by lust and deception. Instead, let the Spirit renew your thoughts and attitudes. Put on your new nature, created to be like God—truly righteous and holy.

Ephesians 4:22–24 NLT

When you began believing in Jesus and were blessed with the Holy Spirit, you became a new woman. You are now to throw off that former nature you were sporting, that way of life you were modeling, and take on the Spirit, allowing Him to give you new thoughts and attitudes.

Every day, seek that renewal. Allow the Spirit to transform you and change your mode of life so you live and act like Jesus did, walking as He walked, loving as He loved, forgiving as He forgave, giving as He gave.

Each day, allow yourself to get your energy and power from the true vine: Jesus. Spend private time with Him. Then, as He builds up His presence within you, you'll begin to see the futility and danger that come from anger, bitterness, and harsh words. And you'll find yourself becoming more tenderhearted, kind, unable to hold a grudge. You'll then become just as God in His love intended you to be—the true you.

I come to You, Jesus, seeking renewal of the Spirit. May You give me the energy and power to be the woman You designed me to be, a loving woman, the true me.

Child of the Light

*Although you were once the personification of darkness,
you are now light in the Lord. So act like children of the
light. For the fruit of the light is all that is good, right,
and true. Make it your aim to learn what pleases our Lord.*
Ephesians 5:8–10 VOICE

You are a new woman, a woman of light. So now you need to act like it. Your life must be as distinct from the world as heat is from cold and light from darkness.

Jesus, the living Word, is the true, bright, shining light. He's the Sun of Righteousness (Malachi 4:2), the one who came with healing in His wings to restore the world to God. It's from Him you're to take the spark and become a light in your own world.

To act like a woman of light—doing and being all that is good, right, and true—feed the spark within you by staying in God's Word, using it to discover what pleases Him, not the world you live in.

Take a dive deep into the God-breathed Bible today. Allow it to fuel your life with its light. Manifest who you are in Christ.

*Through Your Word, Lord, teach me how to be Your light.
Help me learn what pleases You as we walk together, step by
step, day by day, moment by moment, word by word.*

Jeremiah 4:23–5:31 / Ephesians 6 / Proverbs 7:6–27

Woman Warrior

*Be prepared. You're up against far more than you can handle
on your own. Take all the help you can get, every weapon
God has issued, so that when it's all over but the shouting
you'll still be on your feet. . . . God's Word is an indispensable
weapon. In the same way, prayer is essential.*

EPHESIANS 6:13, 17–18 MSG

This spiritual battle between light (good) and darkness (evil) is ongoing. To be able to stand and stay standing against the forces of darkness, you'll need to be prepared. Fortunately, God has not left you to battle on your own. Instead, He provides an arsenal just for you. It contains the belt of truth, armor of right standing with God, shoes of peace, shield of faith, and helmet of salvation.

For weaponry, God provides you with the sword of the Spirit, which is His Word. Immersing yourself in the Word will give you the encouragement to stand your ground.

And sharing the Word will strengthen and buoy your spirit as well as the spirits of those around you.

Last but not least, take up God's weapon of prayer, using it constantly. Pray in every way every day. For yourself and others.

So dig deep, woman warrior. Connect with Christ. Walk through the Word. Pray feverishly. Take up your holy armor. And you will be more than able to stand your ground.

Lord, be with me as I prepare myself to stand strong in Your light.

Jeremiah 6:1–7:26 / Philippians 1:1–26 / Proverbs 8:1–11

At the Crossroads

GOD's Message yet again: "Go stand at the crossroads and look around. Ask for directions to the old road, the tried-and-true road. Then take it. Discover the right route for your souls."
JEREMIAH 6:16 MSG

There you are. Standing at a crossroad, wondering which would be the right way to turn, the path God would have you choose. Before you take another step, ask Him for the old path, the one that will lead to where He'd have you go. For only upon His path will you find peace with Him, as well as His provision and protection. Walking His way, your soul will find its true rest.

So pray, asking God for wisdom and direction. Then dig deep into His Word. Believe He will show you the right road and then go before you, clearing any obstacles that may stand in your way.

Proverbs 8:2 (NLT) says that Wisdom "takes her stand at the crossroads," directing her voice to those who encounter her upon the way. "You'll only hear true and right words from my mouth; not one syllable will be twisted or skewed" (Proverbs 8:8 MSG), says she.

So when you have a decision to make, remember to stop. Stand still. Pray. Seek wisdom in God's Word. And you will find the right road for your soul.

Lord, I have a decision to make. Give me wisdom at this crossroad.

Jeremiah 7:26–9:16 / Philippians 1:27–2:18 / Proverbs 8:12–21

God at Work

*Work out (cultivate, carry out to the goal, and fully complete)
your own salvation. . . . [Not in your own strength] for it is
God Who is all the while effectually at work in you [energizing
and creating in you the power and desire], both to will and to
work for His good pleasure and satisfaction and delight.*

PHILIPPIANS 2:12–13 AMPC

This call to live a godly life, to walk God's way and do His will, is not a journey you make alone. God is with you every step of the way. He's at work within you. He's giving you the energy and the power to take the paths He'd have you take.

God's Spirit desires your heart to remain always open to His promptings, His urgings. He wants you to make the right choices, the ones that will give God delight and further the work He created you to perform. Yet God does not force you to go one way or another. The path you choose is still your decision to make. And if you do walk out of His will, you'll soon know it by outward circumstances.

Even if the course before you seems difficult, remember that God is within you, energizing you "both to will and to work for His good pleasure and satisfaction and delight"!

So, friend, walk on!

*I realize, God, I'm a work in progress. May I remember that
You are working within me and will show me the way to go.*

Jeremiah 9:17–11:17 / Philippians 2:19–30 / Proverbs 8:22–36

Boasting Rights

*"Those who wish to boast should boast in this alone:
that they truly know me and understand that I am the LORD
who demonstrates unfailing love and who brings justice and
righteousness to the earth, and that I delight in these things."*

JEREMIAH 9:24 NLT

God doesn't want a follower to be boasting about her wisdom, her strength, or her riches, what she's stored up on earth. He wants her to be boasting about one thing only: that she knows Him and His Son, Jesus (Philippians 3:7–10). That she understands who He is and what He does.

All the things of this world, all the wisdom you have, strength you wield, and earthly treasures you've gained—including family, friends, home, possessions, IRA, etc.—cannot be counted on. Such things do not make you stand out in God's sight. What He values is you knowing Him. And the best way to do that is to read His Word. To understand that He loved you before you were ever brought into being. And that His love was so strong, rich, and deep that He allowed His Son to be sacrificed so you could be right with Him and live with Him in eternity.

If you insist on boasting, do so about how much you love God and He you. That you know who He is and have given Him credit for what He's done in your life. In that boasting He delights!

*Lord, help me to know You, to understand
You are Lord, a Lord who loves me!*

Jeremiah 11:18–13:27 / Philippians 3 / Proverbs 9:1–6

Pressing On

*But I focus on this one thing: Forgetting the past and
looking forward to what lies ahead, I press on to reach
the end of the race and receive the heavenly prize for
which God, through Christ Jesus, is calling us.*

PHILIPPIANS 3:13–14 NLT

We all have a past, a place where we were before we knew Jesus. We
may have memories that make us cringe with shame. But that's not
where God would have us looking. Because if we're so busy focusing on what's behind us, there's a good chance we'll lose our balance
and stumble on the path before us.

Remember Saul (later renamed Paul)? He persecuted Christians.
Then Jesus showed him the light on the way to Damascus. Afterward,
he became an apostle and a major player in the early church. In the Old
Testament, Rahab was a prostitute but, after finding God, turned her
life around, becoming an ancestress of Jesus! Moses was a murderer.
David was that too, as well as an adulterer. Yet if any of these people
had kept their eyes on their personal history, they would have never
envisioned themselves as the people God already saw: His children
who, with His strength and help, would further His kingdom.

So, dear one, forget the past. Press on to the place to which Jesus
is calling you!

*Help me, Lord, to leave the past behind
and walk in the present Your way.*

Unsurpassable Peace

*Don't be anxious about things; instead, pray. Pray about everything.
He longs to hear your requests, so talk to God about your needs and
be thankful for what has come. And know that the peace of God (a
peace that is beyond any and all of our human understanding) will
stand watch over your hearts and minds in Jesus, the Anointed One.*

Philippians 4:6–7 voice

Imagine what kind of a life you'd have if you'd pray instead of worrying. Truly imagine it. Consider what's on your mind this very moment. Perhaps you're fretting about everything that's on your overloaded plate. Maybe a relationship seems to be going sour. It could be that someone close to you has deserted you.

Whatever is eating away at your joy, gnawing at your heart, weakening your spirit, pray about it. Then leave that particular concern at His feet or in His hands. If the worry comes back, creeping once again into your mind, take it right back to God. Remember that He can do anything.

And while you're praying, thank God for all the good He has brought you. Doing so will spark your love of Him and allow peace to take up the space the problem was hoarding. Ah, how wonderful to live, love, pray, and praise in Jesus!

*Lord, thank You for wanting to hear my worries and
wants. Today I come to You with prayer and praise!
Bless me with Your unsurpassable peace!*

Nary a Dropped Leaf

"Blessed is the man who trusts me, GOD, the woman who sticks with GOD. They're like trees replanted in Eden, putting down roots near the rivers—never a worry through the hottest of summers, never dropping a leaf, serene and calm through droughts, bearing fresh fruit every season."

JEREMIAH 17:7–8 MSG

When you begin to know God, understand Him more fully, and continue to learn about Him, you'll find yourself sticking with Him more and more. You'll truly trust Him with not just your own life but the lives of all those you love and care about.

That trust in God will make you blossom in a way you never imagined possible. You'll be like a tree in the garden—before the snake. You'll begin to put down your roots into the stream of His presence. You'll never worry even though you're living through one of the hottest summers ever recorded. You'll drop nary a leaf, staying calm, cool, and collected during a fire-weather watch. For in God's presence, you cannot help but blossom. Each day, trusting in God, you will increase in strength and begin to bear fruit you never dreamed imaginable.

What are you waiting for? Grow, girl, grow!

Lord, help my trust in You to grow so much so that I become a woman warrior instead of a woman worrier. I will put down my roots in You and rise up to bear You fruit, dropping nary a leaf!

Jeremiah 18:1–20:6 / Colossians 1:24–2:15 / Proverbs 10:6–14

That Firm Foundation

*Now that you have welcomed the Anointed One, Jesus the Lord,
into your lives, continue to journey with Him and allow Him to
shape your lives. Let your roots grow down deeply in Him, and let
Him build you up on a firm foundation. Be strong in the faith,
just as you were taught, and always spill over with thankfulness.*

COLOSSIANS 2:6–7 VOICE

The key to living a godly life lies in allowing Jesus to shape it. That
means not resisting His presence or His way or His wisdom but gladly
welcoming all those things, allowing Him to have full sway, trusting
Him with each and every aspect of your life. It means keeping in step
with Him, walking as He would have you walk, loving as He would
have you love.

Once your roots are deep within Him, you'll be seeking His
perspective everywhere you turn. You'll be asking Him for His advice,
His wisdom, His take on every situation. Then, before you know it,
you'll find yourself overflowing with thanks to Him.

There's coming into the faith. Then there's learning about the
faith. And then there's actually walking in it. What stage are you in?
Are you ready for the next step?

*Lord, help me in my walk with You. Make me eager
to allow You to mold me, to shape me any way
You want me. I want to live my life in You.*

Things Looking Up

*So if you're serious about living this new resurrection life with
Christ, act like it. Pursue the things over which Christ presides.
Don't shuffle along, eyes to the ground, absorbed with the things right
in front of you. Look up, and be alert to what is going on around
Christ—that's where the action is. See things from his perspective.*

COLOSSIANS 3:1–2 MSG

Once you accept Christ, you are a new woman. A daughter of God
Almighty "Whose power no foe can withstand" (Psalm 91:1 AMPC).
You are a part of Jesus' family. Your destiny lies in the heavens not
here on earth. That's why you need to be looking up, eyes fixed on
Jesus' plans and priorities.

That old life you were living is dead. The Message explains it this
way: "Your new life, which is your *real* life—even though invisible
to spectators—is with Christ in God. *He* is your life. When Christ
(your real life, remember) shows up again on this earth, you'll show
up, too—the real you, the glorious you" (Colossians 3:3–4).

Whatever you do, don't worry. The Holy Spirit is here to help
you. Just keep looking up!

*I'm looking to You, Lord. Open my eyes to
Your presence. Help me to understand and
follow the Spirit's lead. I'm all in, Lord. In You.*

Jeremiah 22:20–23:40 / Colossians 3:5–4:1 / Proverbs 10:27–32

Dressed for Success

Clothe yourselves with tenderhearted mercy, kindness, humility,
gentleness, and patience. Make allowance for each other's faults, and
forgive anyone who offends you. Remember, the Lord forgave you,
so you must forgive others. Above all, clothe yourselves with love.

COLOSSIANS 3:12–14 NLT

As a woman chosen by God, you're to be someone who mirrors His Son, Jesus. Rooted in Him, you're to be a woman not just focused on Him but reflecting His personality. It's great to have your nose in the Bible, but then you need to deal with the other humans around you and treat them as Jesus treated others. That means having a tender heart toward them. You're to be merciful and kind, humble, gentle, and patient.

You're also to make allowance for the faults of others. None of us are perfect and all of us deserve forgiveness, the same forgiveness with which God graces us. And above all these things, you're to clothe yourself with love.

This sounds like a tall order. But if you're steeped in the Word, focused on Jesus, praying for strength, and praising God for all He has done for you, the Spirit within you will help you do what sometimes seems impossible. By clothing yourself with Christ's attributes, you will be, in God's eyes, dressed for success.

Help me, Lord, to be like Jesus, to do as He did. Fill me,
clothe me, strengthen me, empower me with
Your presence, within and without.

Open Doors

Pray, and keep praying. Be alert and thankful when you pray.
And while you are at it, add us to your prayers. Pray that God
would open doors and windows and minds and eyes and hearts for
the word. . . . Be wise when you engage with those outside the faith
community; make the most of every moment and every encounter.

Colossians 4:2–3, 5 voice

We are to pray. Constantly. And to have an alert mind while doing so. For we cannot long handle this life on earth without opening ourselves up to God, allowing Him to refill and replenish us with His power, strength, love, hope, light, and grace. We are to pay attention to what He may be telling us in His Word and in our circumstances.

At the same time, we're to pray for others. Although God may not have called us to be foreign missionaries, preachers, or leaders in the church, we can still pray for them. And we can pray that God will open doors of opportunity in every corner of the world, including our own. We can ask Him to open the minds and hearts of unbelievers so the Word can take root in their lives.

This constant and consistent life of prayer will not only keep us rooted in Jesus but help us build a better world for Him to enter. Ready? Let's begin!

Lord, make me a woman of prayer.

Spirit-Infused Message

*What you experienced in the good news we brought you was more
than words channeling down your ears; it came to you as a life-
empowering, Spirit-infused message that offers complete hope
and assurance! . . . You took to heart the word we taught with
joy inspired by the Holy Spirit, even in the face of trouble.*

1 THESSALONIANS 1:5–6 VOICE

The Word does something to you deep down inside, stirring up the
spirit within you, linking it to the power of God's Spirit. It touches
your heart, changes your mind, inspires your soul. Within God's Word,
you find God. You get to know Him. You begin to understand things
in a way you never could before.

When you take God's Word to heart, you begin to find hope
and joy even amid trouble. You find a way to see things from God's
perspective. And from there the view is spectacular. That's why the
Word is there for you to read, to meditate on, to write upon your
heart. That's how you grow into God, sense His presence, feel His
promptings as to your next steps in any endeavor or circumstance.

Today, dip into the Word, allowing it to link your spirit to God's.
Feel its life-empowering message and the joy that comes with it.

Lord, as I open Your Word today, speak to me, Spirit to spirit.

Jeremiah 28–29 / 1 Thessalonians 2:9–3:13 / Proverbs 11:22–26

God Knows

I know the thoughts and plans that I have for you, says the Lord,
thoughts and plans for welfare and peace and not for evil, to give
you hope in your final outcome. Then you will call upon Me, and
you will come and pray to Me, and I will hear and heed you. Then
you will seek Me, inquire for, and require Me [as a vital necessity]
and find Me when you search for Me with all your heart.

JEREMIAH 29:11–13 AMPC

When you base your life on Jesus, when you dig deeply into His Word, you will find hope on the hardest of days. Because there you will discover this truth: God is thinking about you. . .all the time.

God has a plan only you can fulfill. He has a task specifically designed for you to undertake. And He promises that His plan is for your good, to bring you peace and hope in your days.

Your task is to call on God. To go into His presence and pray to Him. Then to be still and listen. When you do, when you enter that secret and holy place, the Lord will hear you. When you seek Him, when you require Him as a relationship you must have, when you look for Him with all your heart, you will find Him.

It happened to Mary Magdalene when she sought Jesus in the garden. It will happen for you.

Lord, I come seeking Your presence as
my vital necessity. Hear my prayer!

Jeremiah 30:1–31:22 / 1 Thessalonians 4:1–5:11 / Proverbs 11:27–31

Everlasting Love

*This is what I, the Eternal One, declare to you: . . . "I have loved
you with an everlasting love—out of faithfulness I have drawn you
close." . . . God Himself has already taught you how to love outside
yourselves. . . . Brothers and sisters, we urge you to love even more.*
JEREMIAH 31:1, 3; 1 THESSALONIANS 4:9–10 VOICE

God loves you. It's as simple as that. He wants nothing more than
to draw you ever closer to Him so that you can feel His love, bathe
yourself in it, lose yourself in His embrace.

Sit with that idea, that truth. That God is constantly drawing you
close to Him. Drink up that love. Allow it to fill your entire being.
Now take that love, that sunshine, that warmth in your heart, soul,
spirit, and mind and allow it to bring you to the point where you
love yourself. Where you let go of all the mistakes you think you've
made and forget all the troubles you've endured because of them.
Love yourself as God loves you.

Now you are ready to branch out. To pour God's love onto others.
To forgive the mistakes of others as God has forgiven you and for
which you have forgiven yourself. To love even more.

That's what you're here for.

*Lord, allow Your everlasting love to fill me to
overflowing, then to splash out into this world.*

Jeremiah 31:23–32:35 / 1 Thessalonians 5:12–28 / Proverbs 12:1–14

Nothing Too Difficult

"Eternal Lord, with Your outstretched arm and Your enormous power You created the heavens and the earth. Nothing is too difficult for You. . . . You rescued Your people Israel out of Egypt with miraculous signs and wonders—with a mighty hand and an outstretched arm, with a power too terrible for words."

JEREMIAH 32:17, 21 VOICE

In the verses above, the prophet Jeremiah praised God's power. In awe, he cites the circumstances in which God has shown in the past that nothing is too difficult for Him. How He performed signs and wonders before His people in Egypt and beyond. Later, in Jeremiah 32:27 (VOICE), God agrees with His prophet, saying, "Look! I am the Eternal, the God of all living things. Is anything too difficult for Me?"

You have God's power within and without. Remember this when you consider the apostle Paul urging you to help the weak and be patient with everyone. To not pay back evil for evil but do good to all. To "celebrate always, pray constantly, and give thanks to God no matter what circumstances you find yourself in" (1 Thessalonians 5:16–18 VOICE).

Remember who you belong to and who works through you: your God, for whom nothing is too difficult!

Lord, help me do all You call me to do. With Your power working within me, I know I can!

Expanding Possibilities

Thus says the Lord Who made [the earth], the Lord Who formed
it to establish it—the Lord is His name: Call to Me and I will
answer you and show you great and mighty things, fenced
in and hidden, which you do not know (do not distinguish
and recognize, have knowledge of and understand).

JEREMIAH 33:2–3 AMPC

Looking for some answers? Pray. Need help deciphering God's Word? Pray. Confused about life, desire direction, can't seem to find your way out of a difficulty? Pray.

God is telling you, promising you that He is the ultimate Creator and generator of answers. He has an imagination you couldn't even begin to understand. He can make confusing things clear. He can reveal that which is hidden. He can solve any enigma. And He is more than accessible.

When you are in the midst of darkness, call on God and He will turn His light upon it, helping you to find your way out. When your thoughts are getting you nowhere, call on God and He will help you think outside the box.

Prayer is essential in this life with God. So take up those hands. Lift up your eyes. And seek God. Talk to Him. Be still before Him. Listen to His reply. Expand your mind, heart, spirit, soul, and possibilities.

Lord, I come seeking Your face and presence, looking for
Your light and revelatory insight. Hear my prayer. Open my
mind, heart, soul, and spirit and expand the possibilities.

Riding Out the Storm

The Lord is faithful, and He will strengthen [you] and set you on
a firm foundation and guard you from the evil [one]. . . . Now
may the Lord of peace Himself grant you His peace (the peace of
His kingdom) at all times and in all ways [under all circumstances
and conditions, whatever comes]. The Lord [be] with you all.

2 THESSALONIANS 3:3, 16 AMPC

God has set you on a firm foundation. His promises, His Words, His love will give you all the strength you need to have a resilient faith. All you need to do is believe. And keep on believing.

When you stay connected to God throughout your day and life, you will reap the benefits of belonging to the Lord and creator of peace. His peace, His kind of calm, will keep you afloat in any and all circumstances, regardless of your finances, family, relationships, work, health, or wealth. No matter what political, worldwide, or natural storms come upon the horizon, you're safe in the harbor with your Lord, who's constantly reminding you to be calm. To be still. To understand that *He* is God. That you need not worry. For you're safe in the ark of His love.

Help me remember, Lord, that You and Your peace, protection,
and power are always with me. That with You within and
without, I can ride out every storm. Harbored in the ark
of Your love, I'm as safe as a babe in arms. Amen.

Good Enough

I thank Christ Jesus our Lord, who has given me strength to do his work. He considered me trustworthy and appointed me to serve him. . . . He filled me with the faith and love that come from Christ Jesus.

1 TIMOTHY 1:12, 14 NLT

Paul hadn't been the best of men. Before becoming an apostle, he'd been a bloodthirsty persecutor of people on the Way. In those days his name had been Saul. He was the one that held the coats of those "pelting Stephen with rocks" (Acts 7:59 VOICE). Saul "was pleased by Stephen's death" then later "went on a rampage—hunting the church, house after house, dragging both men and women to prison" (Acts 8:2–3 VOICE).

Yet, Paul writes to Timothy, "God had mercy on me so that Christ Jesus could use me as a prime example of his great patience with even the worst sinners. Then others will realize that they, too, can believe in him and receive eternal life" (1 Timothy 1:16 NLT).

If you think you're unworthy or just not good enough to follow Jesus, to do His work, think again. Know that with the faith and love that come from Jesus, you are worthy. You are good enough. And God will give you the strength, faith, and love to serve Him well.

Thank You, Jesus, for believing I'm good enough.
Give me the strength, faith, and love to do
what You put in my hands to do. Amen.

Pray

*The first thing I want you to do is pray. Pray every way
you know how, for everyone you know. Pray especially for
rulers and their governments to rule well so we can be quietly
about our business of living simply, in humble contemplation.
This is the way our Savior God wants us to live.*

1 TIMOTHY 2:1–3 MSG

Where is prayer on your list of priorities?

The apostle Paul, writing to Timothy, tells him the first thing he wants Timothy to do is pray. The first thing. Pray. What's the first thing you do in the morning? Is it devotions? Is it exercise? Is it showering, then putting on your makeup?

God told people to pray. To call on Him and He would answer. Jesus also told His followers to pray. He Himself made prayer His number one priority, often going into secluded places so He could have a one-on-one conversation with His Father. Our Father.

Every morning before you turn on the coffee pot, take a shower, eat breakfast, or feed the kids, pray. If you must, wake up early, giving yourself time to pray before the household begins to stir. Pray, every way you know how, for everyone you know. Especially pray for leaders, asking God for those who will lead well. Lovingly. Caringly. Faithfully. Humbly.

*Lord God, help me make prayer a priority, something I do
before I begin my day. Speak. And I will listen. Amen.*

On Your Side

"You don't have to fear the king of Babylon. Your fears are for nothing. I'm on your side, ready to save and deliver you from anything he might do. I'll pour mercy on you. What's more, he will show you mercy! He'll let you come back to your very own land."

JEREMIAH 42:11–12 MSG

God is with you for a reason: to save you. Thus, all those who strike you with fear—prompting your heart to beat wildly, your palms to sweat, your mind to spin out of control—can and should be put aside. After all, they're only mere mortals, whereas God is the supreme power, the master Creator, the one "Whose power no foe can withstand" (Psalm 91:1 AMPC). He is "the all-wise, all-powerful, and ever-present God" (Jeremiah 42:11 AMPC), the one who promises to never leave nor forsake you.

Yet that's not all. The same God who is on your side, who promises to deliver and save you from others, not only will show you compassion and mercy but will arrange things so that the ones you may fear will also show you compassion and mercy!

So let your fears fade away. Consciously live your life knowing you need not be afraid of anyone because you're a woman of God, the daughter of a King. Your fears are for nothing.

Thank You, my Lord, for being on my side, for taking my part, for loving me. You're my knight in shining armor! And I am Your humble servant.

Jeremiah 43–44 / 1 Timothy 4:11–5:16 / Proverbs 13:22–25

Tough Love

Those who spare the rod of discipline hate their children.
Those who love their children care enough to discipline them.

PROVERBS 13:24 NLT

It's hard to discipline our children because we love them more than life itself! Yet if we don't discipline them, they may quickly careen out of control.

Chances are God feels the same way about us. He loves us so much He sacrificed His Son so that we could be reconciled to the Lord. That's an amazing amount of love for any parent to show a child. And in His eyes, that's what we are. Children.

While we're on the subject, let's not confuse our trials in life with God's discipline. When we suffer because of something wrong that we did, that's on us. That's not a trial but discipline. A mode of correction the Father uses to keep us on the straight and narrow.

Remember when David committed adultery with Bathsheba then had her husband, Uriah, killed? Because of David's conduct, God sent Nathan the prophet to tell him the sword would never depart from his house (2 Samuel 12:10). *That's* discipline.

The point is there are consequences to a person's actions. And it's every parent's obligation to try to keep a child on the right road. That's going to take a lot of love but will be worth it in the long run.

Lord, thank You for disciplining me, for keeping me on the right road. Give me the strength to do the same for my own children.

Where the Heart Lies

For the love of money—and what it can buy—is the root
of all sorts of evil. Some already have wandered away
from the true faith because they craved what it had to
offer; but when reaching for the prize, they found their
hands and hearts pierced with many sorrows.

1 TIMOTHY 6:10 VOICE

Today's verse is often misquoted. It's not money itself that's evil. It's the *love* of money. Unfortunately, down through the centuries, many people have become obsessed with getting more. And more. And more.

Yet God would have you live not worshipping the almighty dollar but Him. He's the prize for which we're to be striving, not monetary treasures. As Paul writes Timothy: "A devout life does bring wealth, but it's the rich simplicity of being yourself before God. Since we entered the world penniless and will leave it penniless, if we have bread on the table and shoes on our feet, that's enough" (1 Timothy 6:6–8 MSG).

Consider what you're making a priority in your life—earning money for what it can buy you or spending time with the Lord and sharing His riches. Someday you'll be leaving behind all your earthly treasures and be uniting with the Lord in the heavenlies, going out of this world the same way you entered it: penniless in money but rich in love and light.

Lord, help me to live a life where my heart lies
with You alone, not with making money.

Living the Call

*Stir up (rekindle the embers of, fan the flame of, and keep
burning) the [gracious] gift of God, [the inner fire] that
is in you. . . . For God did not give us a spirit of timidity
(of cowardice, of craven and cringing and fawning fear),
but [He has given us a spirit] of power and of love and of
calm and well-balanced mind and discipline and self-control.*

2 TIMOTHY 1:6–7 AMPC

God has given each of us a gift. And in today's verses, we are reminded
to use our gifts so that we may live out the calling God has put on
our hearts.

Perhaps you have yet to hear your call. If so, pray that God would
reveal how He would have you use your desires and talents to further
His plan for yourself and this world.

Wherever you are in life—whether old or young, rich or not so
rich, married or single, a mother or foster parent, in the city or in the
country—God has equipped you with the strength, power, courage,
love, calm, and control to perform a certain task. Whether that task
be to paint, write, act, sing, teach, preach, nurse, or be a mother, you
can do it. In His power and with His blessing.

What embers will you stir up today?

*Lord, remind me that You have already equipped me
to do what You call me to do. Then help me pursue that
path in Your power, strength, love, and courage.*

Instead...

*Timothy, run away from youthful desires. Instead, direct your passion
to chasing after righteousness, faithfulness, love, and peace, along
with those who call upon the Lord with pure hearts. Excuse yourself
from any conversations that turn into foolish and uninformed debates
because you know they only provoke fights. As the Lord's slave, you
shouldn't exhaust yourself in bickering; instead, be gentle—no matter
who you are dealing with—ready and able to teach, tolerant without
resentment, gently instructing those who stand up against you.*

2 TIMOTHY 2:22–25 VOICE

Here we find Paul's advice to his young friend Timothy. While he is
directing Timothy on what *not* to do, he doesn't just leave it at that.
Paul also gives solid wisdom for what Timothy should do instead.

How often have we adhered to partial advice and not followed
through full circle? Perhaps we *don't* contribute to the gossip at book
club—but we *do* sit and soak it all in. Maybe we *don't* cower in fear
when it comes to chasing our hopes and dreams—but we *do* neglect
to make sure we're on the same page with God before taking that
first step.

Before taking any advice to heart, make sure it aligns with God's
Word. If so, then it's wise to act on it and *follow through*! Not only
will we benefit, but those who are watching will too!

*Lord Jesus, help me to always follow
Your Word—not just parts, but all of it.*

Jeremiah 50:17–51:14 / 2 Timothy 3 / Proverbs 14:28–35

Who's Watching You?

*You. . .know all about my teaching, my way of life, my purpose,
faith, patience, love, endurance, persecutions, sufferings—what kinds
of things happened to me. . . . The Lord rescued me from all of them.
. . . Continue in what you have learned and have become convinced
of. . .how from infancy you have known the Holy Scriptures.*

2 TIMOTHY 3:10–11, 14–15 NIV

Timothy knew all about Paul's life—the good, the bad, and the ugly.
He had listened to Paul teach. He had witnessed Paul's patience, love,
perseverance, and faith in action. And he knew of Paul's persecution
and suffering.

Which part likely had the biggest impact on Timothy?

Think about it. Do you fuss and fume at the barista who gets
your order wrong, or do you extend grace? Do you cut in line, or do
you pray for patience as you wait?

As we think about our faith and how we react to everyday
situations, it would serve us well to remember that someone is *always*
watching—friends, family, and even strangers get a front-row view
of how we handle ourselves. They watch us struggle and overcome,
grieve and celebrate, hurt and forgive.

When we handle life's difficulties with grace, mercy, and
perseverance, that's when others take notice—that's when our faith
is magnified. *That's* when they see Jesus in you!

Lord, help me to live like someone is always watching!

Jeremiah 51:15–64 / 2 Timothy 4 / Proverbs 15:1–9

Real Love

*Proclaim the Message with intensity. . . . Challenge, warn,
and urge. . . . Don't ever quit. . . . You're going to find that
there will be times when people will. . .fill up on spiritual junk
food—catchy opinions that tickle their fancy. They'll turn their
backs on truth. . . . But you. . .keep the Message alive.*

2 TIMOTHY 4:2–5 MSG

Today there's increasing pressure to cave to culture's warped way of thinking. Sadly, many churches and Christians have been swayed to affirm behaviors and ideas that are far from biblical—to spare people their hurt feelings.

Make no mistake, we should *always* be considerate when we share the truth. But when we are feelings-focused, somewhere in the process we end up watering down or even burying God's message. When we're tempted and take even small bites of "spiritual junk food," we hurt our heavenly Father and mar the beautiful message of the gospel.

Unfortunately, the truth of God's Word is often made fuzzy in the name of "love." And so, we must take Paul's teaching to heart. Paul was familiar with the ways of the world. He understood the temptation to give in when faced with criticism and rejection. And yet, he advised to keep going—*with intensity*!

Never stop challenging, warning, urging people toward Jesus. That is *real* love in action.

*Heavenly Father, when it comes to feelings or
truth, help me to always stand for truth.*

The Better Life

*We rest in this hope we've been given—the hope that we will live
forever with our God—the hope that He proclaimed ages and ages
ago (even before time began). And our God is no liar; He is not
even capable of uttering lies. So we can be sure that it is in His
exact right time that He released His word into the world.*

TITUS 1:2–3 VOICE

The day you said yes to Jesus, everything changed. Your loneliness
turned to belonging; your anxiety to calm; your fear to courage; your
insecurity to confidence; your despair to hope. What was lost, found!
Darkness became light!

Life with Jesus is just better! God's Word guarantees it: "I am
the light that shines through the cosmos; if you walk with Me, you
will thrive in the nourishing light that gives life and will not know
darkness" (John 8:12 VOICE).

When you live in the light, that's when you have real hope—an
inexplicable optimism that those without Jesus don't understand. With
hope as your steady companion, you can truly rest and rejoice every
day that you're given on this earth, because you know what your future
holds—you have the "hope that [you] will live forever with [your]
God." Who wouldn't want that kind of assurance?

Say yes to Jesus. Say yes to the better life today!

*Father God, today I am declaring my loud
and clear YES! I choose the better life!*

Lamentations 2:1–3:38 / Titus 1:10–2:15 / Proverbs 15:18–26

God-Filled

God's readiness to give and forgive is now public. Salvation's available for everyone! We're being shown how to turn our backs on a godless, indulgent life, and how to take on a God-filled, God-honoring life. This new life is starting right now, and is whetting our appetites for the glorious day when our great God and Savior, Jesus Christ, appears. He offered himself as a sacrifice to free us from a dark, rebellious life into this good, pure life.

TITUS 2:11–14 MSG

What does a God-filled life look like?

A God-filled life is never lonely because God is always present—24/7, He's there. (Joshua 1:9)

A God-filled life is overflowing with blessings. (Psalm 78:20)

A God-filled life is complete—lacking nothing. (Colossians 2:10)

A God-filled life is aligned with His perfect plan. (Hebrews 13:20–21)

A God-filled life is overflowing with constant conversation with the heavenly Father. (Philippians 4:6)

A God-filled life is abundant in blessings! (John 10:10)

When you compare your life to this checklist, where are you deficient?

If you need to strengthen your relationship with the heavenly Father, ask Him to give you the motivation and determination to keep learning and growing in your faith. When you do, you'll experience "new life"—the "good, pure life" your soul craves.

Heavenly Father, I desire a God-filled life. Thank You for making it possible for me to experience all Your goodness. Help me to keep learning and growing.

Who's Righteous?

The LORD is far from the wicked,
but he hears the prayer of the righteous.

PROVERBS 15:29 NIV

Prayer: Is it a right or a privilege?

News flash: God, the Creator, sustainer, and ruler of heaven and earth, has *zero* obligation to you—or to me. So, it makes sense that there are certain requirements we must meet to receive all the blessings that the *privilege* of prayer has to offer.

Here in the book of Proverbs, it says that God is "far from the wicked," but He "hears the prayer of the righteous." When you're righteous, you're "right" with God.

What must a person do to be "righteous," you might be wondering? After all, God's Word does say, "No one is righteous—not even one" (Romans 3:10 NLT). So, it's quite clear we can't have a right relationship with the heavenly Creator on our own merit—it's impossible. That's the bad news.

But, friend, there's good news—*very good* news indeed! You can be made righteous with a simple, heartfelt *yes* to God's beautiful gift of salvation. If you haven't accepted this gift already, won't you say yes today?

When you say yes to Jesus, you're saying yes to love, to joy, to hope, to peace, to wisdom, to a resilient faith!

God, thank You for the precious gift of Your Son. Through
His death and resurrection on the cross, I can be made "right"
with You. I am ready to receive Your wonderful blessings.

Refreshed Hearts

I always thank my God as I remember you in my prayers,
because I hear about your love for all his holy people and your
faith in the Lord Jesus. I pray that your partnership with us
in the faith may be effective in deepening your understanding
of every good thing we share for the sake of Christ. Your
love has given me great joy and encouragement, because
you. . .have refreshed the hearts of the Lord's people.

PHILEMON 4–7 NIV

Have you ever sent up a prayer of thanks for the Christ followers in your circle? Those people who are there for you through thick and thin, who listen when you need to talk, who love the Lord with everything they have, who also love you well.

These people are true gifts from God. They are the ones you don't want to do life without because their example, their encouragement, their resilience can—and *will!*—rub off on you. Never underestimate their contribution to your faith! They add to our joy, our understanding, and our hope because of our shared beliefs. What blessings these brothers and sisters in Christ are to us!

Truly, when we love others well, it helps to build resilient faith and refreshes hearts in the process!

Who are you thankful for today?

Lord, thank You for those in my circle who have played
a part in encouraging and strengthening my faith.
Help me to be a steady encouragement to them as well.

Save Your Life!

*Get wisdom—it's worth more than money. . . . The road of
right living bypasses evil; watch your step and save your life.
First pride, then the crash. . . . It's better to live humbly among
the poor than to live it up among the rich and famous. . . .
Things work out when you trust in* GOD. *A wise person gets
known for insight; gracious words add to one's reputation.*

PROVERBS 16:16–21 MSG

We buckle up every time we get into a car. We schedule regular
checkups to evaluate our health. We look both ways before crossing
the street. We lock our doors at night. When we think of all we do
to stay safe, it's a lengthy list. We're quite proactive when it comes to
our physical well-being, aren't we? But can we say the same of our
spiritual life?

Proverbs 16 maps out all we need to do to preserve and protect
our spiritual health. Like seek wisdom. Make good choices. Stay
humble. Trust in God. Choose words carefully. All these things add
up to a good reputation and a deeply satisfying life. On the flip side,
anytime we choose the world's ways over God's ways, life gets messy,
misguided, and miserable.

Are you taking the right steps to "save your life"? Chase the right
things that pave the path to eternity today. You'll never regret it!

God, would You please help me to chase the things that matter?

Crown of Honor

Gray hair is a crown of honor, earned by living the right kind of life.
PROVERBS 16:31 VOICE

After spending just a few minutes on social media, it's possible—and likely—you'll fall prey to the comparison trap. You'll come away feeling dissatisfied not just with your looks, but your life. With all the filtering and falsifying of photos and reels, it seems the women popping into your newsfeed are the complete package—they're obviously aging in reverse, have their act together, and are living their best lives. Meanwhile, your "hot mess express" life features a cluttered house, unruly hair (maybe sprinkled with wiry grays), and saggy, blemished skin. Certainly not social media material.

Or so you think.

But, friend, God's Word says otherwise. In His eyes, your life is *better* than social-media-worthy. In fact, He calls your graying hair "a crown of honor." Your beautiful heart makes you stand out from the crowd. You are radiant! Your lovely soul is a product of "living the right kind of life."

> *What matters is not your outer appearance—the styling of your hair, the jewelry you wear, the cut of your clothes—but your inner disposition. Cultivate inner beauty, the gentle, gracious kind that God delights in. (1 Peter 3:3–4 MSG)*

> *Lord God, I am so thankful You call me beautiful. You call me worthy. Help me to nourish my inner beauty and to be satisfied—no, overjoyed!—with the life You've gifted me.*

Ezekiel 8–10 / Hebrews 3:1–4:3 / Proverbs 17:1–5

Distractions

Watch your step, friends. Make sure there's no evil unbelief lying around that will trip you up and throw you off course, diverting you from the living God. . . . Keep each other on your toes so sin doesn't slow down your reflexes. If we can only keep our grip on the sure thing we started out with, we're in this with Christ for the long haul.

HEBREWS 3:12–14 MSG

No matter how many years you've been driving, you've been distracted at some point—by your phone, a stray dog, your audio controls. While these distractions don't always result in traffic accidents, they do often cause mishaps: swerving to avoid hitting another car; slamming your brakes; spilling your coffee; getting a flat tire—all of which are followed by a terrifying, heart-pounding few minutes.

When our reflexes to sin are slowed down, it's a lot like distracted driving. We take our eyes off Jesus (even for a few minutes), and we get tripped up. If we don't veer back on course, the consequences can be comparable to a three-car pileup. We can cause others to "crash" as well. But, when we are dedicated to keeping our gaze on the one who loves us most, He'll keep us safe. He'll keep us beside Him "for the long haul."

Where is your focus today?

Father, I confess I have been living a distracted life. I want to do better. Help me keep my eyes fully focused on You.

Ezekiel 11–12 / Hebrews 4:4–5:10 / Proverbs 17:6–12

Loving Judge

The word of God is alive and active. Sharper than any double-edged sword, it penetrates even to dividing soul and spirit, joints and marrow; it judges the thoughts and attitudes of the heart. Nothing in all creation is hidden from God's sight.

HEBREWS 4:12–13 NIV

Fair or not, women have a reputation for being critical of other women. We tear each other apart, giving our unwelcome opinions about each other's hairstyles, home decor, handbags, and more. And sadly, we often let others' opinions really get to us, sometimes losing sleep over them.

But, at the end of the day, instead of getting in a tizzy over what someone has said about us, we should ask ourselves: Does Judgmental Judy's opinion *really* matter? Judy's just a human being after all—and humans can be, well, petty.

What a comfort to know our heavenly Father doesn't concern Himself with our personal style choices. He instead concerns Himself with *who* we are. He pays close attention to what's in our hearts. And when our hearts and motives align with His Word, nothing else matters.

So, friend, we'd be wise to tune in to the Word of God when we make our life choices. It will never lead us astray. God and His Word are fair, loving judges when it comes to who we are!

God, You are fair. You are loving. And Your Word tells me the best way to live—for You!

Ezekiel 13–14 / Hebrews 5:11–6:20 / Proverbs 17:13–22

The Just One

*God is not unjust; he will not forget your work and the love you
have shown him as you have helped his people and continue to
help them. We want each of you to show this same diligence to
the very end, so that what you hope for may be fully realized.
We do not want you to become lazy, but to imitate those who
through faith and patience inherit what has been promised.*

HEBREWS 6:10–12 NIV

Life isn't fair. You've probably heard this hundreds of times. You've
probably uttered the phrase yourself. Certainly, you've *experienced* it:

You discovered that you make less money than a coworker who's
doing the same job.

You lost a promotion to someone less qualified.

A person you trusted took advantage of you.

Your health-nut friend was diagnosed with a life-threatening
disease.

Your best friend betrayed you.

Unfortunately, there's not much we can do about unfair situations—
stuff happens, and it's typically beyond our control. *But. . .*

We *can* control how we react to every unjust situation we
experience. Instead of melting down, we can always dig deep for
grace and courage. Even more important, we can put our trust in the
only just one. His name is Jesus.

Do you know Him?

*Jesus, I am so glad I know You. I trust You and am "all in" for
You. When life isn't fair, You are—and that's enough for me.*

Quiet Wisdom

*Those with knowledge know when to be quiet, and those with
understanding know how to remain calm. Even a fool who keeps quiet
is considered wise, for when he keeps his mouth shut, he appears clever.*

PROVERBS 17:27–28 VOICE

Wisdom is often demonstrated through words—through the trusted
advice of a friend, family member, or teacher. Words can be good when
they guide in love, soothe hurting hearts, build confidence, and create
connection. However, words can also have a negative impact—when
they lead us in the wrong direction, wound hearts, crush confidence,
and build walls.

Wisdom isn't always displayed through spoken words, though.
In many situations, it's demonstrated through silence. And silence is
always the best choice when words are likely to ignite a smoldering
argument or cause confusion, when our words come from a selfish
place, or when our words aren't guided by scriptural truths. In difficult
situations, we should always *listen* before we respond, *think* before we
react, *pray*, then—and *only* then—if God nudges, we should *speak*.

To speak or to stay silent? It can be confusing. When you feel
unsure, lean into Jesus, the wisdom-giver Himself. He'll grow you
up in wisdom—directing you to speak, to listen, to react, to pray, or
to keep quiet!

*Father, I want to be a living, breathing example of Your
wisdom. Help me to grow and to know when to speak and
when to keep my mouth shut. I trust You to lead me.*

Always

*This new plan I'm making with Israel isn't going to be
written on paper, isn't going to be chiseled in stone; . . .
I'm writing out the plan in them, carving it on the lining of
their hearts. I'll be their God, they'll be my people. They won't go
to school to learn about me, or buy a book. . . . They'll all get to
know me firsthand. . . . They'll get to know me by being kindly
forgiven, with the slate of their sins forever wiped clean.*

HEBREWS 8:10–12 MSG

Write it. Carve it. Chisel it. However we choose to record words,
they're temporary. Paper can be ripped to shreds, wood burned to
a crisp, stones smashed to bits. Over time, materials will decay and
ink will fade.

While nothing in this world lasts forever, one truth remains: God's
Word and His plan, carved into our hearts, is lasting. It's permanent.
Nothing can destroy it because our God is the same yesterday, today,
and forever. And once He calls us His, it's for keeps. Once His Word
is etched into our hearts, it's there to stay—always.

Even better, when God works Himself deep into the center of
our hearts, we get to fully experience Him. We get quality one-on-one
Father-daughter time with the Lord and leader of our life.

*God, my heart is full. You have carved Your Word into its depths,
and it's there to stay. My greatest desire is to know You more.*

Ezekiel 18–19 / Hebrews 9:11–28 / Proverbs 18:8–17

Consequences

"Imagine a person who lives well, treating others fairly, keeping good relationships—doesn't eat at the pagan shrines, doesn't worship the idols so popular in Israel, doesn't seduce a neighbor's spouse, doesn't indulge in casual sex, doesn't bully anyone, doesn't pile up bad debts, doesn't steal, doesn't refuse food to the hungry, doesn't refuse clothing to the ill-clad, doesn't exploit the poor, doesn't live by impulse and greed, doesn't treat one person better than another, but lives by my statutes and faithfully honors and obeys my laws. This person who lives upright and well shall live a full and true life."

EZEKIEL 18:5–9 MSG

Consequences. Good or bad. Love them or hate them, there's no escaping them.

Spend or save?
Relocate or stay put?
Get married or stay single?
Follow the rules or break them?
Chase after God or chase after the world?

Life is full of choices. And every choice leads to a consequence. We've all made choices that led to bad outcomes and had to suffer the consequences. But when we make good choices, what a difference! Life somehow seems easier, more carefree and joy-filled. And, friend, that's the kind of life God has in mind for you.

Do you crave a life of purpose? If that's your desire, then live well! Embrace the consequences of the good life today!

Father God, lead me on the path to the good life You have planned for me.

Ezekiel 20 / Hebrews 10:1–25 / Proverbs 18:18–24

Better Together

*Let us think of ways to motivate one another to acts of love
and good works. And let us not neglect our meeting together,
as some people do, but encourage one another, especially
now that the day of his return is drawing near.*

HEBREWS 10:24–25 NLT

Have you ever made lame excuses to avoid getting together with other
believers? Does your jam-packed schedule make it nearly impossible
to meet with other women for prayer and encouragement?

Be honest with yourself and with God. What's getting in the
way of your participation in Christian community? Is it something
on your calendar? Or is it perhaps just you?

Sometimes it's simply a matter of neglect. We get busy. Our
priorities get turned upside down. And we just can't find the time to
squeeze in one more thing.

But God's Word shows us that we truly are better together.
We can add so much to each other's lives if we only make meeting
together a priority. If we only take time to listen and offer words of
encouragement and sound, biblical advice.

Doing life alone is lonely. Living in community with other believers
gives us purpose, direction, motivation, and hope. God knows it, and
He wants us to know it too: we really are better together!

*Lord, thank You for the Christian women You
have placed in my life. I am thankful for each one.
Help me to always prioritize our time together.*

Ezekiel 21–22 / Hebrews 10:26–39 / Proverbs 19:1–8

The Company You Keep

My friends, we are not those who give up hope and so are lost;
but we are of the company who live by faith and so are saved.
HEBREWS 10:39 VOICE

Are you truly tuned in to the vibes of the company you keep? Are you being honest with yourself?

We sometimes shrug off that sneaking suspicion that we're hanging out with the wrong crowd. Maybe their foul language makes us cringe. Or they gossip just a little too much—yet we find ourselves hanging on every word. Maybe they spend too much time away from their families and they're encouraging us to do the same. Or we've mentioned our faith and they've responded with disinterest or even disgust.

Just because we're hanging out with a group of women who don't think, talk, or act like us doesn't mean *we'll* change and become like them, right? (At least that's the lie we tell ourselves.)

But the truth is, we will only "become wise by walking with the wise" (Proverbs 13:20 MSG), *and* "bad company corrupts good character" (1 Corinthians 15:33 NIV).

Ask yourself: Am I surrounding myself with women "who live by faith and so are saved" or those who "are lost"? Faithful women will help strengthen your faith! They're the *best* kind of company to keep!

Jesus, help me choose my circle wisely. Do I need
to distance myself from any poor influences who
might pull me away from You? If so, show me.

Ezekiel 23 / Hebrews 11:1–31 / Proverbs 19:9–14

Life Worth Living

*The fundamental fact of existence is that this trust in God,
this faith, is the firm foundation under everything that makes
life worth living. It's our handle on what we can't see. The act
of faith is what distinguished our ancestors, set them above
the crowd. By faith, we see the world called into existence by
God's word, what we see created by what we don't see.*

HEBREWS 11:1–3 MSG

The world tells us we can only trust or believe in something if we can see it, hear it, feel it, taste it, or smell it. That we must rely on our senses to assure us that something is real. What's the phrase. . . "*Seeing is believing*"?

As Christians, though, we do the opposite: we believe *without* seeing. When we say yes to Jesus and invite Him into our hearts, when we begin living an authentic Christian life, we no longer doubt that which we can't see. Although we can't see God and we haven't seen concrete, factual evidence of Jesus' life, death, and resurrection, still, we have faith that God exists, that He loves us unconditionally, that He sent His Son to die on the cross for all humanity, and that anyone who accepts His gift of salvation will spend eternity in heaven.

Have you chosen to follow Jesus? Do you trust His Word? When we believe without seeing, that firm faith foundation is what makes life worth living.

Father God, I believe!

Strong Heart, Stronger Faith

*I could speak of faith bringing. . .loved ones back from death and
how the faithful accepted torture instead of earthly deliverance.
. . . Others suffered mockery and whippings. . .placed in chains
and in prisons. The faithful were stoned, sawn in two, killed by
the sword. . .they were penniless, afflicted. . . . They wandered
across deserts, crossed mountains, and lived in the caves, cracks,
and crevasses. . . . These, though commended by God for their
great faith, did not receive what was promised. That promise has
awaited us, who receive the better thing that God has provided.*

HEBREWS 11:35–40 VOICE

Perhaps you've prayed the same prayer and called out to God day
after day, week after week, month after month—and received only
silence. Maybe you've lived a God-honoring life only to experience
one hardship after another, and you just don't understand why God
seems to be ignoring you while He blesses others.

Sometimes the life of a believer is just *hard*.

Understand, though, that while we live in this world, our home
isn't here—it's in heaven. And heaven is the *only* place where life will
be eternally perfect, where we'll live forever in peace and harmony
with Jesus.

So, when hardships come—and they will—keep your focus on
the heavenly promise that awaits! Take courage; don't lose heart.
God's got you!

*Lord, when I'm struggling, strengthen my faith.
Remind me of Your unfailing promises!*

Soul Adrenaline

Jesus. . .both began and finished this race we're in. . . .
He never lost sight of where he was headed—that exhilarating
finish in and with God—he could put up with anything
along the way: Cross, shame, whatever. And now he's there
in the place of honor, right alongside God. When you find
yourselves flagging in your faith, go over that story again.
. . . That will shoot adrenaline into your souls!

HEBREWS 12:2–3 MSG

The chasing of our hopes and dreams often goes like this: We begin with motivation to spare, strong, with stars in our eyes. But somewhere along the way, we become distracted. The journey becomes difficult. Obstacles block our path. Our motivation wanes. We stop dead in our tracks as we lose hope by the minute. No doubt, the temptation to give up is powerful when hope is hard to come by. And sadly, our faith journey sometimes mirrors this unsuccessful race toward hopes and dreams.

But Jesus! He completed His journey with courage and perseverance. He "never lost sight of where he was headed." And so, "he could put up with anything along the way." And, beautiful soul, He did! For me, for you.

When your faith is flagging, give yourself a shot of soul adrenaline: think of Jesus. Keep your eyes on Him so you can finish strong!

Jesus, help me to never lose sight of You as I run my race.

Ezekiel 29–30 / Hebrews 12:14–29 / Proverbs 20:1–18

Glimpses of God

*Work at getting along with each other and with God.
Otherwise you'll never get so much as a glimpse of God.
Make sure no one gets left out of God's generosity. Keep
a sharp eye out for weeds of bitter discontent. A thistle or
two gone to seed can ruin a whole garden in no time.*

HEBREWS 12:14–15 MSG

When scripture instructs us to get along with God, we respond with a resounding *yes!* After all, God is good. He is loving. He is generous. He is nice! God doesn't cause trouble, gossip, or scold the barista at the coffee shop. But when scripture instructs us to get along with other humans? We might raise an eyebrow. People are rude, obnoxious, annoying. They're anything but nice!

People really can be awful. Yet, when we throw our hands up in defeat because we just "can't get along with those people," it diminishes our witness for Jesus. It hurts others, and it hurts us. It causes "weeds of bitter discontent" to flourish. In fact, the author of Hebrews says if we don't work at our relationships with others, we'll "never get so much as a glimpse of God." And that, friend, is motivation to pursue righteous living.

When we work toward holy living—*together*—our faith increases and blessings abound. Let's get some glimpses of God today.

*Lord, please help me when I struggle to love
people well. I want to obey Your Word.*

Demonstrating Love

*Let love continue among you. Don't forget to extend your
hospitality to all—even to strangers. . . . Remember those
imprisoned for their beliefs as if you were their cellmate; and care
for any who suffer harsh treatment, as you are all one body.*

HEBREWS 13:1–3 VOICE

The Christian faith isn't only about following a set of rules outlined in scripture, going to church, or having your sins wiped clean; nor is it just having a thriving personal relationship with Jesus. While these are all very important pieces of the faith equation, there's something more: building healthy relationships with other believers. It means demonstrating love, compassion, kindness, hospitality.

So, if we attend a small group, host an after-church lunch, or teach a Sunday school class, doesn't that check off the "relationship" requirement of our faith? If we're doing any number of these things, we're in active relationship with other believers. Right? Well, yes, but there's more.

God's Word calls us to love everyone well, including strangers and prisoners! God doesn't give us a pass when it comes to people who are outside our circle. Because we are all "one body," we are connected. We are family because we share one heavenly Father. So, let's "let love continue" among us because we truly are better together.

*Father God, thank You for this reminder. I need to
work harder to live out my faith—and demonstrate
my love—for those inside and outside my circle.*

Opportunity for Joy

*When troubles of any kind come your way, consider it
an opportunity for great joy. For. . .when your faith
is tested, your endurance has a chance to grow.*

JAMES 1:2–3 NLT

When we think of opportunities, we tend to think of positive, wonderful things—*happy* things! A chance at a promotion, to earn a quarterly bonus, to travel somewhere exotic, or to meet new people. It just doesn't make sense to equate opportunity with hardship—or *does* it?

In James 1, we're told, "when troubles of any kind come your way, consider it an opportunity for great joy." *What?*

It's human nature to wallow in self-pity when we experience hardship—to feel terribly sorry for ourselves and wonder, *"Why me?"* But perhaps the better way would be to embrace our troubles—to recognize them as opportunities to grow personally and spiritually. The Lord may be trying to teach us some things when we encounter trials—like how to be patient, to persist under pressure, to nurture our relationship with Him, to cultivate a powerful prayer life, to recognize areas where we need to work on ourselves or our relationships.

If you're experiencing troubles today, ask God what You need to learn. Then be still and listen. Trust that His purpose and plan for you are *very* good—always.

*Heavenly Father, thank You for hard times
that pull me closer to You. Help me to embrace
each difficulty as an opportunity for joy!*

Ezekiel 34:11–36:15 / James 2 / Proverbs 21:1–8

The Good Shepherd

*"The Sovereign LORD says: I. . .will search and find
my sheep. I will be like a shepherd looking for his
scattered flock. I will find my sheep and rescue them. . . .
I will bring them back home. . . . I will give them good
pastureland. . . . There they will lie down in pleasant places
and feed in the lush pastures of the hills. I. . .will tend
my sheep and give them a place to lie down in peace. . . .
I will search for my lost ones who strayed away, and I
will bring them safely home again. I will bandage
the injured and strengthen the weak."*

EZEKIEL 34:11–16 NLT

When sheep wander away from the flock, a shepherd does everything in his power to find them. If they're in danger, he rescues them. He makes sure his sheep are well fed and that they have a safe, peaceful place to rest. If they're injured, he bandages their wounds. Whatever the sheep need, the shepherd provides.

This is exactly how our Lord cares for us when we lose our way. Anytime we need Him, He responds, *"I will. . ."* He doesn't look the other way, leaving us to fend for ourselves. Nor does He pass the responsibility to someone else. Our Good Shepherd is always there—protecting, providing, caring, rescuing.

*My Shepherd, thank You for rescuing me when I lose
my way and for providing everything I need.*

Ezekiel 36:16–37:28 / James 3 / Proverbs 21:9–18

Community

*Real wisdom. . .begins with a holy life and is characterized
by getting along with others. It is gentle and reasonable,
overflowing with mercy and blessings. . . . You can develop a
healthy, robust community that lives right with God and enjoy
its results only if you do the hard work of getting along with
each other, treating each other with dignity and honor.*

JAMES 3:17–18 MSG

So many things fall into place in life *if* we're willing to work hard
and be persistent:

We go above and beyond at the office to land that promotion.

We scrimp and save to afford a down payment on a house.

We sacrifice time, money, and energy to earn a degree and land
our dream job.

Once we accomplish these things, we'd certainly say the sacrifice
was worth it, wouldn't we?

But do we place the same kind of value on building relationships
and community as we do our personal accomplishments?

Relationship-building requires hard work and sacrifice to be
successful. Patience, gentleness, understanding, loyalty, and wisdom
don't come naturally. We must work, work, and work some more to get
along with others and create community. But it's so worth the effort!
Because in community, our faith grows and thrives; in community, we
strengthen and support each other. In a healthy community, we flourish!

*Father, thank You for my tribe. Remind me that it's always
worth the work to develop my relationships and create a
community that can flourish with You at its center.*

Ezekiel 38–39 / James 4:1–5:6 / Proverbs 21:19–24

Just a Whisper

Let God work his will in you. Yell a loud no to the
Devil and watch him make himself scarce. Say a
quiet yes to God and he'll be there in no time.

JAMES 4:7 MSG

Have you ever had trouble getting someone's attention? When you have something important to say, nothing is more maddening than when the person you need to talk to isn't listening. Whether her eyes are locked on a screen or the pages of a book or she's lost in her own thoughts, getting the complete focus of another human being can be difficult. We often start speaking softly, our voices growing louder with each attempt, until we're at a full-on yell—which typically elicits an irritated *"What?!"* in return.

While our fellow humans are occupied with other things, it's comforting to know we always have the full focus of the heavenly Creator. We never need to beg or convince Him to listen. Even better, we don't have to raise our voices for Him to look our way. With just a whisper, we have His complete attention.

If you're feeling misunderstood, unheard, overlooked, or unloved today, say a quiet "yes" to God. He'll remind you of your worth, your value, when He responds, "Daughter, I'm listening."

Father God, I humbly come to You on my knees. Thank
You for always listening, for always being available to
me, even when no one else is. You're truly all I need.

Ezekiel 40 / James 5:7–20 / Proverbs 21:25–31

In All Seasons, Pray!

Is anyone among you in trouble? Let them pray. Is anyone happy?
Let them sing songs of praise. Is anyone among you sick? Let them
call the elders of the church to pray over them. . . . And the prayer
offered in faith will make the sick person well; the Lord will raise
them up. If they have sinned, they will be forgiven. Therefore confess
your sins to each other and pray for each other so that you may be
healed. The prayer of a righteous person is powerful and effective.

JAMES 5:13–16 NIV

In life, we experience seasons—some easy, others difficult; some joyful, others sad; some courageous, others fearful; some comfortable, others quite miserable. Life's unique seasons evoke reactions that run the gamut—laughter, tears, humility, grit, persistence, resilience. No two seasons are the same. But there is always one reaction that is appropriate for all seasons, and that is prayer!

Scripture tells us if we're in trouble, we should pray. We should also pray when we're experiencing illness or joy, struggling with sin and temptation. Whatever it is, there's never a time when we shouldn't pray, because prayer brings comfort, recovery, calm, and restoration to our souls. Truly, there's nothing that time with Jesus can't fix.

See for yourself. Whatever season you're in, tell God all about it. Then quiet your heart and listen.

Heavenly Father, thank You for the gift of prayer.
I trust You'll listen in every season of my life.

Saving Faith

*Although you haven't seen Jesus, you still love Him. Although
you don't yet see Him, you do believe in Him and celebrate
with a joy that is glorious and beyond words. You are receiving
the salvation of your souls as the result of your faith.*

1 PETER 1:8–9 VOICE

Do you love Jesus? Think about that for a minute. Most of us will
respond with a quick "Yes, of course I love Him!" But when you think
deeper, isn't it quite astonishing that we claim to love and place our
complete trust in someone we've never met face-to-face?

And yet, that is what is required for the salvation of our souls—a
faith in the unseen. A belief in something—in someone—our eyes
haven't observed and our hands haven't touched. This kind of saving
faith is rooted in 100 percent trust in God's Word.

Even though we didn't see Jesus die on the cross for our sins,
we *believe* it.

Even though we didn't see Jesus rise from the dead, we *trust* it
happened.

Even though we can't physically see Jesus and touch Him, we
know He exists.

That is a saving kind of faith. It's the kind of faith our Lord
requires of me and of you. In the words of Jesus, "Blessed are those
who have not seen and yet have believed" (John 20:29 NIV)!

*Father God, I love You. I trust Your Word is true.
I believe even though I cannot see!*

Say "Yes"

*For you have been born again. . . . Your new life will last forever because
it comes from the eternal, living word of God. As the Scriptures say,
"People are like grass; their beauty is like a flower in the field. The grass
withers and the flower fades. But the word of the Lord remains forever."*

1 PETER 1:23–25 NLT

When you say yes to God. . .when you accept Him as Lord and leader
of your life, you're also saying yes to all the benefits of becoming His
beloved child, including:

A deeper understanding of your purpose (1 Corinthians 10:31;
Psalm 36:7–9)

Forgiveness of sin (Ephesians 1:7; Romans 8:2)

Freedom from guilt and shame (Romans 8:1)

A personal relationship with the heavenly Father Himself (John
14:20; Ephesians 2:17–18)

The Holy Spirit (John 14:26; 1 Corinthians 12)

A community of likeminded believers (Acts 2:42)

Eternal life (John 3:16)

And so much more!

Put simply, life with Jesus at the hub overflows with blessing upon
blessing—and that's a promise! God's promises are sure because His
Word is unchanging; it's eternal and living! Though all things in the
world will fade, one thing is sure: "The word of the Lord remains
forever." Amen!

*Heavenly Father, because of Your living, breathing Word,
I am confident and secure. I have hope for my future.
Thank You for opening my heart and nudging me to say
yes to You. I'll say it over and over again. . .YES!*

Ezekiel 45–46 / 1 Peter 2:4–17 / Proverbs 22:24–29

Where Do You Belong?

*Friends, this world is not your home, so don't make
yourselves cozy in it. Don't indulge your ego at the
expense of your soul. Live an exemplary life in your
neighborhood. . . . Then they'll be won over to God's side
and be there to join in the celebration when he arrives.*

1 PETER 2:11–12 MSG

Do you know where you belong? Perhaps in your women's Bible study group? Yes! Or maybe your workplace? Yes, you belong there. Maybe the corner café is your jam—so sure, you belong there too!

But God's Word tells us another story. We really *don't* belong—not in this world anyhow, not if we've accepted God's gift of eternal life. Scripture tells us that we should be careful not to get too comfortable in this world because when we do, we become more *of* the world than *in* the world (John 17:14–15). We let down our guards, and the temptations of this world tug hard at our souls. But when we immerse our hearts and minds in the Word, our actions will follow suit. And *that* is where we reach lives for the Lord, friend.

So keep in mind where you really belong, dear one. Live today—and every day—with your eternal, heavenly home in mind.

*Savior of my soul, You are my forever home. Plant a desire
within me to indulge in the truth of Your Word all my days.*

Don't Be Fixed on Riches

Do not overwork yourself just to become wealthy;
have enough sense to know when to quit. As soon as you
become fixed on riches, they vanish. For suddenly they sprout
wings and become like a soaring eagle flying high in the sky.
PROVERBS 23:4–5 VOICE

Money isn't evil. There is nothing wrong with finding a well-paying job and being frugal. The Bible tells us it's the *love* of it that causes problems. When it becomes something we obsess over, a line is crossed. And as we live each day fixated on what it could bring, our faith often switches from trusting in Christ to trusting in currency.

But what if, instead, we are intentional to spend time in God's Word, soaking our heart in His promises? What if we connect with Him through regular prayer and choose an attitude of gratitude for what we already have? What if we keep our mind trained on eternal things rather than earthly ones? And what if our attention rests in the divine rather than the dollar? This reallocation of emphasis is how our roots of faith grow deep, cultivating a robust relationship with the only one who can ensure we will always have all we need to live well.

Lord, help my eyes stay trained on You so my faith
matures into something money could never buy.

Durable Faith

Although the king ate only the finest Babylonian fare,
Daniel was determined not to violate God's law and
defile himself by eating the food and drinking the wine
that came from the king's table; so he asked the chief of
the royal eunuchs for permission not to eat the food.

DANIEL 1:8 VOICE

Daniel understood that he was set apart. Even while exiled in Babylon, this young Jewish man chose to be steadfast to God's law. He decided to follow His will and ways rather than surrender to the world's offerings. Daniel's faith was durable to the end.

Every day, you have a choice to make too. Will you give in to the earthly temptations that bombard you daily or will you be steadfast and do what God is asking? Will you make time to be in the Word or continue to push it to the bottom of your to-do list? Will you find time to pray about what's troubling your heart or will you call your bestie for advice instead?

Every intentional decision made to choose a relationship with the Lord matures your faith into something beautiful and steadfast. What choices will you make today?

Lord, help me have the kind of durable faith Daniel had. Help me
reject the sparkles of the world so I can stand in Your brilliance
instead. And let each choice deepen my faith in meaningful ways.

You're Not Alone

Be alert and of sober mind. Your enemy the devil prowls
around like a roaring lion looking for someone to devour.
Resist him, standing firm in the faith, because you know
that the family of believers throughout the world
is undergoing the same kind of sufferings.

1 PETER 5:8–9 NIV

Sometimes just knowing we're not alone in the challenges we're facing gives us strength. It helps to know there are others battling the same trials and temptations, often at the same or an even greater intensity level. And as believers, it brings much needed encouragement knowing we're not the only ones to feel overwhelmed, worried, and scared. The reality is that life is big and the enemy is real.

But today's verse tells us we can resist the enemy and stand firm because others are in the same fight. That knowledge can strengthen our resolve and create a resilience of faith. If we let it, this truth can help us be watchful for the enemy's nefarious plans. And knowing we have community surrounding us brings a boldness to be steadfast, so the enemy's plans don't prevail. Friend, you are not alone. In God's faithfulness, you have all you need to be victorious.

Lord, I know the enemy is prowling and looking for ways to devour
me. I also know my struggles are universal. Along with Your
imparted strength in me, I can stand strong by faith and triumph.

Daniel 4 / 2 Peter 1 / Proverbs 23:26–35

Adding to Your Faith

*For this very reason, make every effort to add to your
faith goodness; and to goodness, knowledge; and to knowledge,
self-control; and to self-control, perseverance; and to perseverance,
godliness; and to godliness, mutual affection; and to mutual
affection, love. For if you possess these qualities in increasing
measure, they will keep you from being ineffective and
unproductive in your knowledge of our Lord Jesus Christ.*

2 PETER 1:5–8 NIV

Resilient faith comes from the pursuit of righteous living. While the Holy Spirit helps to grow you up in faith, this endeavor requires your participation too. And if you're to "make every effort" to add goodness, knowledge, self-control, perseverance, godliness, affection, and love to your faith, it will require purposeful action on your part.

What can you do to grow these qualities in greater measure? Start by opening the scriptures every day and meditating on them. Connect with God regularly through prayer and praise. Set your mind on the things above. Choose to be content with what you have. Create community with other believers. And as you do, a hardy faith will empower you to walk out the work God strategically purposed for you.

*Lord, help me make every effort to add to my faith
what the Word says is important. Give me direction
so I continue to grow deeper roots of resilient faith.*

Steadfast in the Father

If you fall to pieces in a crisis,
there wasn't much to you in the first place.
PROVERBS 24:10 MSG

Although we will experience wonderful mountaintop moments, we will find ourselves walking through our share of dark valleys too. From broken marriages to the loss of loved ones to financial distress, hard times are inevitable. We may struggle with being single or childless. It may be a daunting diagnosis that challenges our peace. We might experience deep betrayal, painful rejection, or unexpected abandonment. Regardless, navigating crises is part of the human condition.

But, friend, strong and sustaining faith is the result of clinging to God when the valleys arrive. Every time you trust, it strengthens you. And as you build on His faithfulness in action, it produces a robust faith that isn't easily shaken. So when the messy moments arrive, you see the situation with spiritual eyes. You know God is already at work, which allows you to surrender every fear and anxious thought. And rather than fall to pieces, your heart is steadfast in the Father.

Lord, make me strong and sturdy so life doesn't easily knock me down. Make me brave and bold because my faith is anchored in Your goodness. And rather than fall to pieces in a crisis, let my heart find calm and comfort knowing You're still on the throne.

Daniel 6:1–7:14 / 2 Peter 3 / Proverbs 24:19–27

Clinging to God's Truth

*Above all, be sure to remember that in the last days mockers
will come, following their own desires and taunting you, saying,
"So what happened to the promised second coming of Jesus? For
everything keeps going just the way it has since our ancestors fell
asleep in death; since the beginning of creation, nothing's changed."*

2 PETER 3:3–4 VOICE

Stay strong and cling to the truths from God's Word. It's His inspired
Word that is alive and active. There's nothing to add to it, nothing to
tweak within it, and nothing to delete from its pages. What was true
then is still true today, and we can trust it to stand the test of time.
But unless we fill our heart and mind with the Bible's teachings, how
will we keep from being deceived?

Now more than ever, it's important to lay our foundation of faith
in His truth. We need to read it, hear it, share it, and meditate on
His promises. Mockers will try to confuse you. They will try to bring
chaos to your heart and mind. But those who have been purposeful to
grow deep roots of faith will have discernment, wisdom, and courage
to know what's true and stand firm in it. They'll be steadfast in their
belief, no matter what life brings their way.

*Lord, help me prioritize reading and
learning the truths in Your Word.*

Daniel 7:15–8:27 / 1 John 1:1–2:17 / Proverbs 24:28–34

Rotten Fruits

*All the things the world can offer to you—the allure of
pleasure, the passion to have things, and the pompous
sense of superiority—do not come from the Father.
These are the rotten fruits of this world.*

1 JOHN 2:16 VOICE

The Bible tells us that all good things come from God, yet so often we look to the world to satisfy us on every level. We put our faith in earthly solutions to fill the emptiness we feel. We place our trust in people, processes, or procedures. We expect things and stuff to fill our heart and settle our spirit. And we invest our time and treasure looking for answers in this material world.

Today's verse says the world only gives rotten fruit. Yet it's only when we spend time growing our relationship with the Lord, by digging in His Word and going to Him in prayer, that we find lasting satisfaction. Only by seeking God do we develop a contented heart that brings true rest and gratitude. At the same time, we learn to trust God will sustain us as we stand in expectation of His eternal goodness.

*Lord, when I begin to look to the world for what only
You can provide, remind me of its rotten fruit so my
heart quickly turns back to You. I know I'll be filled to
satisfaction by Your kindness and generosity.*

Daniel 9–10 / 1 John 2:18–29 / Proverbs 25:1–12

The Power of a Friend's Word

A well-spoken word at just the right moment is
like golden apples in settings of silver. To an attentive
ear, constructive criticism from a truly wise person is
like an earring or jewelry made of fine gold.

PROVERBS 25:11–12 VOICE

One of the sweetest gifts we receive as believers is godly friends. They are the ones who sit with us at the hospital. They cook us meals, pick up groceries, and clean our homes when we're unable to. Friends help us process the ups and downs of life, always pointing us to God. They advocate on our behalf when we cannot. They remind us of the power we have through Jesus and help us wield our warrior sword when necessary. When we cry, they cry. When we rejoice, they rejoice. There are few things better than believing friends.

Today's verse tells of the value a well-spoken word brings at the right time. And it's often our friends who know just what to say. Whether it's wise advice, a kind encouragement, or constructive criticism, God will use the gift of friendship to help mature our faith and make us more resilient. Do you already have these kinds of friends? If so, be grateful for them. If not, ask the Lord to bring some your way.

Lord, thank You for friends who speak the words You've
put on their heart. Help me be one of those friends too!

Who's Your Daddy?

*Everyone who has been born into God's family avoids sin as a
lifestyle because the genes of God's children come from God Himself.
Therefore, a child of God can't live a life of persistent sin. So it is
not hard to figure out who are the children of God and who are the
children of the diabolical one: those who lack right standing and
those who don't show love for one another do not belong to God.*

1 JOHN 3:9–10 VOICE

This is an extraordinary truth that compels a heart check to all who
read it. Simply put, these verses prompt you to ask yourself, *What does
my life reveal?* Take time today to think this through. Be honest with
yourself. Journal it out. Talk to God. If needed, repent. Confess. Ask
the Lord to make the necessary changes to keep you walking His will
and way. Ask Him to reveal any sinful thoughts or behaviors. Invite
Jesus into your life as your personal Savior. Make certain your heart
is right with God and your salvation secured in Jesus.

Friend, scripture says it is easy to know who are God's children and
who are not. The more time you spend in His presence and meditate
on His Word, the stronger your faith will become and the more of His
light will shine within, as well as without. A light others will notice.

*Lord, my heart is committed to following
Your will and ways. I am Your child.*

Loving Your Enemies

If your enemy is hungry, give him something to eat; if he is thirsty, give him something to drink, for your kind treatment will be like heaping hot coals on his head, it may cause a change in heart, and the Eternal will repay you.

PROVERBS 25:21–22 VOICE

Loving an enemy may be one of the hardest things to do, especially when we'd rather hold on to an offense than forgive. Be it a surprise betrayal, a hurtful word, a painful rejection, or an insult to someone we love, collecting transgressions can sometimes be second nature. We don't want the wrongdoer to be let off the hook, and we don't want our pain invalidated. So instead, we hold on to it with fervor.

But the mark of maturity in a believer is the choice to care in spite of the crime. Rather than point fingers we show favor. We choose respect over retaliation. Patience over payback. Forgiving over fighting. But this only comes from cultivating a weighty relationship with God and choosing to see others through His eyes. And it's this deeply rooted faith that makes us resilient and able to release offenses, so they don't pull us down into the pit of unforgiveness.

Lord, grow my faith roots so deep in You that I'm able to love my enemies and forgive them.

Hosea 4–6 / 1 John 4:17–5:21 / Proverbs 26:1–16

You Are Heard

*We live in the bold confidence that God hears our voices
when we ask for things that fit His plan. And if we
have no doubt that He hears our voices, we can be
assured that He moves in response to our call.*

1 JOHN 5:14–15 VOICE

These verses are a breath of fresh air to those wondering if God hears their prayers. Sometimes we feel unheard and unseen, and there may be a little truth to that from a worldly viewpoint. Yet when we cry to God with our hearts aligned with His, we are heard. Believing this enables our faith to grow. But so often, we don't believe, and we find ourselves doubting the Lord will respond to our deepest needs. This creates a disconnect in our relationship with the Lord and keeps us from praying. And the enemy loves it.

Friend, God's Word is true, and every day we must choose to have confidence in it. Each time we do, our faith matures. Yet a strong, sustaining faith isn't instantaneous but rather comes from a journey of growth over time. If the Word says God hears us, then we must unwaveringly stand in that truth and talk to Him at any time about anything.

> *Lord, I know faith ripens little by little over time and
> commitment and that my belief in Your Word is key to
> helping it grow. I boldly believe You see and hear me!*

Knowing the Word

*If any person comes to you with a teaching that does not align with
the true message of Jesus, do not welcome that person into your house
or greet him as you would a true brother. Anyone who welcomes this
person has become a partner in advancing his wicked agenda.*

2 JOHN 10–11 VOICE

As you partner with the Holy Spirit to develop a resilient faith, the
enemy will do all he can to derail those efforts. He wants to bring
discouragement, so you walk away from the Lord. He wants to bring
disappointment to make you feel unsatisfied in your faith journey. He
wants to bring confusion and chaos that destabilize your belief. And
sometimes that comes in the form of being exposed to false teaching.

That's why it's so important to know the truths and promises in
God's Word. Unless we have a solid understanding of scripture, we
won't know when our faith is under attack by well-placed and often
subtle inconsistencies. Little by little, misinformation and blatant
untruths will chip away at our heart until our resilient faith is wounded.
Rather than allow the enemy a foothold, endeavor to saturate your
mind, heart, soul, and spirit in the Word so that your faith will rest
on truth alone.

*Lord, help me protect my heart and mind by knowing what
the Bible says so nothing disrupts my pursuit of developing
a steadfast faith in Your words, truths, and promises.*

The Gift of a Friend's Counsel

*Oil and perfume rejoice the heart; so does the sweetness
of a friend's counsel that comes from the heart.*

PROVERBS 27:9 AMPC

There are times God prompts the heart of a friend to bring you
much-needed encouragement. That's because He created community
to be an earthly support for your eternal pursuits. Isolating yourself
from others removes you from that vital stream of sustenance. It
separates you from the fold of followers strategically placed in your
life to remind you of God's goodness. And it opens you up to pointed
attacks by the enemy.

Friendship is a tool the Lord uses to bring hope and direction.
And when that friend is a strong believer who deeply loves the Lord
and chases after Him daily, she can offer sweet counsel inspired by
God Himself.

Determine to invest in friendships that help you be steadfast
in your faith. Let your friends' confessions that God is active in all
circumstances and can be trusted at all times and in every situation
shore up your confidence and courage. Let them remind you of His
perfect track record in your life and theirs. And ask God to help you
become that kind of friend to the community that surrounds you.

*Lord, thank You for sweet community and the role it plays
in my life. Help me embrace it rather than push it away.*

Joel 1:1–2:17 / Jude / Proverbs 27:10–17

The Center of God's Love

But you, dear friends, carefully build yourselves up in this most holy faith by praying in the Holy Spirit, staying right at the center of God's love, keeping your arms open and outstretched, ready for the mercy of our Master, Jesus Christ. This is the unending life, the real life!

JUDE 20–21 MSG

Today's verses are a beautiful call for us to be at the center of God's love. It's a place of freedom where we can experience Him unhindered. It's a place of expectation because we are certain of His goodness. It's a place where we come alive and encounter joy uncontained. With arms open and outstretched, we're able to embrace a deeper measure of faith as we surrender our will to His. And, friend, this should be our daily prayer.

The reality is, however, that life keeps us focused on the hard, so we don't focus on the heavenly. We give in to worry and fear, trying to find worldly ways to resuscitate our heavy hearts. Rather than take every anxious thought to God, we try to fix each messy circumstance in our own strength.

Today, choose to stay at the center of God's love by training your mind and heart to depend on Him for everything you need. He sees you. He loves you. He's got you.

Lord, rather than fall back into my human tendencies, help me have steadfast faith that stays at the center of Your love.

Joel 2:18–3:21 / Revelation 1:1–2:11 / Proverbs 27:18–27

God Gives and Takes Away

The LORD says, "I will give you back what you lost to the swarming locusts, the hopping locusts, the stripping locusts, and the cutting locusts. It was I who sent this great destroying army against you. Once again you will have all the food you want, and you will praise the LORD your God, who does these miracles for you. Never again will my people be disgraced."

JOEL 2:25–26 NLT

God gives, and God takes away. In His great wisdom He knows our limits and the perfect time to intervene. The Lord can see the whole situation with complete clarity, understanding it fully. And He's able to do what needs to be done, knowing when to add and when to take away. He knows the exact balance that needs to be struck and how to do so with precision. That's why you can take comfort in God. He has your life in His capable hands and will meet every need at the right time and in the right way.

Once you fully embrace this powerful truth, it will change you. It will deepen your faith and reliance on God. You'll be able to find comfort and stand strong in the hard seasons because you recognize God is God, and He's in control. Thank God!

Lord, help my faith be purposeful because Your timing is perfect.

Amos 1:1–4:5 / Revelation 2:12–29 / Proverbs 28:1–8

Boldly

*The wicked run away even when no one is
chasing them; the right-living, however,
stand their ground as boldly as lions.*
PROVERBS 28:1 VOICE

Why is it that the "right-living" can stand their ground? Maybe it's because they trust God has them in His very capable hands. Maybe they realize He's their protector and defender. It could be they have hidden His rich promises within their heart. Maybe they've found hope in the pages of the Bible. Regardless, it's cultivating a strong faith that allows God's children to be unshakable and bold when the storms of life come barreling through.

So how do we develop a strong faith? Well, friend, it's through the million intentional choices we make each day. We dig into and meditate on scripture when times get tough. We carry on a conversation with God throughout the day, sharing with Him our fears and worries. Rather than freak out, we lean in and rest in His presence. We ask Him to calm our anxious thoughts, taking every negative one captive. We wait on the Lord with an expectant heart because we know He is faithful and will always come through. These are the choices that will create a resilient faith, allowing us to stand our ground against the enemy's schemes as boldly as lions (or lionesses).

*Lord, empower me to make the right choices—
the ones that will create in me a steadfast faith
so that when life hits hard, I stand strong.*

Amos 4:6–6:14 / Revelation 3 / Proverbs 28:9–16

He Is Knocking

Those I love I also correct and discipline. Therefore, be shamelessly committed to Me, and turn back. Now pay attention; I am standing at the door and knocking. If any of you hear My voice and open the door, then I will come in to visit with you and to share a meal at your table, and you will be with Me.

REVELATION 3:19–20 VOICE

These verses come from a letter to the church in Laodicea. It's Jesus' final and most persuasive message, calling them out for being lukewarm. Jesus told them, "You claim, 'I am rich, I have accumulated riches, and I need nothing'; but you do not realize that you are miserable, pathetic, poor, blind, and naked. So here is what I suggest you do: buy true gold from Me" (Revelation 3:17–18 VOICE).

Some may argue we've bought into the same lie that tells us we have everything we need in the here and now. We often look to the world to satisfy our longings and desires. But the truth is that we desperately need the Lord. We're hopeless in our own strength.

Jesus is knocking on the door of your heart, waiting for an invitation. He wants to come in to build a personal relationship with you. He is the one who is able to fully satisfy. And when you open the door and embrace His goodness, your faith will begin to grow and strengthen and eventually become robust. It's not about surviving. With the Lord, you will thrive.

Lord, You are my personal Savior and I'm inviting You into every area of my life. Mature my faith in meaningful ways so I can grow closer to You every day.

Amos 7–9 / Revelation 4:1–5:5 / Proverbs 28:17–24

The God Who Is Faithful

Each of these living beings had six wings, and their wings were covered all over with eyes, inside and out. Day after day and night after night they keep on saying, "Holy, holy, holy is the Lord God, the Almighty—the one who always was, who is, and who is still to come."

REVELATION 4:8 NLT

There's some imagery shared in the final book of the Bible that may be difficult to envision. Yet that shouldn't make us doubt God's Word nor throw us for a loop and cause us to question scripture. For God's ways are not our ways, and His thoughts are not our thoughts. And that's a true blessing!

During those times when we struggle to understand the Bible, let's not lose sight of a beautiful truth: God is always faithful. He has always been, always will be, and is still to come. Yes, God is holy. His will and ways are perfect. His timing is precise. That's why we can have a faith that is resilient. And as we choose to stand in this truth, even though we may not fully comprehend the mysteries of His Word, our spirit will settle and our core will strengthen.

Lord, let my faith be secured in Your faithfulness. I don't have to understand everything. I rest in the assurance that because You have the whole world in Your hands, all is and will be well.

Lesson Learned

The word of the Eternal came to the prophet Jonah a second time.
Eternal One: Get up, and go to that powerful and notorious city of
Nineveh, and pass on to them the message I'm giving you. Having
learned his lesson, Jonah yielded to the Eternal's command and
headed on the road to Nineveh. Now Nineveh was an important
city, so large that it took three days to travel throughout it.

JONAH 3:1–3 VOICE

There are times when we need the Lord to discipline us. Just as with
any good parent, it's an act of love when God teaches us a lesson.
And out of such experiences come hard-won wisdom we couldn't
have gotten any other way. Chances are good that many of us end up
having to take a field trip, just like Jonah. It's then we discover we're
experiential learners.

Yet it's through these journeys our faith grows leaps and bounds.
We find depth in our relationship with the Lord. We learn to rely on
Him for everything. Our soul finds rest and peace and comfort in His
hands. And in the end, we choose to follow God's leading because we
have seen His goodness. We know where our strength comes from
and where our future lies.

Lord, thank You for never giving up on me. I confess
my rebelliousness and am now committed to
trusting and obeying Your will and ways.

Micah 1:1–4:5 / Revelation 6:1–7:8 / Proverbs 29:1–8

A Pliable Heart

For people who hate discipline and only get more
stubborn, there'll come a day when life tumbles in and
they break, but by then it'll be too late to help them.
PROVERBS 29:1 MSG

Friend, let today's verse be an encouragement to keep your heart pliable. Why? Because a hard heart makes it impossible for faith to grow. It's stubbornness that keeps us focused on ourselves, trying to remain in our comfort zone at all costs. Rather than living in the freedom of Christ, we stay stuck in our bad habits. And the longer we're inflexible, the harder it becomes to embrace the idea of learning new ways and changing our focus.

Can we agree that no one really enjoys discipline? It's not at the top of the list for fun times, right? But part of growing deeper in faith and closer to God is letting Him make us more like Christ. It's choosing to surrender our will for His. It's giving up control and finding comfort in knowing the Lord is sovereign. And a pliable heart is what helps us become resilient, because it comes from knowing God is at work for our good and His glory.

Lord, forgive me for being stubborn and resistant to
discipline. I want to have a pliable heart that is ready and
willing be transformed into the woman You envision.

Micah 4:6–7:20 / Revelation 7:9–8:13 / Proverbs 29:9–14

A Godly Heart

No. He has told you, mortals, what is good in His sight. What else does the Eternal ask of you but to live justly and to love kindness and to walk with your True God in all humility? The voice of the Eternal cries out to the city of Jerusalem, and the wise fear Your name.

MICAH 6:8–9 VOICE

This chapter of the book of Micah is an imagined conversation between Israel and God. He unpacks their disobedience, and then His people respond with questions, trying to figure out "what is good in His sight." In His faithfulness, God lays it out for them. For us. His response reveals what a godly heart looks like—it's outward (act justly), it's inward (love mercy), and it's upward (walk humbly).

We're to act justly, living with a strong sense of right and wrong and protecting the innocent. We're to love mercy, showing compassion and loyalty to others and God. And we're to walk humbly, which describes our heart's attitude toward Him. Choosing to live this way with the Spirit's help cultivates a deep, enduring faith. Our desire becomes doing what is good in His sight. And that drive keeps our eyes trained on the Lord.

Lord, help my life's focus be doing what is good in Your sight. Let that noble pursuit draw me ever closer to Your heart, creating a weathering faith in me.

Nahum 1–3 / Revelation 9–10 / Proverbs 29:15–23

Avoiding a Hardened Heart

*The rest of humanity, those not killed by these plagues,
did not rethink their course and turn away from the devices of
their own making. Despite all these calamities, they continued
worshiping demons and idols crafted in gold, silver, bronze,
stone, and wood. They bowed down to images which cannot see
or hear or walk. They failed to turn away from their murders,
their sorceries, their sexual immoralities, and their thefts.*

REVELATION 9:20–21 VOICE

What a chilling reality to come! It's hard to imagine such hardened hearts. But unless we choose to invest in our relationship with the Lord and grow deep roots of faith, this could happen to us all!

So how can we avoid this reality? We can rethink our course, turn away from the world, and grow closer to God, worshiping Him alone. To that end, we can make reading and meditating on God's Word a priority each day. We can listen to solid teaching from trusted pastors and speakers. We can pray about anything and everything. We can find a community that consistently points us to God. And we can love others with a humble, servant's heart. These purposeful choices will create a fleshy heart and a robust faith.

*Lord, help me make daily decisions that keep my heart
from hardening toward You. Help my actions be deliberate.
Help my words be thoughtful and measured.*

Habakkuk 1–3 / Revelation 11 / Proverbs 29:24–27

Hinds' Feet

The Lord God is my Strength, my personal bravery,
and my invincible army; He makes my feet like hinds'
feet and will make me to walk [not to stand still in terror,
but to walk] and make [spiritual] progress upon my high
places [of trouble, suffering, or responsibility]!
HABAKKUK 3:19 AMPC

Today's verse describes the blessings we receive as the presence of God comes into our circumstances. When our feet are like hinds' feet, it means we're able—with His help—to live above the situations that threaten to bring us down. The Lord equips us with all we need to thrive. Be it wisdom, confidence, strength, grace, joy, or courage, it will be given so we experience victory. We'll be able to escape enemy plans and stand in freedom. And this is possible because the Lord is our strength.

How does this encourage you today? Where are you struggling to find your footing? What circumstances feel too steep to navigate? Friend, let's remember the gift of God's presence and how it allows us to be resilient in the rockiest times, how each time we trust Him, our faith grows in strength.

Lord, thank You for being my strength, my bravery, and my army.
Thank You for helping me navigate the difficult terrain life brings
my way. I know You will always uphold me, no matter what.

Joyful Singing

The Eternal your God is standing right here among you,
and He is the champion who will rescue you. He will joyfully
celebrate over you; He will rest in His love for you;
He will joyfully sing because of you like a new husband.

ZEPHANIAH 3:17 VOICE

Just a few verses earlier in this third chapter of Zephaniah, we read that God's people were singing to Him. Today's verse reveals the joy He experienced from hearing their voices, causing the Lord to rejoice by singing over them. What a powerful interaction!

There's rejoicing because a time was coming where God's judgement on Israel would end, their enemies would be destroyed, and they'd enter a season of safety. After a time of hardship, God promised to wipe tears and comfort hearts. And this emotional act of love is extended to believers today.

Make sure your faith is secured in the Lord because He is your only hope for rescue. As you look to Him in those tough seasons of life, you will find blessings and abundance. The Lord will strengthen you from within to stand steadfast. In the end, you'll have every reason to sing praises of thanksgiving, because your Father showed up once again. And He always will.

Lord, Your perfect track record in my life is worthy of
praise. I'm humbled in knowing You find joy in singing
over me. Thank You for Your great love.

Be Strong

But don't be discouraged. Be strong, Zerubbabel. Be strong, Joshua
(Jehozadak's son and the high priest). Be strong, all you who once
again live in the land. Keep working on it. For I, the Eternal,
Commander of heavenly armies, am with you! Regarding the
covenant I made with you when your ancestors came out of Egypt,
My Spirit remains with you, living among you. Do not be afraid.

HAGGAI 2:4–5 VOICE

God commanded Zerubbabel, Joshua, and the people of Israel to be strong. This was essential to them finding the internal strength to complete His work. Just like them, we also need courage to ignite action so we're able to accomplish what God has called us to do. And knowing He's with us should bring encouragement. It should strengthen our resolve.

Friend, your faith grows a little more each time you say *yes*. Your willingness to trust God again and again creates a strong and sustaining faith that becomes unshakable over time.

Is God asking you to be strong today? Are fear and worry bringing discouragement? Is there a struggle in your taking the next right step in faith? Be strong! God is with you! As you celebrate the birth of Jesus today, let the realization that He'll never leave you birth a boldness in you to move forward in faith.

Lord, what a blessing to know You are always
with me. Let that promise be what gives me
confidence to follow Your will fully and completely.

Zechariah 1–4 / Revelation 14:14–16:3 / Proverbs 30:17–20

The Apple of His Eye

*For this is what the LORD Almighty says: "After the Glorious One
has sent me against the nations that have plundered you—for
whoever touches you touches the apple of his eye—I will surely
raise my hand against them so that their slaves will plunder them.
Then you will know that the LORD Almighty has sent me."*

ZECHARIAH 2:8–9 NIV

The apple of the eye, also known as the pupil, is one of the most sensitive parts of our anatomy. Today's verse brings that truth into perspective, revealing that whoever assaults God's people, assaults Him. And in response, He will bring judgment on whoever tries to harm His children.

Friend, never doubt that God sees every wrong and destructive action taken toward you, the precious daughter He dearly loves. He's seen the wrong that's come your way, and it feels to Him like a personal attack.

This is why you can trust the Lord to care for you. His love for you is unwavering. His compassion is unending. And He will fight for you. But deepening your relationship with God, growing your faith daily through prayer and time in the Word, is your responsibility. With the Holy Spirit's help, resolve to develop a strong, resilient faith, one that is able to fully embrace God as your fierce defender and tender provider.

*Lord, let me rest in You as You defend me.
I know I'm safe in Your hands.*

Loving and Living Well

Well, the message hasn't changed. GOD-of-the-Angel-
Armies said then and says now: "'Treat one another justly.
Love your neighbors. Be compassionate with each other.
Don't take advantage of widows, orphans, visitors, and the poor.
Don't plot and scheme against one another—that's evil.'"

ZECHARIAH 7:9–10 MSG

Once you accept Jesus as your personal savior—recognizing your need for Him and understanding Christ to be the one and only Son of God who died for your sins and was raised back to life three days later—your salvation is sealed. This act of surrendering, acknowledging your sins, and asking for forgiveness brings you into the family of God. And with it comes the Holy Spirit, whose role is to grow your faith. It's His help that makes mature faith possible.

Today's verses outline how we're to treat others; and it's only through God's power we're able to walk it out. If we don't have faith, we simply won't be able to sustain these lofty actions. We'll never be good enough, especially not in our own strength. But as we deepen our roots in Jesus, our faith will grow up from there. We will be empowered to live and love others according to God's will.

Lord, I know my limitations. I also know that without
a strong and growing faith, it's impossible to please
You because I won't have what it takes. Ripen my faith
more every day. Help me to love and live well!

Zechariah 9–11 / Revelation 17:1–18:8 / Proverbs 30:29–33

A Joy-Sustaining Faith

Cry out with joy, O daughter of Zion! Shout jubilantly,
O daughter of Jerusalem! Look—your King is coming;
He is righteous and able to save. He comes seated
humbly on a donkey, on a colt, a foal of a donkey.
ZECHARIAH 9:9 VOICE

Is your faith full of joy and expectation, especially in hard times? Are you excited to see what God has in store for you each day because you understand and trust His goodness? Do you celebrate all the Lord is able to do in your life? If not, ask Him to grow in you a joy-sustaining faith that can endure the ups and downs life brings.

It takes time and determination to cultivate a willingness to surrender and trust in the Lord. It rarely comes naturally. Just like anything of worth, unless you put forth the effort to deepen your faith, it will stagnate. But when you have a rich understanding of just how wonderful a life of faith can be, when you keep your eyes and heart on Jesus, your faith will grow by leaps and bounds, and you too will cry out with joy and shout with jubilation.

Lord, I want a joy-sustaining faith that is resilient and robust!
Help me see Your goodness in the monstrous and mundane.
Open my heart to receive everything You have for me, helping
to cultivate an attitude of gratitude in me no matter what.

You Are Seen and Known

Speak out on behalf of those who have no voice, and defend all
those who have been passed over. Open your mouth, judge fairly,
and stand up for the rights of the afflicted and the poor.

PROVERBS 31:8–9 VOICE

God sees the deprived and destitute. He recognizes those who are underprivileged. If you're lacking, it's known. If you are in need, it's noted. Friend, God has His perfect pulse on each one of us. He has complete clarity, fully aware of our needs even when we aren't.

Knowing the Father commands believers to surround the poor and afflicted is a heavenly balm that soothes an anxious heart. Today's verse is also a reminder that when others are suffering, we're called to advocate for those who cannot, those who have no voice. The truth is that the more we grow in faith, the more tender our hearts become to what breaks God's heart. And as we are strengthened through prayer and the Word, we begin to receive spiritual eyes to see where we can be His hands and feet, assured that God will empower us to speak up and step up as we rely on Him daily. And we will also become more steadfast as we wait for the Lord to show up.

So dig in deep, friend. And watch how God uses you and comforts you on this supernatural journey of faith.

Lord, thank You for seeing me when I need
hope and sending me out when others do.

Malachi 1–2 / Revelation 19–20 / Proverbs 31:10–17

What Does Your Life Preach?

*She inspires trust, and her husband's heart is safe with her,
and because of her, he has every good thing. Every day of her life
she does what is best for him, never anything harmful or hurtful.*
PROVERBS 31:11–12 VOICE

As women, we have an important role to play in the lives of others.
Our lives preach, whether good or bad. We can be known for being
petty and preoccupied. Or we can be known as someone who is caring
and compassionate. Are we safe or stingy? Do we love or loathe? Do
we inspire or irritate? It all depends on where our focus is.

When we keep our eyes on the Lord and take our faith seriously,
it brings blessings to those around us. Like the Proverbs 31 woman
described in today's verse, a strong faith allows us to confidently
empower others in meaningful ways. We can cheer them on and inspire
them to take a risk. We can create a sense of security that encourages
trust. We can speak value and worth into broken hearts. And as we
look to God to help cultivate a sturdy and sustaining faith, we're able
to bring blessings that motivate others where they need it most.

*Lord, it's both a privilege and a burden to hold places of
influence in the lives of those I love. Help me be a spark
of hope in the right ways and at the right time.*

Malachi 3–4 / Revelation 21–22 / Proverbs 31:18–31

For What Will You Be Greatly Praised?

Charm is deceptive, and beauty does not last; but a woman who fears the Lord will be greatly praised. Reward her for all she has done. Let her deeds publicly declare her praise.

PROVERBS 31:30–31 NLT

The Proverbs 31 woman understands that, as a wife, she is also her husband's partner. And because of that, she has a great deal of influence in his life and work. This chapter also speaks to the ways she inspires her children and functions as a contributing member of society. It's not so much about how she looks or acts or speaks, but rather her resilient faith that's the difference. It makes her a force to be reckoned with because her belief in the Lord is robust. This depth of relationship with the Father makes her praiseworthy, both privately and publicly. It's notable.

Too often, we place our worth in all the wrong things. We exhaust ourselves trying to impress the world, falling prey to what others say is good and valuable. But scripture says it's our faith that allows us to be a blessing. We live by the wisdom of God, not the world. And the more we rest in Him to sustain us, the more resilient we will be day by day and year by year.

Lord, what a privilege to have been led into a more resilient faith this year. I'm ready to journey even deeper next year.

Contributors

Annie Barkley made up her first story at the ripe old age of two, when she asked her mom to write it down for her. Since then she has read and written many words as a student, newspaper reporter, author, and editor. She has a passion for making God's Word come to life for readers through devotions and Bible study. Annie loves snow (which is a good thing because she lives in Ohio), wearing scarves, eating sushi, playing Scrabble, and spending time with friends and family. Annie's devotions appear in January, May, and September.

Donna K. Maltese is a freelance writer, editor, and writing coach. Mother of two children, grandmother of one very active grandchild, and caretaker of two rescue animals, she resides in Bucks County, Pennsylvania, with her husband. When not reading or writing, Donna, an avid knitter and crocheter, can be found frequently wrestling yarn from her cat. You can check out her website at donnakmaltese.com. Donna's devotions appear in the months of February, June, and October.

Kelly McIntosh is a wife, twin mom, and editor from Ohio. She loves books, the beach, and everything about autumn (but mostly pumpkin spice lattes). Kelly's devotions appear in the months of March, July, and November.

Carey Scott is an author, speaker, and certified Biblical Life Coach. With authenticity and humor, she challenges women to be real, not perfect, and reminds them to trust God as their Source above all else. Carey is a single mom with two kids in college and lives in Colorado. You can find her at CareyScott.org. Carey's devotions appear in April, August, and December.

Read Thru the Bible in a Year Plan

1-Jan	Gen. 1-2	Matt. 1	Ps. 1
2-Jan	Gen. 3-4	Matt. 2	Ps. 2
3-Jan	Gen. 5-7	Matt. 3	Ps. 3
4-Jan	Gen. 8-10	Matt. 4	Ps. 4
5-Jan	Gen. 11-13	Matt. 5:1-20	Ps. 5
6-Jan	Gen. 14-16	Matt. 5:21-48	Ps. 6
7-Jan	Gen. 17-18	Matt. 6:1-18	Ps. 7
8-Jan	Gen. 19-20	Matt. 6:19-34	Ps. 8
9-Jan	Gen. 21-23	Matt. 7:1-11	Ps. 9:1-8
10-Jan	Gen. 24	Matt. 7:12-29	Ps. 9:9-20
11-Jan	Gen. 25-26	Matt. 8:1-17	Ps. 10:1-11
12-Jan	Gen. 27:1-28:9	Matt. 8:18-34	Ps. 10:12-18
13-Jan	Gen. 28:10-29:35	Matt. 9	Ps. 11
14-Jan	Gen. 30:1-31:21	Matt. 10:1-15	Ps. 12
15-Jan	Gen. 31:22-32:21	Matt. 10:16-36	Ps. 13
16-Jan	Gen. 32:22-34:31	Matt. 10:37-11:6	Ps. 14
17-Jan	Gen. 35-36	Matt. 11:7-24	Ps. 15
18-Jan	Gen. 37-38	Matt. 11:25-30	Ps. 16
19-Jan	Gen. 39-40	Matt. 12:1-29	Ps. 17
20-Jan	Gen. 41	Matt. 12:30-50	Ps. 18:1-15
21-Jan	Gen. 42-43	Matt. 13:1-9	Ps. 18:16-29
22-Jan	Gen. 44-45	Matt. 13:10-23	Ps. 18:30-50
23-Jan	Gen. 46:1-47:26	Matt. 13:24-43	Ps. 19
24-Jan	Gen. 47:27-49:28	Matt. 13:44-58	Ps. 20
25-Jan	Gen. 49:29-Exod. 1:22	Matt. 14	Ps. 21
26-Jan	Exod. 2-3	Matt. 15:1-28	Ps. 22:1-21
27-Jan	Exod. 4:1-5:21	Matt. 15:29-16:12	Ps. 22:22-31
28-Jan	Exod. 5:22-7:24	Matt. 16:13-28	Ps. 23
29-Jan	Exod. 7:25-9:35	Matt. 17:1-9	Ps. 24
30-Jan	Exod. 10-11	Matt. 17:10-27	Ps. 25
31-Jan	Exod. 12	Matt. 18:1-20	Ps. 26
1-Feb	Exod. 13-14	Matt. 18:21-35	Ps. 27
2-Feb	Exod. 15-16	Matt. 19:1-15	Ps. 28
3-Feb	Exod. 17-19	Matt. 19:16-30	Ps. 29
4-Feb	Exod. 20-21	Matt. 20:1-19	Ps. 30
5-Feb	Exod. 22-23	Matt. 20:20-34	Ps. 31:1-8
6-Feb	Exod. 24-25	Matt. 21:1-27	Ps. 31:9-18
7-Feb	Exod. 26-27	Matt. 21:28-46	Ps. 31:19-24
8-Feb	Exod. 28	Matt. 22	Ps. 32
9-Feb	Exod. 29	Matt. 23:1-36	Ps. 33:1-12
10-Feb	Exod. 30-31	Matt. 23:37-24:28	Ps. 33:13-22
11-Feb	Exod. 32-33	Matt. 24:29-51	Ps. 34:1-7
12-Feb	Exod. 34:1-35:29	Matt. 25:1-13	Ps. 34:8-22
13-Feb	Exod. 35:30-37:29	Matt. 25:14-30	Ps. 35:1-8
14-Feb	Exod. 38-39	Matt. 25:31-46	Ps. 35:9-17
15-Feb	Exod. 40	Matt. 26:1-35	Ps. 35:18-28
16-Feb	Lev. 1-3	Matt. 26:36-68	Ps. 36:1-6
17-Feb	Lev. 4:1-5:13	Matt. 26:69-27:26	Ps. 36:7-12
18-Feb	Lev. 5:14 -7:21	Matt. 27:27-50	Ps. 37:1-6
19-Feb	Lev. 7:22-8:36	Matt. 27:51-66	Ps. 37:7-26
20-Feb	Lev. 9-10	Matt. 28	Ps. 37:27-40
21-Feb	Lev. 11-12	Mark 1:1-28	Ps. 38
22-Feb	Lev. 13	Mark 1:29-39	Ps. 39
23-Feb	Lev. 14	Mark 1:40-2:12	Ps. 40:1-8
24-Feb	Lev. 15	Mark 2:13-3:35	Ps. 40:9-17
25-Feb	Lev. 16-17	Mark 4:1-20	Ps. 41:1-4
26-Feb	Lev. 18-19	Mark 4:21-41	Ps. 41:5-13
27-Feb	Lev. 20	Mark 5	Ps. 42-43
28-Feb	Lev. 21-22	Mark 6:1-13	Ps. 44
1-Mar	Lev. 23-24	Mark 6:14-29	Ps. 45:1-5
2-Mar	Lev. 25	Mark 6:30-56	Ps. 45:6-12
3-Mar	Lev. 26	Mark 7	Ps. 45:13-17
4-Mar	Lev. 27	Mark 8	Ps. 46
5-Mar	Num. 1-2	Mark 9:1-13	Ps. 47
6-Mar	Num. 3	Mark 9:14-50	Ps. 48:1-8
7-Mar	Num. 4	Mark 10:1-34	Ps. 48:9-14
8-Mar	Num. 5:1-6:21	Mark 10:35-52	Ps. 49:1-9
9-Mar	Num. 6:22-7:47	Mark 11	Ps. 49:10-20

Date	Old Testament	New Testament	Psalms
23-May	1 Sam. 28-29	John 7:25-8:11	Ps. 83
24-May	1 Sam. 30-31	John 8:12-47	Ps. 84:1-4
25-May	2 Sam. 1-2	John 8:48-9:12	Ps. 84:5-12
26-May	2 Sam. 3-4	John 9:13-34	Ps. 85:1-7
27-May	2 Sam. 5:1-7:17	John 9:35-10:10	Ps. 85:8-13
28-May	2 Sam. 7:18-10:19	John 10:11-30	Ps. 86:1-10
29-May	2 Sam. 11:1-12:25	John 10:31-11:16	Ps. 86:11-17
30-May	2 Sam. 12:26-13:39	John 11:17-54	Ps. 87
31-May	2 Sam. 14:1-15:12	John 11:55-12:19	Ps. 88:1-9
1-Jun	2 Sam. 15:13-16:23	John 12:20-43	Ps. 88:10-18
2-Jun	2 Sam. 17:1-18:18	John 12:44-13:20	Ps. 89:1-6
3-Jun	2 Sam. 18:19-19:39	John 13:21-38	Ps. 89:7-13
4-Jun	2 Sam. 19:40-21:22	John 14:1-17	Ps. 89:14-18
5-Jun	2 Sam. 22:1-23:7	John 14:18-15:27	Ps. 89:19-29
6-Jun	2 Sam. 23:8-24:25	John 16:1-22	Ps. 89:30-37
7-Jun	1 Kings 1	John 16:23-17:5	Ps. 89:38-52
8-Jun	1 Kings 2	John 17:6-26	Ps. 90:1-12
9-Jun	1 Kings 3-4	John 18:1-27	Ps. 90:13-17
10-Jun	1 Kings 5-6	John 18:28-19:5	Ps. 91:1-10
11-Jun	1 Kings 7	John 19:6-25a	Ps. 91:11-16
12-Jun	1 Kings 8:1-53	John 19:25b-42	Ps. 92:1-9
13-Jun	1 Kings 8:54-10:13	John 20:1-18	Ps. 92:10-15
14-Jun	1 Kings 10:14-11:43	John 20:19-31	Ps. 93
15-Jun	1 Kings 12:1-13:10	John 21	Ps. 94:1-11
16-Jun	1 Kings 13:11-14:31	Acts 1:1-11	Ps. 94:12-23
17-Jun	1 Kings 15:1-16:20	Acts 1:12-26	Ps. 95
18-Jun	1 Kings 16:21-18:19	Acts 2:1-21	Ps. 96:1-8
19-Jun	1 Kings 18:20-19:21	Acts 2:22-41	Ps. 96:9-13
20-Jun	1 Kings 20	Acts 2:42-3:26	Ps. 97:1-6
21-Jun	1 Kings 21:1-22:28	Acts 4:1-22	Ps. 97:7-12
22-Jun	1 Kings 22:29- 2 Kings 1:18	Acts 4:23-5:11	Ps. 98
23-Jun	2 Kings 2-3	Acts 5:12-28	Ps. 99
24-Jun	2 Kings 4	Acts 5:29-6:15	Ps. 100
25-Jun	2 Kings 5:1-6:23	Acts 7:1-16	Ps. 101
26-Jun	2 Kings 6:24-8:15	Acts 7:17-36	Ps. 102:1-7
27-Jun	2 Kings 8:16-9:37	Acts 7:37-53	Ps. 102:8-17
28-Jun	2 Kings 10-11	Acts 7:54-8:8	Ps. 102:18-28
29-Jun	2 Kings 12-13	Acts 8:9-40	Ps. 103:1-9
30-Jun	2 Kings 14-15	Acts 9:1-16	Ps. 103:10-14
1-Jul	2 Kings 16-17	Acts 9:17-31	Ps. 103:15-22
2-Jul	2 Kings 18:1-19:7	Acts 9:32-10:16	Ps. 104:1-9
3-Jul	2 Kings 19:8-20:21	Acts 10:17-33	Ps. 104:10-23
4-Jul	2 Kings 21:1-22:20	Acts 10:34-11:18	Ps. 104:24-30
5-Jul	2 Kings 23	Acts 11:19-12:17	Ps. 104:31-35
6-Jul	2 Kings 24-25	Acts 12:18-13:13	Ps. 105:1-7
7-Jul	1 Chron. 1-2	Acts 13:14-43	Ps. 105:8-15
8-Jul	1 Chron. 3:1-5:10	Acts 13:44-14:10	Ps. 105:16-28
9-Jul	1 Chron. 5:11-6:81	Acts 14:11-28	Ps. 105:29-36
10-Jul	1 Chron. 7:1-9:9	Acts 15:1-18	Ps. 105:37-45
11-Jul	1 Chron. 9:10-11:9	Acts 15:19-41	Ps. 106:1-12
12-Jul	1 Chron. 11:10-12:40	Acts 16:1-15	Ps. 106:13-27
13-Jul	1 Chron. 13-15	Acts 16:16-40	Ps. 106:28-33
14-Jul	1 Chron. 16-17	Acts 17:1-14	Ps. 106:34-43
15-Jul	1 Chron. 18-20	Acts 17:15-34	Ps. 106:44-48
16-Jul	1 Chron. 21-22	Acts 18:1-23	Ps. 107:1-9
17-Jul	1 Chron. 23-25	Acts 18:24-19:10	Ps. 107:10-16
18-Jul	1 Chron. 26-27	Acts 19:11-22	Ps. 107:17-32
19-Jul	1 Chron. 28-29	Acts 19:23-41	Ps. 107:33-38
20-Jul	2 Chron. 1-3	Acts 20:1-16	Ps. 107:39-43
21-Jul	2 Chron. 4:1-6:11	Acts 20:17-38	Ps. 108
22-Jul	2 Chron. 6:12-7:10	Acts 21:1-14	Ps. 109:1-20
23-Jul	2 Chron. 7:11-9:28	Acts 21:15-32	Ps. 109:21-31
24-Jul	2 Chron. 9:29-12:16	Acts 21:33-22:16	Ps. 110:1-3
25-Jul	2 Chron. 13-15	Acts 22:17-23:11	Ps. 110:4-7
26-Jul	2 Chron. 16-17	Acts 23:12-24:21	Ps. 111
27-Jul	2 Chron. 18-19	Acts 24:22-25:12	Ps. 112
28-Jul	2 Chron. 20-21	Acts 25:13-27	Ps. 113
29-Jul	2 Chron. 22-23	Acts 26	Ps. 114
30-Jul	2 Chron. 24:1-25:16	Acts 27:1-20	Ps. 115:1-10
31-Jul	2 Chron. 25:17-27:9	Acts 27:21-28:6	Ps. 115:11-18
1-Aug	2 Chron. 28:1-29:19	Acts 28:7-31	Ps. 116:1-5
2-Aug	2 Chron. 29:20-30:27	Rom. 1:1-17	Ps. 116:6-19
3-Aug	2 Chron. 31-32	Rom. 1:18-32	Ps. 117

Scripture Index

OLD TESTAMENT

New Testament